Anonymus

Transcript of Shorthand Writers Notes of Proceedings

Anonymus

Transcript of Shorthand Writers Notes of Proceedings

ISBN/EAN: 9783742816825

Manufactured in Europe, USA, Canada, Australia, Japa

Cover: Foto ©Suzi / pixelio.de

Manufactured and distributed by brebook publishing software
(www.brebook.com)

Anonymus

Transcript of Shorthand Writers Notes of Proceedings

MANDEVILLE INQUEST.

RETURN to an Order of the Honourable The House of Commons,
dated 13 August 1888;—*for*,

COPY

OF

TRANSCRIPT

OF

SHORTHAND WRITERS' NOTES OF PROCEEDINGS.

(*Mr. Arthur Balfour.*)

Ordered, by The House of Commons, to be Printed,
13 August 1888.

LONDON:
PRINTED BY HENRY HANSARD AND SON;
AND
Published by Eyre and Spottiswoode, East Harding-street, London, E.C.,
and 32, Abingdon-street, Westminster, S.W.;
Adam and Charles Black, North Bridge, Edinburgh;
and Hodges, Figgis, and Co., 104, Grafton-street, Dublin.

CONTENTS.

TRANSCRIPT of SHORTHAND WRITERS' NOTES of the PROCEEDINGS at the CORONER'S INQUEST on the Body of the late MR. JOHN MANDEVILLE, held at *Mitchelstown*, County *Cork*, July 1888.

Mitchelstown, 18th July 1888.

I BEG to state that the following is a transcript of the shorthand notes of evidence, &c., at an Inquiry by Coroner Richard Rice and a Jury, as to the cause of death of Mr. John Mandeville, of Clonkilla, near Mitchelstown, who was some time ago released on the expiration of his sentence from Tullamore Prison, and who died at his residence on 8th July. The inquiry commenced in the Court House here on 17th July, at 11.30 a.m. The MacDermot, Q.C., and Mr. T. Harrington, M.P., instructed by Mr A. Mandeville, deceased's brother, represented the next of kin, and Mr. E. Murphy, M.P., instructed by Mr. St. Leger, appeared on behalf of the Prisons Board. At the opening of the Court, the Coroner complained that the constabulary had not rendered any assistance towards the holding of the inquiry, and Mr. Seymour explained that all the assistance required was given, that the jury had been summoned immediately on receipt of Coroner's precept, but that as he did not initiate the proceedings, did not intend for the present to produce witnesses. After this the inquiry commenced, and the evidence gone into.

John Cameron,
Sergeant 31906.

FIRST DAY.

Tuesday, 17th *July* 1888.

MRS. MARY MANDEVILLE, Clonkilla, Wife of the Deceased, was sworn, and Examined.

The MacDermot, Q.C.

1. ARE you widow of the deceased?—Yes.
2. What was his Christian name?—John Mandeville.
3. When were you married to him?—In 1880.
4. How long had you known him before you were married to him?—About nine or ten years.
5. Can you state about what age he was at the time he died?—About 38.
6. Prior to your marriage in 1880, was he a strong, healthy man?—He was very healthy.
7. Now, he was sent to prison on the 31st October 1887?—Yes.
8. Now, between your marriage and the time he was sent to prison, did he continue a strong, healthy man?—He did.
9. When you say he was strong and healthy, do you want to convey to the jury that he was not in the habit of being confined to his bed from illness, or suffering from ill health?—I never remember his being in bed for one day.
10. You said he was a strong man, and had a healthy appetite?—Very fair.
11. You remember the day he went to prison?—Yes. I did not go to prison with him; I went to Cork, and parted him at Midleton.
12. He was well off, and able to supply himself with what he wanted?—He had everything comfortable.

The MacDermot, Q.C.—continued.

13. During his marriage life he was not accustomed to hardship?—No.
14. Was he a man of temperate habits?—Yes.
15. Did you see him in prison?—Never.
16. You remember the day he returned from Tullamore Prison?—The 24th December; Christmas Eve.
17. Did he appear much altered?—Very much; his lips were quite blue.
18. Had he become pale?—Yes.
19. Did he appear thin?—Yes, very thin.
20. Was there anything wrong with his sight when he came back?—He could not read small print.
21. Did his sight appear to have grown weak?—Yes.
22. Before he went to prison, did he write a good hand?—Yes, a firm hand.
23. Was there any change in his handwriting when he returned?—He was very shaky for the first month; he could hardly write.
24. Now, with regard to his clothes, did he find the weight of his overcoat become oppressive to him?—He was always complaining of the weight of his overcoat after he came from prison. He complained

The MacDermot, Q.C.—continued.

complained of the weight of his boots after he came from prison.

25. Not before?—No.

26. Your residence is about a mile from here?—Yes.

27. Did he find any difficulty after coming from prison in walking that mile?—Yes.

28. Can you mention any incident connected with yourself or otherwise showing how strong he was?—He used to carry me upstairs.

29. Did he try to do it after?—I think he did, and he said I had grown heavy.

30. He died on Sunday, 8th July, at 2.30. During the six months that intervened between his leaving prison and his death, did he complain of anything?—Sometimes he complained of sore throat and bad cough. He said he had never recovered his strength.

31. Did his throat become very sore within a month before he died?—He was complaining of having a bad tooth, and he complained of his throat being sore, and of weakness.

32. Had he a good appetite?—Not so good as formerly. He did not eat some things; he required more delicacies.

33. How long before he died did he grow very much worse?—I do not know; I do not remember now.

34. When he came back from prison did he tell you anything about his prison life?—Yes, he spoke to me of his whole prison life, more to me than to any person in the world.

35. Will you just tell what he said of his prison life?—First of all, he told me that in Cork prison the doctor ordered him heat, flannel, and that he was not allowed it; consequently, his teeth were chattering going out in the morning, and for food. He got to Tullamore about 10 o'clock in the morning, and they got no food till the middle of the day, whatever time the prisoners were served, I think about one o'clock.

36. Can you tell about what hour he left Cork Gaol in the morning?—I think about 4.30.

37. What else did he tell you about his treatment in Tullamore?—He complained that his throat was sore nearly the whole time he was there.

38. Did he tell you anything about the punishment he received?—He complained that the doctor did not believe he had sore throat, and certified he was fit for punishment.

39. Do you know that doctor's name?—Yes, and that he told him one time that his throat was sore when he was on three days' punishment diet, and that he could not eat the brown bread or take the cold water. He told me brown bread and cold water was the punishment diet, and he took nothing for more than twenty hours. He said that one of Tang prisoners gave him a rope and he tied it round his waist, and as he suffered more and more from hunger he tightened it. He said to me that Dr. Moorhead said he was seriously ill, and that Dr. Ridley seemed to think he could stand punishment.

40. Dr. Moorhead was a visiting justice?—Yes——

The MacDermot, Q.C.—continued.

The MacDermot.] Go on.

Witness.] He told me when he was very hungry his mind wandered; and he told me that he prayed to God that he might die rather than go mad.

41. Was this the time the doctor certified that he was fit for punishment?—Yes.

42. Did he tell you whether he succeeded in getting a scrap of meat or anything else?—They had to take him off the punishment before he was discharged, and then he was removed to his ordinary cell. I asked did he get better food there, and he said he only got the ordinary food. He did not get milk, he only got the ordinary diet.

43. Did he say how far he was able to take ordinary diet that time?—He told me always that on coming off punishment that he could not eat.

44. Did he tell you anything about getting a scrap of food from any person?—He told me one evening there was an ordinary warder, and he must have been eating his meal outside the door, and he threw him in a scrap of meat, and he said he never enjoyed anything so much.

45. Did he say anything about putting on the prison clothes?—He told me that he was offered to be put into hospital if he would put them on, and he would not.

46. Did he say by whom that offer was made?—I do not remember.

47. Did he tell you anything about a delusion he was under?—He told me that he thought he was a boy again, and lying on a mountain near his own dear home, and that I was lying dead beside him, and that he was feeling for my dead body with his hands, and he thought that he saw the Crucifixion going on. He said to me that he thought the delusion was caused by hunger and weakness.

48. Did he mention whether he had been suffering from diarrhœa?—Yes, he complained to me that he got stirabout and vegetable soup, and he remarked to the doctor that no old woman would allow a patient suffering from diarrhœa to be fed on such food.

49. Did he say anything about the food he was using before he was released?—Bread and water.

50. Did he say anything to you about his cell?—He said that when he stretched his arms out he could touch each side with the tips of his fingers; and he said the light was very bad, and that he could not see to read the small print of the Bible. He told me the punishment cell was flagged, and that they were compelled to wear slippers so thin that their limbs were frozen.

51. Did he say whether he suffered from rheumatism?—He told me that the plank bed in the punishment cell was permanently fixed opposite the door, and that only he covered his head with the blanket or rug at night he would get inflammation of the lungs. He spoke to Dr. Moorhead about the draught of the door, and he had it greatly remedied by stuffing the places which were bad. He did not tell me where the draught

The MacDermot, Q.C.—continued.

draught came from. He said the cell was very small and cold, and that Dr. Moorhead tried the temperature, and he said it was several degrees below the regulation height.

52. Did your husband continue, after he left the prison, a sober man till he died?—Yes.

53. Did you notice any incident—(*remainder of question not heard*)?—He dined in my father's house on Monday after coming out of prison, and we noticed that he fell asleep just before dinner, and he felt so awfully weak after dinner was over that he asked me to come home as he felt weak, and we drove home about six o'clock.

Cross-examined by Mr. *Murphy*, B.L.

54. Your husband was a man of very large frame?—Yes.

55. Some years after you were married he remained very much at home?—Yes.

56. You remember when it was he first took an active part in a political movement?—He always took an active part.

57. He took a more active part about two years ago?—He took a more public part.

58. At that time was he away from home more frequently?—No, he was never absent unless a few times, I think. Of course, naturally, he used to be out in the daytime.

59. Was he in the habit of remaining out late at night?—Sometimes.

60. Was there a marked alteration in his habits within the last two years from what they had been?—Yes, naturally, under the circumstances.

(Mr. Harrington here objected to this line of cross-examination, but Mr. Murphy persisted in his right to proceed without being interrupted, and went on.)

61. Did he, within that period of two years, get a habit of remaining out up to a late hour at night?—Yes.

62. Was there a marked alteration in his habits?—Up to that time I never remember my husband being away. The time of the political excitement he might have been away one or two nights in the week.

63. From that period was there any alteration in his habit as to the amount of drink he took?—He had taken a pledge, and it expired some time in January 1887, and he renewed his pledge about a month before he died. I cannot exactly remember the date.

64. The pledge which expired in January was not a total abstinence pledge?—It was only a pledge against whiskey. He was at liberty to take any other kind of drink. Before he took the pledge he used to drink very seldom.

65. When it expired did he take whiskey?—Sometimes, but not often, for the reason that he said to me he could not afford it.

66. When he used to return late at night did you observe symptoms of liquor on him?—No, never, except on one occasion, and on that he walked home himself. He had a great horror of drink. I think it was about seven weeks ago he took this pledge, which was also a pledge against whiskey.

Mr. Murphy, B.L.—continued.

67. What was his habit with regard to wearing an overcoat on ordinary occasions?—He generally wore an overcoat.

68. Before he went to prison had he an affection of his throat?—Once or twice he had a sore throat, an ordinary sore throat. He always doctored himself.

69. Did he ever tell you that if he accommodated himself to the prison rules he would have avoided a punishment cell?—Yes; but he said that he had a conscientious objection to associate with ordinary criminals.

70. Did he tell you that if he accommodated himself to the prison rules he would not have got a punishment cell?—He said once, of course, if he accommodated himself to the rules, I suppose, they would not have punished him.

71. When he returned from Tullamore in December 1887, did he recommence to take part in the political movement that was going on in the district immediately?—No; the political movement was nearly over. He said to me he was not strong enough. He was not going about and attending to his ordinary business. I believe he went to Fermoy and Mitchelstown. He went to Cork on the 23rd or 24th of January, and only stayed a few hours in Cork.

72. What time did he leave home to go to Cork?—He went from Ballyhooly about 8.30 a.m.

73. Did he leave for Dublin about that time?—Yes. He went to Tullamore on the way, and he went to Dublin from that. I do not remember how long he was in Dublin.

74. Did he take medical advice while there?—No.

75. Did he take medical advice in Cork?—He took medical advice from Dr. Ahern, of Killworth. He always went to Dr. McCraith for anything he wanted if he did not feel well. He believed in Dr. Ahern as an oculist, and he examined his eye and prescribed for him. He got glasses and wore them, and continued to wear them up to the time of his death, on bad days. They were the weakest smoked glasses. I think Dr. McCraith treated him. He took bottles that were given to him by Dr. McCraith. Dr. McCraith often saw him.

76. What was the last occasion on which you saw him take them?—He had one about six weeks before he died.

77. You are aware there has been a movement in this district about the Leahy tax?—Yes.

78. Was your husband taking an active part in that movement?—He took an active part in everything of the kind.

79. Did he consider this movement about the Leahy tax a political movement, and was he in the habit of going about in reference to it, attending meetings?—Yes, he felt very strongly about the Leahy tax.

80. How long before his last illness did you hear him complain of sore throat?—He complained of his throat. It seems to me since he came home he was always complaining about one thing

Mr. *Murphy*, B.L.—continued.

thing or another, but that was the principal thing.

61. Do you remember his going to Fermoy any part of the week before last?—Yes.

62. What day was it?—I think it was Monday, 2nd July.

63*. What time did he leave home?—I think about 10 or 11 o'clock. I think he did not drive his own trap to Fermoy.

63. Do you know who he went to Fermoy with?—I think he went with Mr. Collinane, of Barnah.

64. When did you next see your husband after he left you that morning?—I cannot tell the time. I think I retired about 10 or 11 o'clock, and I was asleep when he returned, and cannot remember how long I was in bed. It might have been three o'clock in the morning. It must have been an advanced hour. He said nothing about the night. He simply said something to me about Mr. O'Brien. I did not notice that he had got wet.

65. When you came down in the morning did you observe whether it had been raining the previous night?—I did not. I did not inquire what kept him so late, but he told me he stopped with a few friends in Fermoy. He did not say to me what business he went to Fermoy on on that day. I did not even know that he was going to Fermoy. Before he went to Fermoy he was suffering from toothache. He was several days complaining before he ever said to go to Fermoy.

66. Was his face swollen before he went to Fermoy?—I do not remember his being subject to toothache. He said to me that he had not had a toothache for years till he got this one. He got up next day, I think, about 10 o'clock, and came down to breakfast.

67. Did he breakfast?—He did.

68. Did he complain of anything that day?—He complained of the tooth, but he said it was better than it was, but that it was troublesome still. He went to Mitchelstown that day, and returned about three or four o'clock. He did not complain of anything then, and he spent the evening reading. He did not stand to a late hour. We went to bed early; I think about nine o'clock or 10. He was not complaining that evening about his tooth. Next day I came down to meet my brother early, and he told me to tell the servant to have some milk, and complained that he could not eat solid meat. He came down and ate his breakfast that day and complained of a difficulty in swallowing. He said to me he would have the day at home on the farm. He dined at my father's about two o'clock. That is about a mile off. He got home about three o'clock. It was not raining that day. I do not remember that he complained that evening of any affection of his throat. We retired early that night, about nine. He first complained next morning of not being well at his breakfast. He said I do not feel well, and said, Shall I go to Mitchelstown, to the board of guardians? I said, You had better not. He stayed at home the whole day, and did not go about the place. He complained of his tooth, and said he had neuralgia, and had pains in his head, throat, and shoulders. I did not observe that he had any difficulty in swallowing when taking his breakfast. I think he complained of a difficulty in swallowing towards evening. He was lying down part of the day, and reading during the evening. On Friday morning, I do not exactly remember the time, he complained of his throat. He did not get up to breakfast on Friday; he remained in bed, assigning as a reason that his throat was sore. He made a remark that he felt very weak, and I made a remark that neuralgia always made one weak. I think he got up about 11 or 12 o'clock that day, and took a drive to Dr. McCraith's. I think he went about 12 or one o'clock, and returned at two; I did not go with him. He went to bed then. Dr. McCraith did not come to see him that evening. He said Dr. McCraith had given him a draught and gargle, and ordered him to take milk and beef-tea.

69. Did he bring the bottles for this draught and gargle with him?—Yes.

70. Did you see them?—Yes. He took a draught that evening at the hour fixed by Dr. McCraith. He went to bed immediately that he came home. He used the gargle during the evening. He had also a linseed meal poultice put on during the night or that evening. He did not sleep that night. I remained dressed on the outside of the bed in his room. Next morning (Saturday) he sent for mother early in the morning; I think, before five o'clock. Mrs. O'Gorman came about five. Dr. McCraith came out at once, after being sent for. Dr. McCraith got out about six o'clock, and he said he would go to Dr. O'Neill. He said that leeches should be applied to the patient's throat, and that he could not apply them himself. He went for Dr. O'Neill, and they came back in a short time, and they applied the leeches, and sent for more leeches. I think they applied about half-a-dozen more afterwards. They were not all applied outside; some were applied externally and some internally. They also gave him some medicine. I telegraphed to Cork for Dr. Cremen. I think the second lot of leeches were applied before Dr. Cremen arrived. The second lot of leeches were applied about 12 or one o'clock. Dr. Cremen arrived about three o'clock. Dr. Aherne adopted the treatment of Dr. Cremen. Dr. Cremen seemed to make a long examination of him. Dr. O'Neill and Dr. McCraith came that evening, after the consultation, about nine o'clock. No visit was made again till early in the morning. The end came about half-past two. I am not certain whether Dr. O'Neill was in the room then. I never heard of an operation being performed before that time.

71. When was the subject of this inquiry first broached to you?—I cannot tell; I do not remember.

72. Did you express your objection to this inquiry to anyone outside your own family?—I do not think so; anything I said it was to my own family; I have got a brother, and I know he visited Tullamore. I do not know the date of his visit; I think it was some time in November.

73. By

Mr. *Murphy*, B.L.—continued.

93. By *The MacDermot*.] You were asked whether you objected to the holding of this inquiry?—Yes.

94. Was there any suggestion made to you by anybody that there should be a post-mortem examination made of your husband?—I am not quite sure, but I thought there was to be a post-mortem examination. I objected to it at first, as I did not think the sanctity of death should be disturbed, and I did not like the idea of a post-mortem examination. I disliked having the body touched; I then thought if it threw any light on his prison treatment poor John would like to have it done. That is the reason I consented to the inquest.

At the time this witness' deposition was being read, she stated in reply to questions put to her by Mr. Murphy, the suggestion of holding an inquest was first made to her by her brother, and that she first gave up her objection to the holding of it on Monday.

Mr. WILLIAM O'BRIEN, M.P., Examined.

Mr. *T. Harrington*, M.P., B.L.

95. You knew the deceased?—I did.
96. You knew him before his imprisonment and afterwards?—I did.
97. He and you were taken into custody at the same time?—Yes.
98. Where were you arrested?—At Mitchelstown.
99. He for a term of two months, and you for three?—Yes.
100. After being taken into custody were you conveyed together or separately to gaol?—We were brought to Cork together in a close carriage by rail.
101. Had it the appearance of a prison van?—No.
102. Had you made any public statement before your arrest as to prison treatment?——

(Question objected to by Mr. Murphy, and allowed; note of objection refused by coroner.)

Witness.] I had made a public announcement as to what my course in prison would be six weeks previously.

103. Had that reference to imprisonment under the Crimes Act of the present day?——

(Question objected to by Mr. Murphy, and allowed by coroner.)

104. Did Mr. Mandeville while in custody have any conversation with you about prison treatment?—Yes; while being conveyed to Cork prison we discussed what our course in prison should be; having regard to the public announcement I had made that I should not wear convict dress, nor associate with criminals, nor perform any menial prison work, Mr. Mandeville said that he would do whatever I did, no matter what the consequences. I urged on him to do nothing of the kind, but to leave the fight to me at first, at all events. I do not know whether I should mention a conversation I urged upon him; I think it may be important; I mentioned to him what Mr. Wilfrid Blunt had told me——

(Here again Mr. Murphy objected, but his objection was overruled by coroner, who again refused to note it, and the witness was allowed to go on.)

Mr. *T. Harrington*, M.P., B.L.—continued.

Witness.] I said that probably it would be a life and death struggle, and I pointed out to him that as I was a Member of Parliament they would probably have more hesitation about maltreating me than him, and that in any event, whatever happened me, the facts were sure to transpire. I urged upon him that as he was a man of such magnificent physique they would probably experiment upon him to any extent——

(Mr. Murphy objected to this conversation being given in evidence, but the coroner allowed it, and refused to note objection, and threatened counsel with removal from court if repeated.)

Witness.] As another reason, I pointed out that as he was not a Member of Parliament they would probably use brutalities against him with less scruple, and that if he died the officials alone would be able to tell the tale, and that his wife and family would suffer. Nothing would induce him to yield as to two of the points; association with criminals and the performance of menial work. He very reluctantly agreed to yield to the question of prison dress, not to carry his resistance to anything beyond a protest.

105. Were there any efforts made that evening to deprive you of your clothes?—None whatever.

106. You were not even asked to put on prison dress that evening?—No.

107. You do not say anything with regard to Mr. Mandeville that evening?—No.

108. When did you see him next?—Next morning, when I refused to exercise with the criminals, and was allowed to exercise by myself, and on that morning had also been allowed to exercise by himself.

109. All that day was spent in the Cork gaol?—Yes.

110. When did you meet Mr. Mandeville next?—At four o'clock the following morning.

Mr. *T. Harrington*, M.P., B.L.—continued.

111. That was not the usual hour for rising in the prison?—No; a very extraordinary occurrence.

112. In winter I believe the usual hour for rising in the prison is seven o'clock?—A quarter to seven.

113. At what hour were you called that morning?—The clock had struck three when the deputy governor, Mr. Oxford, and I think the head warder, unbolted my cell and entered with a lantern. The deputy governor said, "Get up, Mr. O'Brien; you are going." I said, "In God's name, where?" He said, "We know no more than yourself." We were roused out of our beds. I got up and got out on the corridor, and there met Mr. Mandeville.

114. Do you know how he was dressed?—Yes, he was dressed in his own clothes.

114*. Had you then, or subsequently to that day, a conversation with him as to whether he had been deprived of his clothes that day?—On our journey to Tullamore, Mr. Mandeville informed me that about 12 o'clock the previous night the deputy governor and a party of warders entered his cell and obliged him to take off his clothes, which were under him in bed. They left the prison clothes behind. I should say he mentioned that, in accordance with our agreement, he had made no resistance beyond a protest. He told me, when he was called in the morning, the deputy governor said, Mr. Mandeville, we have brought you back your clothes. I think I should add that he then said they have now themselves acknowledged the distinction, by giving me back my clothes; and nothing on earth can induce me to give them up again without a struggle. I at last agreed with him in that, and said, As they have now given you back your own clothes, and as they are bringing us to Tullamore in a first-class carriage, they will find it hard to kill us now for insisting upon this distinction, which they have themselves acknowledged.

115. This conversation occurred in a railway carriage?—Yes.

116. At the time you were called, or up to the time you met Mr. Mandeville on the corridor, did you know where you were to be brought?—No, not the smallest. Nor he? I remarked to him: Did you ever see anything more like a midnight murder? And he said, I believe that is just what they are up to. Major Roberts, the governor of the prison, was waiting for us in the dark, at the outer gate, and I said to him, "In the name of God, what is the meaning of all this?" He shook his head and said nothing. I reminded him that the Mayor of Cork was a member of the Visiting Committee, and that I had requested that the mayor and Dr. Moriarty should be present whenever any attack should be made upon me, and I asked whether they could be communicated with before we left. One of the prison rules themselves require a certificate from the doctor that prisoners can be removed without injury to health before they are removed to another prison. The governor said, It is impossible for me to do anything now. This was after 10 o'clock at night. The rule to which I refer is Rule 11 of the General Prisons Board.

Mr. *T. Harrington*, M.P., B.L.—continued.

117. Are you aware, of your own knowledge, that the rule was complied with in Mr. Mandeville's case?—I am afraid not.

118. When you reached the gate, was the prison van there?—No; a close carriage.

119. And still, on entering the carriage, you were not informed where you were going to?—No.

120. Mr. Mandeville and you were both conveyed in the same carriage?—Yes. I might say that after that conversation with the governor, Mr. Mandeville and I managed to chat.

121. To what station were you conveyed?—To the Dublin terminus.

122. Who did you meet there?—The resident magistrate and county inspector, and there were parties of policemen along the streets. Before leaving the prison we got something to eat, what they call a porringer of tea, and some white bread. Mr. Mandeville was suffering a little from diarrhœa. I remember he made the remark, it would take a good deal to kill him. He was one of the most uncomplaining men I ever met.

123. At this time was there a train waiting for you?—Yes.

124. Into what kind of carriage were you and he brought?—A first-class carriage.

125. Are you aware that that is not the usual conveyance for prisoners?—It never happened before, to my knowledge, in the case of convicted prisoners.

126. Was it at this time you first learned you were going to Tullamore?—When, at the train, I overheard a police officer in charge of our carriage say, You know your orders, Tullamore. I then said to Mr. Mandeville, I know now what it all means. They are bringing us where there will be no witnesses. The blinds of the carriage were pulled down, although it was dark, and no stopping up to Ballybrophy to take water.

127. When you reached Tullamore what conveyance met you?—There was a carriage.

128. And that carriage conveyed you to the gaol?—Yes.

129. By whom were you met at the gaol?—The governor, resident magistrate, and police officer. I do not recollect the name of the resident magistrate; Blosse, I think.

130. At what hour in the day was it?—I think it must be 10 a.m.

131. You and he were then conveyed to separate cells?—Yes.

132. Was there any immediate examination by the doctor?—Yes.

133. You were allowed to bid one another good-bye?—Yes; I said good-bye, God bless you, and he said, good-bye, God save Ireland.

134. Did you see Mr. Mandeville subsequently in prison?—Yes, I saw him next day. On that day I was asked to exercise with what they call the "Class." The "Class," I take it, means persons convicted under the same conditions as in my case and Mr. Mandeville's; persons committed without hard labour; I refused.

135. On that day did you get any exercise during the entire day?—No.

136. Next

Mr. T. Harrington, M.P., B.L.—continued.

136. Next day did you meet Mr. Mandeville?—I did, and the head warder intimated to me that Mr. Mandeville and I would be allowed to exercise alone, and we were.

137. Were you out afterwards that day, or did you get two hours exercise together?—I cannot remember.

138. Are you aware what was Mr. Mandeville's food?—Cocoa and milk, bread and water, and soup.

139. Were you ot be weighed?—Yes.

140. Were you weighed at Cork?—Yes.

141. And at Tullamore?—Yes.

142. Had you reduced in weight?—Yes; seven pounds in six days.

143. Do you know whether Mr. Mandeville was then wearing his own clothes?—His own, certainly.

144. Had you any conversation with the governor that day on the question of prison clothes?—The previous day I had.

145. What was the conversation?—I told him that I was sorry to have to trouble him, that as to prison privations of any description he would never hear a murmur from me, but that as to two or three points of what I regarded as active degradation I could never give way.

146. Did you hear the governor saying that he had got any orders in reference to prison discipline?—No; on the 2nd day he was in Dublin in the morning; upon the 3rd day he came to my cell and asked me, "Do you refuse to put on prison clothes?" I said I do not suppose I have any necessity for repeating what I told you already. Well, he said, "I will have to force you. I have got my orders, and I cannot help it." I said all right, you know your duty, and I know mine. I said I make a formal application to you that the doctor and prison chaplain should be present at any attack made on me of personal violence. He listened and said nothing. He returned in about half-an-hour with the head warder, and said, to my very great surprise, "I will sentence you to 24 hours' bread and water." I said all right.

147. Did you meet Mr. Mandeville next day?—I did. That was Saturday, and Sunday we met at Mass.

Mr. T. Harrington, M.P., B.L.—continued.

148. Was he able to make any communication to you?—Yes.

149. Did you learn how he was treated at that time?—Yes; he had been also on bread and water, and he was still suffering from diarrhœa, but as usual laughed it off, and said they might do their worst to him. As well as I remember, on that day we were confined. On the following day we again exercised together, and he still wore his own clothes; we exercised alone together for three days more. He appeared a bit pulled down, but spoke lightly. He appeared to be very much more concerned about me than about himself.

150. After three days were you exercised again together?—No; after those days I was weighed, and the doctor insisted upon my going to hospital.

151. How much did you reduce in weight?—It was 7 lbs.

152. Did you see him after you were released, and were you able then to form any opinion as to the effects of his imprisonment?—Oh, yes, he was a different man, unhealthy looking, bluish, extremely nervous; a man who apparently never knew he had nerves at all; frequently trembling. He appeared to me before to be as magnificent a specimen of a man as ever I laid eyes on, and when I saw him in Tullamore after my release he appeared to a large extent a broken man.

153. I suppose of his treatment in gaol you were able to learn very little?—Very little.

154. When the chaplain mentioned to me that Mr. Mandeville was on bread and water again and as I was determined that there should be no difference in treatment, I refused to take hospital fare, and went back to my ordinary plank bed, but both the governor and head warder said to me that I was mistaken that Mr. Mandeville was put on punishment diet, that his punishment was over him, and that he was doing very well, and I never knew what the poor fellow had to endure. The only thing I learned was the midnight attack upon him.

Adjourned at 5.30 p.m. till 11 o'clock next day.

SECOND DAY.

Wednesday, 18th *July* 1888.

Mr. O'Brien's Examination was resumed.

Mr. *Harrington*.

155. You had a good deal of intercourse with Mr. Mandeville before and subsequent to his imprisonment?—Yes, and such a cool-headed man I never met. I saw him under circumstances of great excitement, and I never saw the smallest sign of drink on him. I never heard a suspicion of such a thing until I heard it here, or rather until I heard it some three days ago as having been thrown out by the police, by District Inspector Seymour.

156. Do you recollect what day you were sent to hospital?—Yes.

157. On what day?—I think I can fix it within a day or two. It was either the 7th or 8th of November. I did not keep an exact record.

158. What day were your clothes taken?—If I went to hospital on the 7th, it was on the 10th; if I went on the 8th, it was on the 11th.

Cross-examined by Mr. *Murphy*, Q.C.

159. Before your arrest you appear to have made yourself acquainted with the prison rules as to the particular subject of dress?—Generally.

160. Did you read an Act of Parliament dealing with the subject?—No; I may have read it but I did not study it.

161. Were you aware that there was a statute of attainment with reference to this matter?—Certainly.

162. You are a Member of the Legislature?—I am.

163. And for how long have you been?—About five years.

164. I suppose you are aware that it is the duty of every subject of Her Majesty to obey the law?—I am aware that it is the duty of a people to obey laws which they make themselves, and not their duty to obey laws which their enemies make for their own advantage.

165. Was Mr. Mandeville, so far as you know, aware of the prison rules with regard to the clothing of prisoners?—In a general way, I should say yes.

166. Did he and you determine that he and you should resist those rules?—I told you yesterday in his case he distinctly agreed not to do so, and not only agreed but carried out his agreement, and surrendered his clothes, under protest, without a struggle.

167. Have you any cause to complain of your treatment while in prison by any of the officers?—Certainly not. It seemed to me that their duties were revolting to them; but that does not prevent me from saying that they carried out

Mr. *Murphy*, Q.C.—continued.

those duties even though they involved very gross barbarities.

168. Now that word gross barbarities is your expression?—It is.

169. You never heard any officer of the prison make use of it?—I do not think that they used it, I know very well that in ten thousand ways they intimated their shame of the duties they were performing. They seemed to consider themselves more guilty parties than the prisoners they were dealing with.

170. Mr. Mandeville was in Tullamore the day you were discharged?—He was.

171. Did he go with you to Dublin?—Yes.

172. Did he go down with you afterwards to Mallow?—I think he did not go down for a week after.

173. How many days after you saw him in Tullamore was it when you saw him again?—I saw him next day; I saw him on the 31st.

174. Did he leave Dublin then?—He called with Mr. Condon at the hotel where I was stopping.

175. You were in Mallow on the 28th January?—Yes.

176. There was a banquet there?—Yes.

177. Was Mr. Mandeville there?—He was.

178. Did you hear him make a speech there?—No; I was rather ill and had to go away after speaking myself; but Mr. Mandeville came to my room before I left.

179. Did you read his speech in the papers?—I daresay I did.

180. Do you remember an expression in it that his imprisonment had not knocked a feather out of him?—I do not.

181. When next did you meet him?—I do not think I met him till I came down here to Mitchelstown.

182. On the 2nd of April, was it?—About that time.

183. Was Mr. Mandeville sitting near you at the banquet?—He was sitting at the head of the table near me; I do not know his position.

184. And in good spirits?—Well, yes; his spirits seemed to me never so buoyant; but he appeared to me to be making a hard struggle to appear cheerful.

185. Did he remain after you?—He did.

186. What time was it you saw him afterwards?—I left about 9 o'clock and I saw him at 10.

187. Did he tell you that he made speeches at the table?—I do not think so. The next place I saw him was at the Mitchelstown meeting.

188. He

Mr. *Murphy*, B.L.—continued.

188. He attended that meeting, and spoke at it?—Yes, he did; a short speech.

189. When did you meet him next?—At Tullamore.

190. Do you remember the date of that?—Well, it must have been three weeks after he accompanied me there.

191. Did he speak there?—He did. Now I remember when dining together that evening at the presbytery his hair had grown grey.

192. Can you say whether his hair had grown grey before?—No, I never observed whether his hair was grey before; that was the first time I noticed that he had grey hair.

193. Will you say he was not grey before he went to prison?—No.

194. You are not in a position to make a comparison, then?—No.

195. Did he at that meeting at Fermoy object to speak on the grounds of any delicacy of his throat, or anything of that sort?—No.

196. When did you meet him again?—I rather think I saw him in Dublin after that.

197. Did you meet him between that and the 3rd of June?—I think I met him in Dublin in May, and in Cork on the 3rd of June, at a meeting there.

198. Was he long in Dublin?—No, he was only a bit of a day. He spoke at the meeting at Cork Park; I heard him. It was an open air meeting, and the meetings at Mitchelstown and Fermoy were in the open air. He was always brief in his speeches.

199. At that meeting at Cork on the 3rd June did he complain of any difficulty of any affection of his throat?—No, he never complained. It seemed to me a torture to him to refer at all to his complaints, chiefly and entirely because of the base use that was made by our opponents of every reference to it.

200. Did he tell you that was the reason he did not complain of any delicacy?—Certainly not. He did not put it in that way, but fifty times over he referred to them, and distinctly told me that one of his troubles in prison was to know what to say in reply to visiting justices as to whether he had any complaints, inasmuch as every word of ours might be tortured by the scoundrels into whining.

201. He never assigned it to you as a reason of any complaint to you, personally, that anything he communicated to you could be tortured in that way?—Certainly not.

202. When asked to speak, he never complained that he had a delicacy of the throat?—No. I did not see him after the 3rd June.

203. Did you visit this district afterwards?—He died on the 8th July, and I came to this district the morning of the funeral, last Thursday.

204. Did you previously to that in any way suggest the holding of an inquiry on his remains?—Certainly, I suggested an inquiry to everyone I met.

205. Did you suggest it to any of the family?—I communicated with Mr. Ambrose Mandeville, asking what was the date of the funeral and inquest; that was the only way I suggested it to him.

206. How did you send that communication?—By wire; early in the day I got a message of his death, and on the Monday following Mr. Mandeville's death I sent a wire from the House of Commons, I think after four o'clock.

207. What time does the House of Commons meet on Monday?—Half-past three or four.

208. Were you informed in that message that Mrs. Mandeville had some objection to holding an inquest?—I was. I got that communication on Tuesday. That communication was made to me by wire also, and I replied to that by telegram to Mrs. Mandeville direct. I telegraphed to Mrs. Mandeville something to this effect, that I felt deeply how naturally she objected to post-mortem examinations, but that I would earnestly press her to overcome her objection in order that the particulars of her husband's treatment might be authenticated on oath.

209. Did you send that on Tuesday night or Tuesday evening?—I rather think I sent it late on Tuesday night, and that it came to her on Wednesday morning. I was wrong; I must have wired on Monday night, as I was a day in Dublin before I came to the funeral.

210. You were informed that a telegram sent late at night would not be delivered till morning?—I was.

211. Were you aware that Mr. Mandeville had instituted an action in reference to his prison treatment?—I was.

212. You were aware then that action was instituted?—Yes.

213. Were you concerned in it?—No.

213. You are aware that it never was prosecuted?—I am.

Witness.] With reference to this threat of Mr. Seymour's, I mean it was a threat to his family not to take these proceedings; a threat which I consider worse than the prison treatment.

Mr. *Murphy*.

214. You said that the District Inspector used threats; were you present?—No; my authority is Mr. Mandeville's brother, whom he threatened with ugly disclosures.

16 *July* 1888.

Dr. Moorhead, of Tullamore, Member of the King's and Queen's Colleges, Ireland; Licentiate of the College of Surgeons, and Justice of the Peace for the King's County; Examined.

Mr. Harrington, M.P.

215. Do you remember having made application in your capacity as Justice of the Peace to visit the prisoners in Tullamore Prison?—I did.

216. Can you recollect the date of that application?—It was the day of Mr. O'Brien's committal to jail.

217. Did you obtain admission on that occasion?—No.

218. Whom did you meet?—I asked to see the governor, and was taken to him. I made my application to visit the prisoners as a justice of the peace, and he refused to give me that authority. He said I had no authority.

219. Did you subsequently visit the prison again until you got a communication from the prison?—No, I got a communication on the morning of the 7th November from the governor.

220. I believe that communication conveyed to you that you had a right to visit as a justice?—Yes.

221. Did you immediately, then, visit the prison?—I did that morning.

222. Did you see the deceased, Mr. Mandeville, during that visit?—I did.

223. Had you any conversation with him?—I had, but I have no notes of that conversation. Mr. Mandeville was in the cell. The governor was with me. He seemed bright and cheerful, and was undergoing a bread and water punishment. I asked him if he had any complaints. He said he had bread and water and plenty to eat.

224. Was he then wearing his own clothes?—He was.

225. I believe the questions you were allowed to ask him were very limited; what were they?—Whether the prisoner had any complaints to make as regards his treatment or any abuses.

226. Did the governor caution you in any way as to the questions you were to ask?—He said they were confined to these.

227. And even these limitations were confined to a certain day?—Yes.

228. Was there any visitors' book kept in the gaol on that first day?—No.

229. You also visited Mr. O'Brien and other prisoners that day?—Yes.

230. Did you also visit the prison on the 8th?—I did.

231. Did you see Mr. Mandeville in the course of your visit on the 8th?—I did.

232. Do you remember whether he made any complaint to you on the 8th?—He made no complaint.

233. Was he still wearing his own clothes?—He was.

234. Do you know whether he was allowed to exercise at that time?—I think on the 8th he was allowed to exercise; but on the 7th, when on punishment diet, he was not.

235. When you visited him on the 8th, was he in his cell?—He was.

236. Can you give me a description of his cell?—About 6 feet wide, 10 or 12 feet long, and about 10 feet in height in the centre.

Mr. Harrington, M.P.—continued.

237. This was an ordinary cell?—Yes.

238. It was not a boarded cell?—It was a flagged cell.

239. Did you make any report as to his condition on the 8th?—I did not. I made no report of his condition until the 10th. The governor was with me on the occasion of my visit on the 8th also.

240. Are you aware how long a prisoner is confined in such a cell as you describe?—When not on punishment a prisoner is confined 22 out of 24 hours, and when on punishment he is confined the entire 24 hours, as long as the punishment lasts. I am speaking now of that particular gaol, the only one I have ever seen.

241. As a matter of fact had you not a controversy with the governor as to his interpretation of the rule with regard to that?—Not that time.

242. Do you remember, when you found Mr. Mandeville on punishment diet, on the 7th, what he was punished for?—No.

243. Did you visit the prison also on the 9th?—I did; I saw Mr. Mandeville on the 9th.

244. Do you recollect at what hour you saw him?—No. I think it was in the morning; the doctor was with me on the 9th, and the governor was present at any questions I asked, and the governor frequently objected to the questions I asked and the information I received.

245. Were you ever threatened by the governor?—Yes, threatened with the termination of my visits.

246. On what occasion?—On the same occasion.

247. Were you ever threatened to be deprived of the commission of the peace?—No.

248. You made no report on the 9th as to Mr. Mandeville's condition?—No; I also visited on the 10th.

249. Can you recollect where you found Mr. Mandeville on that occasion?—I *found* him in his cell.

250. Was he still wearing his own clothes?—He was.

251. Did he on that day make any complaint to you of his treatment?—He complained of sore throat.

252. Did you make any entry in the visitors' book of the prison on that day?—I did.

252. With reference to Mr. Mandeville's condition?—Yes.

253. You have an extract of that report with you, I believe?—I have.

254. Will you kindly read that extract for the coroner?—"November the 10th, I found Mr. Mandeville in the same cell as formerly. It is a small stuffy apartment for a man of his size. He complained of sore throat, and his breathing is embarrassed. He also had had no change of linen since his being in gaol; I would recommend a larger and better ventilated cell for him, and also a change of flannel shirts for him and Mr. O'Brien."

Mr. *Harrington*, M.P.—continued.

255. Did you at all, Doctor, come to the conclusion that that recommendation was necessary for the prisoner's health; I mean the change of clothes?—Yes.

256. Apart from the complaint of Mr. Mandeville, had you evidence yourself of his having sore throat?—No.

257. But you had evidence of the condition of his breathing?—Yes, because it was apparent.

258. Did you ask on that occasion to be allowed to see the prison doctor's report as to Mr. Mandeville?—I asked on that or some other occasion to be allowed to see the entry in the surgeon's book as to Mr. Mandeville's condition and treatment.

259. Were you refused?—Yes.

260. Can you say whether you visited the prison on the 11th?—My impression is that I visited nearly every day.

261. You are certain you visited on the 12th?—Yes.

262. You found Mr. Mandeville in a different cell?—Yes.

263. Did you make any entry on that day in the prison's book as to his condition?—I did. (The *Witness* read the extract of entry, as follows:—)

> "November 12th found Mr. Mandeville removed from former cell to cell previously occupied by Mr. O'Brien. The light was very bad, and he complained that he could not read the small print of the Bible, and that his eyes were suffering much from the long confinement. His throat was better, and he is under medical treatment. In my opinion he should be removed to hospital while undergoing medical treatment."

264. Do you remember whether the governor accompanied you to Mr. Mandeville on that day?—Yes.

265. On that occasion also did he wear his own clothes?—Yes.

266. The cell that he was removed into was, I believe, a flagged cell?—Yes.

267. Can you recollect whether he said anything about his exercise?—No.

268. At the end of your entry there is a reference made that he should be removed to hospital whilst undergoing medical treatment; did you recommend that on several occasions in the course of your report?—I did.

269. During the whole course of the imprisonment did you ever see Mr. Mandeville in hospital?—No.

270. Can you say, as a matter of fact, that he was not there?—I can.

271. During the progress of your visits there, was it evident to you as a medical man that his health was suffering and his constitution failing?—It was.

272. Was it your observation of that that induced you to make frequent recommendations of his removal to hospital?—It was.

273. And these frequent recommendations were disregarded?—Yes.

274. Did the governor know you personally for a long time; he knew you as a medical officer attending the local workhouse?—Yes.

275. And he knew you as a doctor in practice in the town of Tullamore?—Yes.

276. The prison doctor knows you well, does he not?—He does.

277. I believe you were personally acquainted?—Yes.

278. Was there any conversation between you and the prison doctor by which he could learn of these recommendations of yours?—No.

279. At all events you know they were brought under the notice of the Prison Board?—I do not.

280. Did you, as a medical doctor, consider the removal to hospital essential for Mr. Mandeville's health?—I did at periods of his imprisonment.

281. Can you recollect whether you visited the prison on the 13th?—No, I visited it on the 14th.

282. Did you on that occasion see Mr. Mandeville?—I did.

283. Can you recollect whether he made any complaint to you on that occasion?—I can; he made a complaint to me on that occasion.

284. You made an entry of it in the visitors' book, and you have an extract of that entry?—Yes. (The *Witness* read the extract, as follows:—)

> "November 14th visited Mr. Mandeville in the cell. He complained of being sentenced by the governor to three days' punishment on bread and water for refusing to wear prison dress. He complained of sore throat, for which there was a garg'e prescribed by the prison doctor, who, I was informed, had given a medical certificate of Mr. Mandeville's fitness to undergo punishment. I regard his sore throat as evident, and I would recommend Mr. Mandeville to be removed to hospital for medical treatment."

285. When you visited on the 12th, was Mr. Mandeville under medical treatment?—Yes.

286. When you visited on the 14th, was it Mr. Mandeville or the governor that informed you that the doctor had certified Mr. Mandeville's fitness for punishment?—It was the governor.

287. Did you visit the prison on the 15th?—Yes.

288. Was he still on punishment diet?—He was on bread and water, and confined in his cell.

289. Are you aware of the quality of the bread?—Yes, brown bread.

290. He was still suffering his term of three days' bread and water?—Yes.

291. He made a complaint that he was suffering from diarrhoea on the 15th, which he attributed to the treatment he was getting, and I need scarcely ask you whether bread and water is food calculated to produce diarrhoea?—Yes, when given as sole food.

292. And if that is the case with bread and water, I suppose it is the case with brown bread and water?—Yes, it is in a greater degree.

293. Did you make any observation of his condition yourself on that occasion?—I did.

294. And recorded it in the visitors' book?—Yes.

Mr. *Harrington*, M.P.—continued.

295. Have you an abstract of your report for that day?—I have. (Reads extract.)

> "On the 15th November I visited Mr. Mandeville, whom I found undergoing three days' punishment on bread and water, inflicted by the governor for a breach of prison discipline by not wearing prison clothes. He complained of diarrhœa, and seemed to me to be rapidly decreasing in weight. He ought, in my opinion, be moved to hospital department for medical treatment."

296. It was not as a result of any statement made, but as a result of your own observation that you made this record?—It was the result of my observation.

297. Did you consider him fit to be treated with bread and water when suffering from diarrhœa?——

298. Can you say whether he was visited by Dr. Ronayne?—No.

299. Now, Doctor, from your observation of Mr. Mandeville at that time, I ask, in your opinion, was that three days of bread and water punishment calculated to produce a bad effect upon his constitution?—It was calculated to injure him very much. It might not produce a fatal, but it was calculated to produce a pernicious effect on his constitution.

300. From what you know of gaol arrangement, would you consider a prisoner's ordinary cell a dangerous place to keep a prisoner suffering from diarrhœa?—In close confinement I certainly would.

301. You are aware that while he was so confined he was not taken out of his cell during the entire time unless by asking?—Yes.

302. He was not taken out for exercise during his punishment?—No.

303. Are you aware of the arrangement by which he had to ring if he required to be taken out of his cell?—Yes.

304. Are you aware that there was only one warder to attend to such a call?—I understand that on each landing there was a warder to attend to a call.

305. I suppose you are aware that prisoners are locked up at eight o'clock?—I am not really aware.

306. Did you visit again on the 17th?—And saw Mr. Mandeville. I think the governor was present. I made a report as to his condition.

307. Have you an extract of that report?—Yes. (Witness reads extract.)

> "On the 17th November I saw Mr. Mandeville. He complained of being weaker after his punishment of bread and water, and his sight was failing fast. This punishment I think is in excess of the governor's jurisdiction under Rule 56, the general rule for prisoners, and I think he (Mr. Mandeville) ought to be removed to the infirmary, and placed under medical treatment."

308. At the date of that visit, was he still wearing his own clothes?—He was.

309. Are you aware that from the period of his imprisonment, 31st October, up to that day, 18th November, he had got no change of underclothing?—I cannot say that.

310. Did you visit him on the 19th?—I think I did, but I have no note of it.

311. When have you next a note of a visit?—I have a note of the 23rd November.

312. Did you visit on that occasion, and did you see Mr. Mandeville?—I did.

313. Can you recollect what time on the 23rd you visited him?—On the morning of the 23rd.

314. Describe his condition?—He had no clothing on him.

315. Not even a shirt?—No, he was wrapped up in a quilt and sheet. He complained of his clothes being taken from him the previous evening. He told me he was awakened out of his sleep by several warders, and after a struggle the clothes were taken from him. He protested against the treatment, and demanded his clothes.

316. Do you remember whether portions of his body were uncovered?—His chest and arms, legs, and feet.

317. I need not ask the description of weather we had on 23rd November?—The usual weather.

318. The governor was present when these complaints were made?—He was.

319. You made an entry in the book that day?—I think I did, but I have not an extract.

320. Can you say whether you visited the prisoner again next day?—Yes; he was then attired in prison garb.

321. Can you recollect that he made a special complaint that he had been left perfectly nude?—On the following day, the 24th, he told me that these articles, the quilt and sheet, had been taken from him, and that then he put on the prison clothes.

322. Can you recollect whether you visited him on the 26th?—I think I did; the next extract of notes I have is of a visit on the 30th.

323. Where did you find him on the 30th?—In his cell.

324. Did he make any complaint to you on that occasion?—He complained that he was suffering from rheumatism.

325. I suppose you were not surprised to hear that complaint?—No.

326. Can you recollect whether you were told by Mr. Mandeville how long he remained from the time his own clothes were taken from him?—He thought he said 24 hours.

327. It was winter weather?—It was.

328. Did you make an entry in the visitors' book on the 30th?—I did.

329. You have an extract of that entry?—I have. (Reads extract.)

> "November 30th found Mr. Mandeville in his cell. He complained of rheumatism, for which the prison doctor had not prescribed. His cell was close, dirty, and offensive smelling from the presence of excreta not removed. He told me the governor asked him to cleanse his cell, which he refused to do. He was also ordered by the governor to take exercise with ordinary criminals, which he declined doing, and, in consequence, had been confined for the last 24 hours to this close unhealthy cell. The

continuance

Mr. Harrington, B.L.—continued.

continuance of such treatment would break down the constitution of the strongest man, and would probably develop into a malignant type of disease in Mr. Mandeville's case. Such a state of affairs calls for immediate remedy."

330. You have been visiting the prison continuously since the 7th?—I think so.

331. Was that the first occasion you heard of any demand on him to cleanse his cell?—It was.

332. Are you aware that he would not to do it?—Yes.

333. During the time you visited before this, did you hear anything of punishment for refusing to associate with criminals?—Except the loss of exercise which it entailed.

334. During his imprisonment did he ever cleanse his cell?—Not that I am aware of.

335. Did you visit on the 29th; where did you find him on the 29th?—He was in his cell.

336. Did you observe his appearance?—I did.

337. Did you observe upon his condition and appearance in your report in the visitors' book?—I did.

338. You have an extract of that report?—I have. (*Hands extract.*)

> "November 29th was in his cell; was chilled from the bread and water treatment. He also had a distinct tremor in both hands. He complained of the long confinement to his cell, now four days without exercise. He pointed out that the visiting justices and the governor had power under Rule 10 of the regulations for the treatment of convicted prisoners to relax the strict observance of the prison rules. I think under the circumstances, and as the enforcement of the rules has proved injurious to Mr. Mandeville's health, they ought to be relaxed at once, and healthy open air exercise permitted to be taken, which is so essential to his health."

339. I suppose that that was disregarded as well as the other recommendation?—I am not aware that it was followed by any amelioration whatever.

340. You visited the prison continuously after that day?—I did, and made entries which I have not the extracts of.

341. The first report of which you have an extract is the 21st December?—Yes.

342. Can you recollect whether between that and the intervening period Mr. Mandeville had to complain to you of any other punishment?—No, I have no recollection.

343. You visited 21st December and saw Mr. Mandeville?—Yes.

344. Were there a large number of prisoners about whom you made entries?—Yes.

345. Where did you find Mr. Mandeville when you entered the prison on the 21st?—I found him in a punishment cell.

346. Was this a special cell for special punishment?—Yes, so I understand.

347. You are aware that this was within two or three days of his release?—Yes.

348.

Mr. Harrington, B.L.—continued.

348. Is that the first time you had seen a punishment cell?—Yes.

349. Is it the only time you have seen a punishment cell?—He was the only prisoner I have seen in a punishment cell.

350. Would you describe that punishment cell?—Yes, the punishment cell is a separate cell on the ground of a separate building from where Mr. Mandeville had been previously confined. The cell door opened directly on the outside yard by an iron door, a small yard. It was a flagged cell. The plank bed permanently fixed opposite the door at a distance of about 8 feet from the door. The cell was whitewashed and very badly lighted. The only light was a small aperture of stained glass over the door. The door fitted very badly and unevenly in stone jambs, and, as a consequence, the cell was draughty in the extreme; the ventilators too low down. It was on the morning of the 21st I saw Mr. Mandeville there. He had been there all night, and he was still there when I visited him on the 22nd.

Mr. Harrington.

351. What luxurious diet had he at that time?—Bread and water.

352. Can you tell me what quantity of bread he was allowed during that time?—I think the greatest quantity was 16 ounces for the 24 hours.

353. Ordinarily it would be brown bread?—Yes.

354. Are you aware that a tin left in a cell of that kind with water in it for a day would be likely to rust?—Unless the tin was enamelled.

355. Read extract of 21st December?—"21st December. Found Mr. Mandeville in his punishment cell undergoing a sentence of 48 hours of bread and water and solitary confinement. He complained that he was brought before the prison resident magistrate, Mr. Heath, yesterday evening, and charged with a breach of prison rules in refusing to clean out his cell, which he acknowledged, and was sentenced to 48 hours close confinement on bread and water. He said he protested against the magistrate as not being a county justice of the peace or a member of the committee of visiting justices, but a paid Government official; also that his case was then *sub judice*, having complained to the visiting committee, but did not receive an answer. He replied he was satisfied he had power to act. He said he complained of the cold and draught in his cell, and that he slept very little in consequence of it. He said, 'My rheumatism is worse this morning. I complained to the prison doctor and said it was no place to send me. He did not examine me and did not prescribe for me. My feet are famished, walking in slippers on the cold flags. I have had these sentences seven times, and have been ill on each occasion afterwards from three to six days.'"

Mr. Harrington.

356. Now, Doctor, I will ask you for your opinion as to the effect of that treatment on a man's constitution?—I think, with regard to the treatment, it is calculated to undermine the constitution of the strongest man.

357. Is

Mr. *Harrington*, M.P.—continued.

357. Is it your opinion, Doctor, that it undermined and injured his constitution?—I have no doubt it did.

358. Mr. Mandeville said to you that he had complained to the visiting committee?—Yes.

359. As to his being relieved of the duty of cleansing his cell?—Yes.

360. Did he tell you that no answer was given to his application before the resident magistrate adjudicated on his case?—He did.

361. The resident magistrate was not a member of the visiting committee?—No.

362. Did you know the members of the visiting committee?—I did.

363. Was Mr. Ridley a member of the visiting committee?—He was.

364. Does he live near Tullamore?—He lives in the town.

365. You visited again on the 22nd?—Yes.

366. You know as a matter of fact he was released on the 21st?—Yes.

367. And you know that this punishment was within a few days of his release?—Yes.

Cross-examined by Mr. *Murphy*, Q.C.

368. How long are you a visiting justice?—About two years.

369. Did you up to November 1887 exercise your functions as such?—No, never.

370. How did you become aware that you were entitled to go in on the first day you went to the prison?—I got no information whatsoever. I merely thought I was entitled to go there.

371. You said a while ago you did not know you had a right as a justice of the county?—Certainly.

372. When did you find out that you had that right?—I went to see Mr. O'Brien.

373. What suggested to your mind the fact that you had a right, as justice of the county, to go into the prison?—I do not know.

374. Is it a fact that you did not know up to the 3rd of November that you had a right, as a justice of the peace, to go into the prison?—I did not know it.

375. Did anybody give you any information on the subject prior to the 3rd or 4th of November?—No.

376. You went on the 7th, and you told us you found Mr. O'Brien and Mr. Mandeville, Mr. O'Brien in one cell and Mr. Mandeville in the other?—Yes.

377. There was a plank bed and no mattress?—Not that I saw.

378. At any time did you observe a mattress in Mr. Mandeville's cell?—(*No answer.*)

379. Will you undertake to say that upon any of your visits there was no mattress?—On those days of punishment there would be no mattress in the cell.

380. Do you mean to convey by that that the man never got a bed or anything of that sort?—(*No answer.*)

381. You observed that they were all flagged cells; are you aware that there is nothing else in prisons but flagged cells; in this prison are there any but flagged cells?—I never saw any but flagged cells.

382. Have you gone through every division of the prison?—No.

Mr. *Murphy*, Q.C.—continued.

383. How many of them have you visited?—A great portion along the side of the infirmary.

384. Did you observe whether the cell floors were covered in any way?—Yes.

385. What is the covering?—Fibre, cocoanut fibre.

386. On every occasion you were in Mr. Mandeville's cell was it covered with matting?—I understand it was.

387. You did not expect to see Brussels carpet there?—No.

388. The governor informed you that you were restricted to certain questions?—Yes.

389. Did you satisfy yourself that that was a statutable provision?—I did.

390. You were also aware that you were not entitled to visit the prison, except in presence of one of the prison officials?—Yes, I think so.

391. You never made any medical examination of Mr. Mandeville during his imprisonment?—No.

392. You knew by the provision of the statute you were not entitled to interfere?—Yes.

393. You never had an opportunity of making such an examination as a physician would in reference to this attack of diarrhœa?—No.

394. Except from statements of Mr. Mandeville to you, you never had an opportunity of judging what his condition was?—Yes, those statements coupled with the appearance of the man.

395. Would you know without examination whether a man had diarrhœa or not?—You might infer from his appearance, coupled with his statement.

396. Could you form an opinion as to the condition of his throat without any medical examination?—No. I had no reason to doubt his statements from his appearance.

397. Would a man with full habits, and who led an active life, suddenly transferred to prison, be likely to get a blanched appearance?—I never noticed a very blanched appearance on Mr. Mandeville. I observed a blueness in his colour.

398. Did you not tell me you drew your conclusion from what he told you, and from his blanched appearance?—(*Not answered.*)

399. When did you make this manuscript that you produced here to-day; did you make it in Mr. Mandeville's presence, and afterwards put it in the book?—I wrote it first on some sheets of paper, and afterwards in the book.

400. There were several newspaper correspondents in Tullamore about that time?—There were a great many.

401. Did you know them all?—No.

402. Did you know any of them?—I did.

403. Which of them did you know?—Some of them called on me; I knew the "Freeman" reporter, but I did not know him till he called on me.

404. When did he call on you first; did he call on you soon after your first visit?—That day.

405. Did he call on you on several subsequent days?—He did.

406. Did you always communicate to him the purport of any note you made in the prison book?—No, but I did it on some occasions.

(Mr.

Mr. *Murphy*, R.L.—continued.

(Mr. Harrington here objected to Mr. Murphy's questions. Mr. Murphy said he would proceed with his cross-examination till stopped.)

407. Did you see the purport of these communications recorded every morning in the "*Freeman*"?—I suppose I did.

408. Did you also send the purport of these notes to anybody else?—I may have.

409. Did you send them away yourself by post or otherwise?——

The *MacDermot*, Q.C., here objected, and said these documents being in writing they could be only evidence themselves.

Mr. *Murphy* said in that case he should ask for an adjournment of the inquiry so as to have the documents produced.

The *MacDermot* withdrew his objection, and the cross-examination proceeded.

410. By Mr. *Murphy*.] Did you send the purport of these notes to any person other than to a correspondent of the "*Freeman*"?—I may have; I swear that at the present moment I cannot say.

411. Did you send them to anybody else?—I may have.

412. Did you?—I probably did.

The *Coroner*.] I think if you performed that duty you were bound to let the public know all about it.

The *MacDermot*.] It was the duty of everyone to make the public aware of these things.

Cross-examination resumed.

413. When you visited Mr. Mandeville, what questions did you put to him?—As a rule they were in the stereotyped order.

414. Did you ever suggest anything to him in this way: "Have you been suffering from diarrhoea"?—No, I think not.

415. Have you examined the prison dietary?—Yes.

416. And you saw the dietary for ordinary prisoners under circumstances such as Mr. Mandeville was?—Yes.

417. And you know whether there is a large number of prisoners in Tullamore gaol?—I do not know; I believe there are.

418. How many prisoners have you visited upon a day there?—I have visited 15 or 18.

419. Were they male prisoners?—Yes.

420. And they appeared to be in ordinary health on the diet they were getting?—Well, fairly.

421. The ordinary diet is such as would keep an ordinary man in fair health?—Well, a man who was not accustomed to luxuries, it would keep him well.

422. And, of course, Dr. Moorhead, we all know that a man who has a repugnance to prison food, the necessary result must be that he will lose weight to some extent?—Yes.

423. Do you attribute any delicacy you observed in Mr. Mandeville to prison diet; that is in connection with close confinement?—I attribute it to punishment diet, close confinement, deprivation of exercise, and general prison surroundings.

424. Do you attribute in any special degree the delicacy you noticed in Mr. Mandeville to the punishment system?—It was a large factor in his delicacy.

425. And the absence of this punishment would have diminished to a considerable extent the development of these symptoms?—I would say so.

426. Of course you are aware that if he conformed to the prison rules no punishment would be inflicted on him?—Yes.

427. When you first saw him in prison he looked like a man who could go through a considerable amount of hardship?—Yes; a strong man.

428. Do you think the observance of the ordinary prison rules would have injured his health in any way?—I do not think it would have undermined his constitution.

429. When was the last occasion on which he complained to you of any delicacy or affection of his throat?—About 10 days before he was discharged.

430. You never saw Mr. Mandeville after he was discharged?—I did on the occasion of Mr. O'Brien's release in January.

431. You never saw him afterwards?—No.

432. Do you know how the prison is heated?—It is heated by hot water.

433. What do you consider a reasonable temperature to live in?—About 60 degrees.

434. Do you not think for a big man 60 would be inconvenient at times?—I consider 60 a regular temperature.

435. Mr. Mandeville did not consult with you as to his health when leaving the prison?—No.

436. Nor upon the occasion of his subsequent visit to Tullamore?—No.

437. Do you know what the process is of exercising prisoners in these yards?—Yes, walking exercise.

438. The prisoners walk round the yards?—Yes.

439. And are not in close contact?—No.

440. At considerable distance between?—Yes.

441. Are you aware whether there is a warder there to prevent any communication?—Yes, I have always seen a warder.

442. So there is no contact between them in those yards?—No.

443. They do not walk near each other?—No, they are about 10 or 15 yards apart.

444. Have you been in the prison frequently since Mr. O'Brien and Mr. Mandeville left it?—Yes.

445. You do not go there every day?—No.

446. Or once a week?—I was there on last week.

447. What prisoners did you see on that occasion?—I think Mr. O'Brien, of Cappoquin, and Mr. Byrne.

448. You do not go there unless there are special prisoners?—Well, I have nothing to do with ordinary prisoners.

449. Do you think the "class" diet laid down for ordinary prisoners very fair?—I do.

450. I suppose you have no doubt if they persist in disobeying the rules they will be subjected to the same course as Mr. Mandeville?—No.

THIRD DAY.

Thursday, 19th *July* 1888.

Dr. Edward M'Craith, Mitchelstown; Examined.

The *MacDermot*, Q.C.

451. *Witness.*] I am a physician and surgeon.

452. Have you been for many years practising as such?—Yes.

453. How many years?—For many years I was practising in Cork.

454. I believe, doctor, you are the doctor of the dispensary?—Yes.

455. And, I think, also doctor of the constabulary?—Yes.

456. Did you know the late John Mandeville?—Yes, for a number of years.

457. For how many years did you know him, doctor?—I don't know exactly; in fact, since I came to reside here he was an intimate friend of mine.

458. During that time you had frequent opportunities of seeing him; was he a strong man?—He was, I would say, a very strong, able man, of fine physique.

459. Was he healthy?—Yes, up to the time he went to prison he was healthy.

Mr. *Murphy*.] He said up to his last illness he was healthy.

460. Did you see him while in prison?

Mr. *Murphy*.] With great respect the doctor said, up to his last illness he was healthy.

The *MacDermot*.] Up to his last illness he was healthy?

Witness.] Yes.

461. You did not see him in prison?—No.

462. How long before he went to prison did you see him?—I saw him in Mitchelstown the day he and Mr. O'Brien were sentenced to be sent to Cork Gaol, in the police barrack.

463. Up to that day, so far as you can form an opinion, was he a healthy man?—Yes.

464. A strong man?—Yes.

465. Was he a man of joyous temperament or morbid?—Joyous temperament.

466. Did his nervous system appear to you to be strong or feeble?—Strong.

467. Did he consult you medically up to the time he went to prison?—No. He might have occasionally asked me for a couple of pills.

468. He may have asked you for medicine?—Yes, pills, but very rarely.

469. Did he complain to you of any affection of his throat before he went to prison?—No.

470. So far as you know, had he any medical attendant or take medical advice from anybody except yourself?—Not that I am aware of.

471. Was he a sober man?—He was.

The *MacDermot*, Q.C.—continued.

472. I suppose he sometimes dined with you?—Yes, when he came to town he would run in and dine with me.

473. So far as your knowledge went would it be just or unjust to charge him with intemperance?—So far as my knowledge goes it would be unjust to charge him with intemperance.

474. Now, doctor, before I come to the next time you saw him, I want to ask your medical opinion on a few matters. You know what a punishment cell is?—I know, but I have never been in them.

475. Punishment would be bread and water and confinement; would you consider that proper treatment for a patient with diarrhoea?—I would think it very improper.

476. Would you think it proper for a patient who had been nourished as you knew Mr. Mandeville to be, would you think it treatment calculated to produce increased diarrhoea?—Certainly I would.

477. It was stated here in evidence Mr. Mandeville remained without food for 30 hours.

Mr. *Murphy*.] Who stated that?

The *MacDermot*.] It was stated by his wife and Dr. Moorhead.

478. (*To Witness*.) I am not trying to alter the evidence that was given, I am only asking your opinion; but assuming that Mr. Mandeville remained without food for 30 hours, when he refused to take bread-and-water diet, when he used a rope, tightening it around his waist, to enable him to bear the pangs of hunger.

Mr. *Murphy*.] Don't answer, doctor.

The *MacDermot*.] Assuming; I will not ask you, is it so.

Mr. *Murphy*.] I object.

479. The question I ask you on that assumption, would such a state of things be injurious to the health and constitution of Mr. Mandeville?

Mr. *Murphy*.] I object to that question, and I ask you to take a note of my objection.

The *MacDermot*.] And I ask you to take a note of it; it is one of those questions it is better to object to. Assuming that state of things to have taken place is the question.

Mr. *Murphy*.] The question is, would all this be injurious to the constitution of Mr. Mandeville as known to you?

The

The *MacDermot*, Q.C.—continued.

The *Coroner*.] You are entitled to get a medical opinion. You are entitled to get the opinion.

Witness.] It would have an injurious effect on any man.

480. Assuming that Mr. Mandeville was suffering from sore throat.

Mr. Murphy.] I object to this question.

The *Coroner*.] I have the assumption, but have not heard the question yet.

481. Assuming Mr. Mandeville was suffering from a sore throat and occasionally from diarrhœa, would remaining for about 24 hours in his cell without any covering except such as was afforded by a sheet and quilt, with his chest bare, his legs bare, his throat bare, in this cell in the winter season, would this be calculated to injure his constitution and undermine his health.

Mr. Murphy.] I object.

The *MacDermot*.] Put down objection from Mr. Murphy.

Mr. Murphy.] I say that there is no evidence.

The *MacDermot*.] Not if what was stated in the presence of the governor is not evidence.

The *Coroner*.] Although there is no evidence given I may receive this, as there may be evidence.

482 (To *Witness*.) Would it damage his constitution and undermine his health; I only ask you opinion about it?—It would.

483. Assuming that Mr. Mandeville was confined on the 20th December at night of the 20th December in a punishment cell, on a plank bed, the bed being opposite an iron door within three feet of it; the door opening in the outer air; the stone jambs being uneven and badly fitted in; the draft coming in so that the prisoner found it difficult to sleep; would that be suitable treatment for a prisoner suffering from rheumatism and sore throat, and fed on bread and water. Would that be suitable treatment?

Mr. Murphy objected to the question, and his objection was entered on the depositions.

The question was allowed.

484. (To *Witness*.) Would it be calculated to injure his health?—In my opinion it would be calculated to injure his health.

485. Doctor, in your opinion, would it be calculated to give a shock to the nervous system a number of warders arousing a man from his sleep and engaging him in a struggle for the clothes. Would it be likely to give a shock to his nervous system.

Mr. Murphy objected to the question.

Witness.] Most certainly it would if he resisted.

486. Well, now tell me one other question on that head and I will pass from it. Do you consider it would be injurious to the health of Mr. Mandeville as a matter of hygiene to have to remain for 24 hours in a cell uncleansed.

Mr. Murphy objected.

Witness.] It would in a hygienic sense.

487. How soon after he left Tullamore Prison did you see Mr. Mandeville?—I suppose a couple of days after coming down here, perhaps the next day. I took no note of it.

488. You saw him a few days after?—Yes.

489. Did he seem to you as healthy as he used to be?—He did not.

490. Did his nervous system appear to you to be the same?—At that time I did not observe his nervous system; that was the first few days after.

491. Later on did you?—Later on I did by his asking something from me, I did notice that he was in a low, nervous, excitable state.

492. Mrs. Mandeville stated, as a matter of fact, that for a month after he came out he could scarcely write, though he formerly wrote a good hand, his hand trembled; would that indicate damage to his nervous system?—Certainly.

493. Inability to write from trembling of the hand would indicate injury to his nervous system?—Yes.

494. It was proved, as a matter of fact, that his sight had grown feeble; what would that indicate?—Affection of the nervous system.

495. It was stated by the same lady that her husband found it difficult to carry his outside coat and boots as in former times?—That would indicate physical debility and loss of strength.

496. It was also stated as a fact by Mr. O'Brien and Mrs. Mandeville that they observed a bluish tint about the lips; would that indicate that his blood had been rendered less normal?—It would show that his blood had got into an abnormal state.

497. Would it show that the circulation of his blood had been impaired?—It would show that something had gone wrong with the circulation of his blood.

498. Did you observe, doctor, whether Mr. Mandeville, between the time he left prison and his death, seemed to have lost size and weight?—I remarked to him that he had grown thin. He pulled out his vest and said yes, showing the space between his vest and his body.

499. What would that loss of weight in a man of his constitution as you are acquainted with indicate?—It indicates loss of muscular strength and the nervous system being injured.

500. Now, doctor, were you consulted by him in any way medically, or as a friend after he left prison?—He came to me as a friend one day, I should suppose about a month or six weeks previous to his death, complaining of a sore throat.

501. Did you then examine his throat?—I did not examine it, but I gave him a gargle.

502. You think he may have come twice to you?—I think he might, but I am not sure. He subsequently came to me and asked for a cough mixture, which I gave him. He sent back the bottle and had it repeated.

503. Now,

The MacDermot, Q.C.—continued.

503. Now, with that exception, did you prescribe for him before he died?—No.

504. Or furnish him with any medicine?—No.

505. Now, doctor, did he personally consult you during the week before he died; did he come to you?—He came to my house.

506. Do you remember what day that was?—It was between two and three o'clock on Friday the 6th July. He drove up to my house in a covered car; I saw him pass the window and I went out and opened the door for him; he came in wrapped up in a large frieze coat up to his ears, and a muffler besides around him. I opened the door for him, and I said, "John, what is the matter with you?" He replied that "he got a sore throat and could not open his mouth." I then took him into the surgery and found no enlargement of the glands in the neck, and getting my finger into his mouth I pressed his tongue with my finger and saw the pharynx swollen, red, and congested. I found the voice husky. I said, "You are very sick and should not have come out to-day." I then gave him a draught and some gargle, recommended him to go home at once, to use the gargle frequently, apply hot stupes to his throat of bran and warm water, and to inhale the steam of warm water, to go to bed early, to put his feet in warm water and take a sweating draught, and to take fluid nourishment in the shape of beef-tea, and to let me know in the morning how he would feel.

507. Now, doctor, were you sent for early next morning?—Next morning about seven o'clock a covered car drove up to my house. I got up and dressed. The man told me he was worse. I proceeded to his house and found him worse. He could not articulate. I could not understand what he was saying. The glands of the neck hard and swollen. I said it would be advisable in my opinion to apply leeches, but that I would not undertake to do anything unless I had another doctor with me, because seeing his state I got uneasy; I would not undertake to apply the leeches without the assistance of another medical man. I drove back to town at once and brought out Dr. O'Neill with me and two leeches which I had. He made me apply the leeches at once. I gave him three teaspoonsful of salts before applying the leeches. I had to put it down with a spoon; he could not open his mouth. It was then proposed to get more leeches, and Mr. O'Gorman sent for them to Fermoy. I think it was Dr. O'Neill suggested it. We came downstairs and Mr. James O'Gorman there asked me would it be advisable to send for a Cork doctor. I said by all means; Mr. Mandeville is well known in the political world.

508. That will do; you telegraphed for him?—I came into town and telegraphed for Dr. Cremen.

509. Could you say about what time he arrived?—He arrived about half-past three o'clock, the leeches had arrived in the meantime. At about 12.30 I went out and found him worse and the tongue swollen. That was about one o'clock; I applied two leeches under the tongue and the other four around the neck externally.

510. Well, what hour do you say Dr. Cremen arrived?—Dr. Cremen arrived about half-past three.

511–12. The whole three of you then met there?—Yes, and we there had a consultation. Dr. Cremen had a very unfavourable opinion of him. We tested his urine and found albumen in it. We administered to him tincture of iron and chlorate of potash and another sweating mixture.

513. Did Dr. Cremen approve of the treatment you gave him?—Yes, I told him exactly the history of what I did, and he approved of it.

514. Well, what happened next?—We then went away. Dr. Cremen went home to Cork, Dr. O'Neill came to town and came back about nine o'clock. We recommended beef-tea and nourishment to support the system, and a little brandy and water and hot steam to be inhaled, and besides quinine to be applied to the throat. We then left and came home. We went out again at seven in the morning. We found him in the same state and continued the same treatment. I may mention that after the application of the leeches to the tongue they reduced it temporarily. We went out again after mass about one o'clock. We still found no improvement; in fact, worse. Dr. O'Neill and I had to go a few miles farther on, and when we returned in about an hour we found him dead.

515. You never saw him again alive?—No.

The Coroner.

516. Were you present when the jury viewed the body?—I was.

517. Whose body was that?—It was the body of John Mandeville.

The MacDermot.

518. Now, doctor, what was the immediate cause of death?—Failure of the heart's action was the immediate cause.

519. Arising from what?—From a diffused septic inflammation of the glands.

520. Did that septic inflammation amount to poisoning of the blood?—Yes.

521. Was there a secondary symptom again of the albumen?—Yes, there was albuminuria as a secondary symptom. I may mention that on Saturday night or Sunday morning I punctured with an exploring needle the pharynx and there was a mixture of blood and matter came from it.

522. Now, you were saying that when Dr. Cremen was there in consultation, you there came to the conclusion that if the swelling increased to endanger suffocation, you were to scarify?—If he was threatened during the night by swelling we were to lance it with a knife so as to prevent suffocation. The operation was performed with the exploring needle and gave him relief.

523. Well, doctor, you knew Mr. Mandeville before he went to prison, and you saw him after he came from prison?—Yes.

524. And I have already drawn your attention to a good many matters. What is your medical opinion as to what was the cause, I am not talking of the immediate cause, but what was the cause that led to the death of Mr. Mandeville?—I should

The MacDermot, Q.C.—continued.

I should say the first cause was the lowering of his nervous and physical system from the treatment received in prison, by the change of the normal condition of his previous life. He was used to good food, pure air, and good exercise. He was rendered more susceptible of getting disease, and less able to resist it.

525. Then I understand you to say the lowering of the vital powers renders the patient more liable to disease and less able to resist it?—Yes.

526. Now, from what you knew of Mr. Mandeville before he went to prison and from what you saw of him after he came from prison, and the circumstances and cause of his death, in your opinion, as a medical man, having a medical knowledge of Mr. Mandeville, would Mr. Mandeville have been alive now if he never went to Tullamore Prison?—In my opinion as a medical man, knowing his general history, and the circumstances of his death, in the natural course of events, he would be alive now. It is the treatment in Tullamore Prison I am taking into account, and the hardships he was exposed to.

527. Doctor, there is one question I omitted to ask you. On any of the occasions you saw him after he left prison, did he wear glasses?—I saw him once or twice in the street and I was astonished to see him with glasses, and a muffler around his throat. That was about a couple of months before his death. On two occasions I saw him with the muffler, and on the first occasion I saw him with the glasses. I said, "John, why are you wearing those blue glasses?" He replied that his sight got weakened in Tullamore Gaol.

528. You said you were surprised at his wearing his muffler?—Yes, because he appeared to be a good strong man, and I was astonished to see him wearing a muffler.

529. Could you form any opinion, doctor, as to whether the germ of the throat disease was formed or contracted?—I don't know, except in Tullamore. What I intended to say is, that the germ of the disease was contracted when he was exposed in the cold cells. In my opinion it was there the throat got affected for want of warm clothing and exposure to draughts.

530. Do you consider want of proper food would also render him more susceptible to this; would it be increased by the want of proper cleansing of the cell and proper hygienic conditions?—Yes.

531. Would you consider, doctor, a post-mortem examination necessary?—No.

The Coroner.

532. In your treatment of the disease, did you apply the best medical skill that your knowledge would furnish?—I did, and that treatment was concurred in by the other doctors.

Cross-examined by Mr. *Murphy*.

533. Now, doctor, you are a physician; what diploma do you hold?—The diploma of the Royal College of Surgeons and Physicians, Edinburgh, and the diploma of the Apothecaries' Hall of Ireland.

534. I presume you got the Apothecaries'

Mr. *Murphy*—continued.

diploma before you got the other?—No, subsequently. I served my time to an apothecary in 1849 and 1850.

535. When did you get this diploma from the Apothecaries' Hall?—I forget the year.

536. When did you get the diploma in Edinburgh?—I could not exactly tell you; I think in 1854. I was never regularly practising as an apothecary. Having completed my medical education in Ireland, I then went and took out the other diplomas.

537. Your diplomas in medicine and surgery, are they got for attending at the school or by passing an examination?—By regular terms; you must attend such a number of sessions in Edinburgh, or elsewhere.

538. Did you take out any in Edinburgh?—I did, and in Cork.

539. After getting your diplomas, where did you go?—To the East.

540. You had been there previously?—I had.

541. What were you at?—I was acting as assistant in Smyrna and at Ephesus.

The Coroner.

542. Your brother is a physician there of known eminence?—He is. I may tell you that I had charge of 8,000 men there.

543. When did you return?—It is a good many years ago.

544. Did you settle down in Mitchelstown?—Not immediately, but I came back to Mitchelstown and settled down about 14 years ago.

Mr. *Murphy*.

545. When did you become dispensary doctor of Mitchelstown?—I am dispensary doctor about 18 years; I have a dispensary for my own private use.

546. You saw Mr. Mandeville after returning from prison?—Yes.

547. You remember the day he returned?—Yes, it was some time in or before Christmas.

548. You are aware he made a speech in Mitchelstown about that time?—I heard he did. I passed by a back lane and saw a number of people, and was told Mr. Mandeville was speaking.

549. That was the 26th of December?—I don't know. It was in December.

550. Immediately after he came down he delivered an address here; was it on the square?—I heard he spoke from Ahern's window. It is on the square.

551. If a man had any delicacy of the throat do you think speaking in the open air in December would assist to relieve it or to develop it?—It would not benefit it.

552. I suppose you are aware, doctor, that speaking in the open air is rather trying upon anybody's throat?—If you have a sore throat and speak for any time it won't serve it.

553. Are you aware of any other occasion he made an open air speech in Mitchelstown?—I don't know.

554. You never heard him speak yourself?—I did, but it was previous to his incarceration.

555. Are you aware of what Mr. Mandeville's practices were with regard to going about the country?—No. I would frequently knock

against

Mr. *Murphy*—continued.

against him in the town, but anywhere about the town at meetings I have never met him.

556. You don't know whether he used to attend meetings in other parts of the country or not? - I don't know.

557. If a man had a sore throat would the fact that he was out at a late hour of the night in such seasons of the year, would it tend to develop the disease?—It would not benefit it. It would be owing to certain conditions.

558. A man driving on an outside car in winter labouring under some delicacy of the throat, would that have a tendency to develop rapidly any disease of the throat?—It would, if he did not take precautions to have himself well muffled, he would have a tendency certainly to take the disease.

559. And a disease of that sort, would it not develop very rapidly?—It may or may not. It depends on circumstances.

560. In what class would you place the disease from which Mr. Mandeville ultimately died?—Diffused septic inflammation.

561. Now, what do you mean by septic inflammation?—Poisoning of the blood. It is like diphtheria.

562. Are you well versed in this theory of disease?—No; I am not in the germ theory of disease.

563. Was Mr. Mandeville up to the occasion of his last illness suffering from specific or inflammatory disease?—Inflammatory.

564. As distinguished from specific; do you know what I mean?—No. He was suffering from inflammatory disease.

565. Then you cannot tell me whether he was suffering from a specific disease or not?—It was specific inasmuch as it was poisoning.

566. But if you remark, there is a difference between specific and inflammatory; can you tell me which Mr. Mandeville died of?—Inflammatory.

567. You have stated that you attribute the germ of the disease of which Mr. Mandeville died to be acquired in Tullamore?—Yes.

568. Upon your oath, do you mean to say that inflammatory diseases arise from a germ?—I don't know. The origin I say.

569. What do you mean by the origin?—I mean that by the way he was treated in prison, his nervous system undermined, his muscular system undermined, his physical strength undermined; thereby lowering the debility and affecting his whole constitution, which rendered him afterwards very susceptible of disease with very little power of resistance; when the system is in that state it won't resist disease.

570. Did you mean to convey that he had the germs of throat disease when you gave that answer to Mr. M'Dermott that he got the germs of throat disease in Tullamore?—I mean as to his having suffered from sore throat in prison left the throat in a state very likely to become sore again from any excitement.

571. Do you know anything as to whether he had a sore throat in prison or not?—I don't know.

572. When did you form the opinion that it was attributable to his having suffered from a sore throat in prison?—When I heard the evidence given here. I only formed the opinion on the evidence.

573. If a man were suffering or labouring under a delicacy of the throat do you think he could with impunity have travelled much at night in the open air in winter?—No; without wearing a muffler. With a muffler I should suppose he could have done it safely.

574. With the risk of a wetting?—Oh, that would be different.

575. Would he run the extreme danger of constantly getting this affection if he was driving about at night in winter with the risk of a wetting and other things that a man incurs in winter?—He would run the risk of developing a disease already existing if not protected by a muffler or something to heat the air before entering the mouth.

576. I presume the risk would be greater the shorter the interval between the attack in the prison and the exposure to the open air?—The more dangerous, the more would be the risk.

577. Have you ever known, in the course of your experience, an affection of the throat such as this develop in a man rapidly who never had been affected by throat disease before?—I did.

578. I suppose the cold air of a December or January night would have a greater tendency to develop the pre-existing tendency than the air of a June or July night?—Certainly.

579. Or the east winds of March or April?—Yes.

580. Are the east winds prevalent here in the spring?—I could not say.

581. Did you ever treat a case similar to that which Mr. Mandeville was suffering from before?—I had one case somewhat similar.

582. Was it in Mitchelstown you treated it?—No; it was in the district.

583. How long ago?—I think it was last October or November. It was not exactly the same in every detail; the man went to death's door.

584. Before that particular attack did you ever treat a case for throat disease before?—No.

585. So far as you know that particular attack was the first occurrence?—Yes.

586. As I understand, it is not an unusual thing for acute throat inflammation to occur to a man who has never had any delicacy of the throat before?—Oh, constantly.

587. It is not an unfrequent occurrence?—No.

588. You knew Mr. Mandeville very well, and from the time he returned from prison you saw him going about as he had been going about before?—Just the same.

589. You told me you observed he was a little reduced in flesh; previously he was a very large man?—He was a very large man in physique.

590. You are aware that such men are anxious to take down their weight?—Sometimes.

Mr.

Mr. *Murphy*—continued.

Mr. *Harrington*, M.P.] Not on bread and water.

Mr. Murphy.

591. Was he rather reduced before he went to prison?—He was.

592. That may be reduced without danger to a man's health?—Yes, by air and exercise.

593. Surely the development of fat in the system won't tend to reduce him?—No.

594. He did not consult you after he came out of prison, professionally?—No.

595. Nor as a friend?—No.

596. You met him constantly?—Yes.

597. Was he in your house?—He was.

598-9. Mr. Mandeville was in the habit of going to your house?—After leaving prison; not very frequently, perhaps once a week or once a fortnight. I would say once a fortnight.

600. Independent of that you met him every day?—Not every day.

601. He was frequently in your house, and you and he were great friends?—Great friends.

602. Were you the medical attendant of his family?—No, he had no family except his wife and brother.

603. Up to the time that you have mentioned that you gave him this gargle he never mentioned to you that he was suffering from any throat disease?—No, he was a reticent man.

604. What was the date of his coming to you in reference to this sore throat?—I could not fix the date, because he came as a friend; I gave him a gargle, and subsequently gave a bottle.

605. Did you charge him for the gargle?—No.

606. Consequently, you have no entry of it?—No; it was about a month or six weeks before his death.

607. You subsequently gave him a cough bottle?—Yes.

608. Have you any entry of that?—No, I gave it as a friend.

609. Did you ascertain had he a cough?—He told me so.

610. Did you examine him?—No; for the cough I gave him some spirits of chloroform and other things. It was about a fortnight afterwards I gave him the cough mixture.

611. Was it in your own house he asked for the cough mixture?—It was.

612. You made no examination of him then?—No.

613. Did you ascertain what the nature of his cough was?—No, I simply gave him a cough bottle.

614. Did you think it important to ascertain if the cough was coming from the irritation of the throat for which you gave him a gargle before?—I did not.

615. Did you ascertain in any way the nature of the cough you were prescribing for or what it proceeded from?—No.

616. Did he on that occasion complain of any ill-treatment in Tullamore?—No.

617. You had never, except the few pills you gave him occasionally, any professional intercourse with him until Friday, the 6th July?—No.

Mr. *Murphy*—continued.

618. Do you keep a supply of those pills on hands?—Of course I do.

619. Any fellow who goes in for a pill you have them ready?—Oh, no; there is no druggist in town, and the doctors here keep their own medicines.

620. On the 6th July, about two o'clock, he came to your place?—Yes.

621. You took him into the surgery?—Yes.

622. You had good light there?—Yes.

623. You examined his throat?—As well as I could.

624. Did you observe any swelling?—The glands both sides.

625. And under the chin?—Yes.

626. And inflammation was fast setting in?—Yes.

627. Was there considerable swelling under the chin?—No.

628. Was there considerable swelling of the glands of the throat?—Not considerable.

629. Were they hard?—They were hard, and getting hard.

630. You opened his mouth?—I opened his mouth so that I might look as well as I possibly could with the light.

631. He turned himself to the light?—Yes.

632. He experienced a difficulty, then, in opening his mouth?—Yes.

633. How did you get his mouth open?—By putting my finger in and depressing the tongue.

634. Was the tongue swollen at that time?—No, it may be swollen a little; there was a smell from his breath, a strong smell.

635. This smell that you observed from his breath, would that indicate the existence of inflammation for some time before?—No, it would not.

636. Tell me, when you depressed the tongue, the portions of the throat and mouth you were able to observe?—I saw the pharynx.

637. Behind that were you able to see?—No, I saw the uvula.

638. The whole of it?—Yes.

639. Now, unless the tongue was considerably swollen, would you not see much farther back than that?—I could not open the mouth.

640. You did not try, at all events?—I did not use more force than was necessary.

641. Would it not have been easier for the patient to have used the handle of a spoon than your finger?—I think not.

642. Was not it necessary that you should see clearly what was the matter before you treated it?—What I saw was sufficient to know that the mischief was there.

643. Could you by introducing anything else besides your finger have seen more of the throat than you did?—I don't think I could.

644. The introduction of no other instrument would have enabled you to see more of the throat behind?—I don't think so.

645. Did not you think it was necessary for you to make a fuller diagnosis of his case before you treated him?—I don't think so; I saw enough to guide me.

646. You said the pharynx was red and congested?—Yes.

647. Was there swelling of the pharynx?—There was.

Mr. *Murphy*—continued.

648. Did you observe it?—I did.

649. You gave him a gargle?—Yes.

650. What did that gargle consist of?—Borax and decoction of bark.

651. Was that the same gargle you used previously?—Yes, I find it very useful in all affections of the throat.

652. When you gave him that gargle what portions of the throat did you observe affected?—The pharynx.

653. You are dealing with a particular affection of the throat; tell me what portions of the throat you thought were affected?—The pharynx and palate all round.

654. Did you suppose at that time that the tonsils were affected?—Something struck me that there might be a beginning of inflammation of the tonsils.

655. And you considered that when you were administering this gargle?—Yes, because the voice was husky.

656. You know a disease called tonsillitis?—Yes.

Mr. *Harrington.*] I think I see a gentleman here who should be above lending himself to this, an English doctor.

Mr. *Murphy.*] I think the remark is very unseemly, to say the least of it.

657. (To *Witness.*) You say there are two sorts of tonsillitis?—Yes.

658. Did you suppose you were treating Mr. Mandeville for tonsillitis?—No; for the general inflammatory state that was there.

659. You were not treating him for tonsillitis?—Not for simple tonsillitis.

660. Did you form any opinion as to the time, doctor, which he had been suffering from the effects you observed in his throat?—I should think, judging now, that it might have been a couple of days that the first inflammation was observed.

661. When you made the examination at two o'clock on Friday the 6th, did you form any opinion as to what standing this inflammatory tendency was?—About two days, I am inclined to believe, at least. It may have been more or less.

662. I suppose the use of a gargle requires certain muscular action of the throat?—Certainly.

663. Did you think his throat was in a proper condition for it when you gave it to him?—Certainly.

664. You sent him home?—I told him to go home at once; I think I told him to go to bed. I told him to go home, to put his feet in warm water, and to inhale the steam of hot water.

665. What effect did you think the inhaling of hot water would have on him?—A soothing effect.

666. You are not sure that you told him to go to bed at once, or to go to bed early?—I am not sure.

667. You did not see him until the next morning?—No.

668. Did you consider the case a serious one on Friday?—I did not know; something struck me there was something peculiar in the case, but I did not then think it serious.

669. Did you ask him whether he had been subjected to any exposure?—No.

Mr. *Murphy*—continued.

670. Or did you inquire what could be the possible cause of this?—It struck me that it should be cold or chill, or some exciting cause, but I could not say.

671. Is not it usual in the profession to ascertain the cause of a case of this sort?—Well, he was a reticent man, and I did not ask him.

672. You did not ask him whether he had been subjected to any exposure, or try to ascertain the approximate cause of this affection?—No.

673. Is not it usual for a physician dealing with a case of that kind to ascertain how the cause was brought about?—Well, I would not like to ask an old friend, were you out last night, were you drinking last night?

674. You don't think it would insult a man to ask him did he get a wetting?—No.

675. Is not it usual in a case of the sort for the physician to ascertain the approximate cause of the affection from which they are suffering?—It generally takes place. It is usual.

The *Coroner.*

676. You first told us that he came and asked you himself; why did not you ask him?—I did not like to be throwing a doubt upon a man as to whether he got a wetting or was out last night.

677. You knew the man?—Oh, well.

678. And his habits?—Yes.

Mr. *Murphy.*

679. A wetting, if he got it within a few days before, might be the approximate cause of this disease?—Oh, certainly.

680. Did you think it would insult or offend any man if you asked him if he got a wetting?—It did not strike me.

681. You saw him the next morning, on Saturday?—Yes.

682. At what time?—About eight o'clock.

683. Was he in bed?—He was.

684. Did you examine his throat that morning?—I merely felt the throat, and seeing the state he was in I then proposed to bring up Dr. O'Neill.

685. You felt his throat, you told us?—Yes.

686. Did you look at it as well?—No.

687. You felt the glands of the throat; were they much more swollen than the previous day?—They were to a marked extent, and harder.

688. Did you observe that he was much more swollen under the chin?—I did not.

689. You did not examine that part?—I felt it and found it hard.

690. That was not its normal condition?—Oh, certainly no.

691. Was there a marked increase in the dangerous symptoms?—No.

692. Was it more than the previous day?—It was perceptibly more.

693. Under the lower jaw and chin?—Yes, the glands at both sides and under the jaw.

694. You then went for Dr. O'Neill?—Yes, and the instructions I gave him he obeyed and carried out to the letter.

695. You came to the conclusion he was worse?—Yes.

696. In a marked degree?—On the third morning he was worse in a marked degree.

697. You

Mr. *Murphy*—continued.

697. You brought Dr. O'Neill?—Yes.

698. What time did you and Dr. O'Neill arrive there?—About nine o'clock.

699. Did you make a more minute diagnosis with Dr. O'Neill?—I then made a more minute examination of the mouth.

700. You say you examined the mouth, what was the condition of that, describe it?—The mouth was all inflamed, and tongue swollen.

701. You could not then see down his throat, I suppose?—I could not.

702. How far back in his mouth could you see?—I could see the pharynx.

703. Did you see the pharynx?—Yes.

704. They were considerably more inflamed?—They were.

705. You had then a consultation with Dr. O'Neill, and as the result of that did you adopt any remedy for the man except two leeches?—The two leeches and steam, and giving him the salts.

706. When you talk of the steam in this connection, do you mean inhaling it as well?—Yes.

707. Then you determined to send for the other leeches to Fermoy?—Yes. Dr. O'Neill's prognosis was unfavourable at that time.

708. Did you consider with Dr. O'Neill whether any surgical operation should be performed?—Oh, no; we considered what was done sufficient under the circumstances.

Mr. *Murphy* (to the *Coroner*).] I have put a specific question, and I want to get a specific answer.

The *Coroner*.] You will have any question answered which you require.

Mr. *Murphy*.

709. (To *Witness*.) Did you discuss directly, or indirectly, the advisability of resorting to a surgical operation at that stage?—No.

710. Did you, in your consultation with Dr. O'Neill, determine to defer the ultimate decision of the course to be taken until Dr. Cremen came?—No. I sent for leeches.

711. Did you agree with Dr. O'Neill that the gentleman was in a dangerous condition at that time?—I was not so much alarmed as he was. We did not entirely agree.

712. Was the suggestion that two leeches should be applied first and four afterwards your suggestion, or Dr. O'Neill's?—I brought out the leeches before Dr. O'Neill had seen the patient.

713. Was not Dr. O'Neill there when you applied the leeches?—Yes.

714. Did you tell Dr. O'Neill you were going to put on the leeches?—Yes; and he agreed with me.

714. Did he agree with you that the application of these leeches was an adequate measure to meet the condition he was in?—He did.

715. Was Mr. James O'Gorman in the room when you applied the leeches?—I think he was.

716. He came down stairs with you?—He did. It was he, when he came downstairs, said, what do you think of sending for Dr. Cremen.

Mr. *Murphy*—continued.

717. You left with Dr. O'Neill and returned about three o'clock?—That was the following day.

718. After you applied the two leeches you came back and applied the six leeches?—In the meantime they had sent for the leeches to Fermoy. Dr. O'Neill and I then went out. At twelve o'clock he got a call and I went out by myself. The inflammatory symptoms of the disease had increased since I was there in the morning about nine o'clock.

719. Had they increased to a marked degree?—The tongue had increased.

720. You then had the six leeches with you?—They were there before me, and I applied them.

721. Did you at that time consider him in a critical condition?—At that time I began to get uneasy.

722. The tongue was more swollen than it was in the morning?—It was.

723. Was the glandular swelling increased?—No.

724. Was there at that time diffusion of matter?—No.

725. You applied two of those leeches under the tongue?—Yes.

726. How did you get them in?—Opened the mouth and put them in.

726. Dr. Cremen then arrived?—Yes; I then applied the other four leeches.

727. Did you consider that that was an adequate step to take in the condition you found him at half-past twelve?—I did.

728. What would be the medical description of the man's condition then?—Suffering from septic diffused inflammation.

729. That was about one o'clock?—Yes.

730. You saw him again when Dr. Cremen arrived?—Yes.

731. And that was about half-past three o'clock?—Yes.

732. You and Dr. O'Neill were there?—Yes.

733. Did Dr. Cremen examine him?—Yes, very minutely.

734. Did he come to the conclusion that it would terminate fatally?—Yes, he did.

735. Did Dr. Cremen say anything at that time as to the advisability of having previously or then or afterwards applied the knife?—Dr. Cremen did say that if during the night any urgent suffocating symptoms should set in that I ought to scarify it; that is, use the knife. He said, send for me if any suffocating symptoms set in, and you are then to scarify it with a knife.

736. Was that said in consultation?—Yes; and I think in the hearing of Mr. Mandeville.

737. Is not it the usual practice with physicians when in consultation to be alone?—Yes; and so we were alone.

738. Did Dr. Cremen suggest the use of the knife in any other case except this suffocating you mentioned?—No.

739. Did you express your readiness to perform that operation if the necessity arose?—I had not the tracheotomy tubes.

740. What were the symptoms that were to justify tracheotomy?—The tongue swells, and he could not breathe.

741. Did Dr. Cremen suggest at all that relief might

Mr. Murphy—continued.

might be obtained by an opening in front under the chin?—No.

742. Did you tell Dr. Cremen if the occasion arose you would try to perform this operation of tracheotomy?—I said I had no tracheotomy tubes.

743. Did you indicate to Dr. Cremen whether or not if the occasion arose you would perform this operation?—I don't know that I did.

744. So you would not like to perform this operation?—No; but if necessity arose I would be bound to do it.

745. I suppose you never had to perform the operation?—I never had.

746. Dr. Cremen and you and Dr. O'Neill came to the conclusion that there was danger of suffocation?—No; but that there might be, possibly.

747. Did you, furthermore, come to the conclusion that it would be probable?—It might be.

748. Would you adopt the word "probable"?—I would not.

749. You all came to the conclusion that he was in a very critical condition; how far is Mr. Mandeville's house from Mitchelstown?—About a mile, or a mile and a half. It is counted an Irish mile.

750. A man would be easily suffocated before a messenger could come here and you be got out?—Yes.

751. Was there, when Dr. Cremen was there, any difficulty in his breathing?—Not in his breathing.

752. No difficulty about his breathing?—No.

753. You were there again that night?—Yes.

754. About nine o'clock?—Yes.

755. Was there any difficulty in his breathing then?—No.

756. Having regard to the determination which you came to on the advice of Dr. Cremen, that if suffocation did supervene, and the probability was present to your mind that such suffocation might supervene, did you consider it advisable to remain with the patient all night?—No, because there was no urgent symptom.

757. Did you consider that night that he was in a very critical condition?—Yes.

758. And that possibly he might die before morning?—That might be.

Mr. Harrington.

759. Did you consider that he might die before morning?—I did not.

Well, that is the question you ought to answer.

Mr. Harrington (to the Coroner).] The reason I stopped him was, because the Doctor had been unfairly asked the remainder of a question without being asked the beginning.

Mr. Murphy.

760. Did you know, having regard to the critical state he was in, that the fatal end might come before morning?—I did not believe the fatal end would come before morning.

761. Did you consider whether there was a possibility of suffocation supervening before morning?—No, I did not.

Mr. Murphy—continued.

762. Was that matter discussed between you and Dr. O'Neill, at nine o'clock, the possibility of such a thing occurring?—I do not remember at all.

763. When did you apply the exploring needle?—I think it was on Sunday morning or Saturday night.

764. Now which was it, Sir?—I think it was on Sunday morning.

765. Was Dr. O'Neill present?—He was.

766. You said, in your direct examination, that it was either on Saturday night or Sunday morning. Are you certain now?—I think now it was on Sunday morning.

767. Was it on your first visit on Sunday morning you applied the exploring needle?—I think so.

768. You know it is a very remarkable circumstance, and it is not so long ago; can you not fix accurately?—It was on Sunday morning at the first visit, about seven or half-past seven.

769. Were there any symptoms of suffocation then?—No; but the swelling was there when I used the exploring needle.

770. Was this a substitute for the knife that Dr. Cremen had suggested?—It was a substitute.

771. Was it in pursuance of that determination come to that you applied the exploring needle?—It was.

772. Now, Sir, was it not agreed, in consultation, that such a course should not be adopted, except suffocation should come on?—Yes, that I should use the knife but not the exploring needle. I did not use the needle for the same operation that Dr. Cremen had recommended the knife.

Here there was a discussion between Counsel regarding Dr. M'Craith's answer to this question in his direct examination.

Mr. Murphy.

773. At the consultation with Dr. Cremen, was there any suggestion as to the use of the knife or other instrument in the throat except in the case of suffocation supervening?—Certainly, if suffocation supervened, if the extent of inflammation went on, then he recommended that it should be scarified. That did not arise.

774. Was anything said at the consultation with Dr. Cremen as to using of this exploring needle or any other instrument?—No.

775. You saw him again on the Sunday, after mass?—Yes, about one o'clock.

776. Now, Sir, are you clear whether it was at the visit at eight o'clock in the morning or at the half-past one o'clock visit that you used this exploring needle?—Oh, it was in the morning.

777. Are you certain of that?—Perfectly.

778. Where exactly did you puncture with this needle?—In the pillar of the pharynx.

779. Did you take any means to observe the course the needle was taking?—Yes; I observed the course of the needle. There was a discharge of blood and matter followed.

780. Did you take any steps to keep the opening made by this exploring needle open?—Yes, by applying hot or tepid water.

781. You mentioned about albuminuria; what was it caused by?—By the disease.

782. By

Mr. *Murphy*—continued.

782. By the particular disease in the throat?—Cold will cause that; it was a secondary cause in consequence of his condition.

783. What time did you leave the house before the poor man died?—About an hour. I left to visit a patient, and when I came back in an hour's time he was dead.

784. You told us it was failure of the heart?—Yes.

785. You were not present when the poor man died?—No; Dr. O'Neill was.

786. Immediately before his death, when you left, was there any difficulty of breathing?—No.

787. No gurgling, or anything of that sort?—No.

788. You cannot say whether that came on after you left, before he died?—It might come on.

788. You are only giving what Dr. O'Neill said, that it was failure of the heart?—His heart was very weak.

789. He was a very stout man?—Yes.

790. Are stout men more liable to be cut off by these acute diseases than men of spare habits?—They are.

791. Had Mr. Mandeville fatty degeneration of the heart?—I never examined him.

792. A post-mortem examination; would it have assisted in ascertaining the immediate cause of death?—I don't know that it would.

793. If it had taken place before the body decomposed?—I don't think it would throw any light on it.

794. Even though it took place before decomposition set in?—I don't think so.

795. Would it indicate whether he had been properly treated or not?—I don't think it would throw any light on that.

796. In your intercourse with Mr. Mandeville subsequent to his discharge from prison, did you ever observe any tremor in his hands, or anything of that kind?—No; I always looked upon him as a powerful athletic man.

797. Subsequent to his discharge from prison?—I did not.

Dr. CHARLES RONAYNE, Youghal; Examined.

Mr. *T. Harrington.*

798. ARE you a surgeon?—Yes.

799. I believe you are a medical inspector for the Board of Trade?—Yes.

800. You were also, until recently, a justice of the peace for the County Cork?—Yes, until a recent occasion, when I endeavoured to preserve the public peace.

Mr. Murphy objected to him proceeding in this strain.

801. While justice for the County of Cork, were you also for years a member of the visiting justices for the gaol?—I was for 18 years a visiting justice.

802. In your capacity as justice of the County Cork, did you visit Mr. Mandeville as he was there in Tullamore Gaol?—I did.

803. On what date did you visit Mr. Mandeville?—The 16th of November last year.

804. I ask, Doctor, whether you had the good fortune to find him when he was not undergoing punishment?—He was then undergoing a term of punishment.

805. Did you know the nature of that punishment?—I did; bread and water for a period of three days.

806. May I ask, Doctor, whether before, in your experience as a visiting justice of the prisons, you had found a person undergoing three days' bread and water?—Never.

807. Would you describe; do you know anything about the quantity of bread allowed?—Yes; I used to know prison diet pretty fairly. I think it is 24 ounces of bread.

808. Did Mr. Mandeville complain to you of being suffering in consequence of that punishment?—He did.

809. That complaint, I presume, was in answer to a question of yours?—Yes.

810. What was your own opinion of his appearance, as a medical man?—I formed a bad opinion of his condition from his appearance. He had a peculiar flabby look, bluish lips, suffused and congested eyes, rapid and shallow breathing, and all the marks of either heart failure or want of proper oxidation, owing to the air; not having proper air or a proper amount of air.

811-12. You are aware, Doctor, that during the punishment he was allowed no exercise in the open air?—He complained to me. From his appearance I at once suspected that this condition was owing to heart failure, or want of proper air supply, and I asked him, Have you been ordered any exercise by the doctor, Mr. Mandeville, and he said, No. This was in presence of the Governor. I asked him, had he been ordered any additional or open air exercise, and he said No. What I implied by my question, and what he certainly implied by his answer, was that he had neither air nor exercise at all.

813. Did you say, Doctor, in a subsequent visit to the gaol, that in Tullamore the punishment carried with it want of exercise; did he complain of his sight to you?—Yes; he told he was hardly able to read a Bible he was supplied with, though I thought it of fair type. He noticed his sight getting weak.

814. Do you remember, did he complain of being suffering from anything else at the time?—Yes; he complained of diarrhoea and a sore throat, particularly of a sore throat, and I would have known by his voice that there was something wrong with his throat.

815. I believe, Doctor, he told you he had got some treatment for the sore throat?—Yes; he pointed out a bottle to me, and told me the doctor gave him gargle.

816. Did he tell you whether he had got any treatment for the diarrhoea?—No; he was particularly distressed with some test the doctor applied

Mr. *Harrington*—continued.

applied to him. He complained of a peculiar annoyance he had from it. He complained more of the annoyance and pain he suffered from, and that nothing was done for him.

817. At all events, he complained that nothing was done for the diarrhoea?—Yes.

818. What is your experience in the profession?—Twenty years, more or less.

819. Would you, after twenty years in the medical profession, consider the test a very peculiar one for a man fed on a limited supply of bread and water?—I never heard of such a medical test, except those that were often used to examine stools. The impression made on me was that the doctor thought Mr. Mandeville was shamming, and treated him so, and I think Mr. Mandeville thought so, and intended to convey it to me, too.

820. Did he make any statement to you as to the frequency of those attacks?—Turning to the Governor he said, I wish to complain to the Governor that I have been attacked about 12 times since one o'clock. It was then about six o'clock.

821. At what hour would that conversation have been?—About a quarter-past six.

822. Did you, either in Mr. Mandeville's presence or any other time during your visit to the prison, draw the Governor's attention to the severity of the punishment of Mr. Mandeville?—I turned to the Governor, in Mr. Mandeville's presence, and I asked him by what prison rule or available authority did he punish Mr. Mandeville with three days on bread and water, as I am sure you have exceeded your power, I said. I am aware that you have only power to give 24 hours' prison punishment. The Governor said that he had, and that it was according to the prison regulations. I asked him where were they. He pointed them out on the wall. We went over and looked through them. I suppose there were about 80 rules, and it could not be found.

823. Now, Doctor, did you express to the Governor any opinion as to the effect that treatment was likely to have upon Mr. Mandeville's health?—I did, down in the office.

824. And not in Mr. Mandeville's presence?—No. The poor man, I found him seriously damaged by the treatment. I formed that opinion at the time. I said to the Governor, This poor fellow's case is very distressing and very sad to see, this fine able man in this condition. I said to him they were going too far with him, and to take care that there would not be a sudden collapse. I am not too clear whether it was in a report which I was then writing or when speaking to the Governor. I said, Take care you don't have a repetition of the scandal of Kilkenny Gaol here.

825. By that, Doctor, did you refer to the case of Larkin, who was found dead in his cell from diarrhoea?—Under the same circumstances. The picture came to my mind, and I think it right to say that the Governor seemed to feel the responsibility of his position very keenly. He struck me as a man who was honestly trying to carry out a duty which he believed was a very dangerous and a very irksome one.

Mr. *Harrington*—continued.

Mr. *Murphy* objected to these impressions of which was passing in another man's mind being put on the depositions.

The *Coroner*.] If I find there are certain features in this case in favour of the Governor I think it would not be fair to shut them out.

826. Did you ever, in the Governor's presence, or in your report, make reference to the danger of undermining Mr. Mandeville's constitution?

The *Coroner*.] In your report?

Mr. *Ronayne*.] I don't know which, Sir. (*Here the prison book was produced.*)

827. You are sure the report?—Yes.

Mr. *Murphy*.] As a matter of regularity this man cannot refer to a report without reading it.

Mr. *Harrington* objected.

Mr. *Murphy* applied for a ruling.

The *Coroner* ruled that the report would be read.

828. Now, Doctor, are you satisfied that that expression of yours with reference to the danger of Mr. Mandeville's constitution being undermined was made in the presence of the Governor?—I am satisfied that in my conversation with the Governor I cautioned him of the certain impairment of Mr. Mandeville's health they were leading to by this treatment.

829. Had you a consultation with any other medical gentleman who had, about the same time, an opportunity of observing Mr. Mandeville's condition?—I had a consultation that night with Dr. Moorhead.

The *Coroner*.

830. Was it a consultation or a conversation you had with Dr. Moorhead?—It was not a professional consultation. It was a formal consultation.

831. Had Dr. Moorhead also seen Mr. Mandeville that day?—I don't know about that day, but he had seen him in prison.

Mr. *Murphy*.] I object to any conversation, or the purport of any conversation.

832. Mr. *Harrington*.] Was that before or after you left the prison?—After. (*The prison book was here handed to Dr. Ronayne.*)

833. That report is in your handwriting?—Yes. (*The Witness then read, as follows*):—"I also visited Mr. Mandeville. He states that he is again on bread and water punishment for three days for not wearing prison dress, and that he is now labouring under an attack of diarrhoea for the past 12 hours, and that the doctor has not done anything for him, although he complained to him. He also states that he has no change of linen since his imprisonment. This is very sad. He is losing his fine ruddy complexion, getting blanched and flabby, and I noticed, short-breathed. I think he should be put under medical treatment, and removed to the infirmary, with a view to arresting his malady and mitigating his miseries."

834. The Governor of the prison was standing by, I presume, while you were writing that?—He

Mr. Harrington—continued.

He had to go to dinner, but came back before I finished.

835. That book, at all events, was in his custody?—Yes.

836. You were in court while Dr. Moorhead was giving evidence?—The last part of yesterday.

837. I believe you did not visit Mr. Mandeville again?—On my next visit he had been discharged.

838. Did you hear Dr. M'Craith examined to-day?—I did.

839. Assuming that Mr. Mandeville was treated in prison as was mentioned in the questions to Dr. M'Craith to-day by The M'Dermott, do you agree with his answer that that treatment had a tendency to lower his constitution, or injure it?—Certainly, I agree with him. It was calculated to lower his constitution and permanently damage his health. I formed that opinion myself even before I heard Dr. M'Craith's evidence.

840. You knew him, Doctor, before he was in prison?—No.

841. You saw him?—Only in prison.

842. Would repeated punishments on bread and water diet, at short intervals, confinement for several successive days from air and exercise, added to the general treatment of a prisoner in gaol, with violent taking away of clothes and covering, and consequent exposure in a flagged cell, in your opinion, create an injurious effect and undermine a man's constitution?

> Mr. *Murphy*.] I object on the grounds that that is a hypothetical question, and assumes a lot of matters that have not been proved.
>
> The objection was entered on the depositions, but question allowed.
>
> Dr. *Ronayne*.] I have got no doubt but all these circumstances would lead to the very serious impairment of the vital state and future health of any man, especially in a man who previously had been living under circumstances the very opposite of all these.

843. Do you agree in the opinion expressed by Dr. M'Craith, that it would render him more susceptible to disease and less able to resist it, particularly the suppurative disease he afterwards succumbed to?—I do.

FOURTH DAY.

Friday, 20th July 1888.

Dr. RONAYNE, cross-examined.

Mr. *Murphy.*

844. You were a visiting justice of the Cork prison?—Not of the Cork prison, but the Youghal local prison in the County Cork.

845. A bridewell in the ordinary term?—It is a local prison.

846. A very small number of prisoners?—We have a good many there sometimes. I have seen, I would say eight; five at one side and three at the other.

847. It is what would be called under the old system a bridewell?—Yes.

848. And only used for the temporary detention of prisoners?—Yes; it has the same rules and regulations, and cell arrangements as an ordinary prison. It is part and parcel of the prison system of Ireland. I was appointed to it in 1874 or 1875, and I was from that up to the time of my supercession a visiting justice.

849. Have you had any experience as a visiting justice or otherwise, of one of the large prisons of the country?—Yes, I have visited Cork Gaol by virtue of my office, and I know the prison system of Ireland, and prison rules and statutes well.

850. Not very frequently?—Not very frequently.

851. You are aware of the regulations of the prison as to dietary, &c.?—Yes.

852. In the discharge of your duties; did you satisfy yourself as to whether the ordinary prison dietary was able to keep a man in ordinary health?—Yes, and I think so.

853. Did you ever form any opinion as to whether the prison regulations for putting a man on bread-and-water when refractory or disobedient, or decline to obey the prison rules, is calculated to injure him?—I cannot say that I did. I don't suppose I did previous to this case. I think not.

854. Did you ever in the course of your past experience come across a case of a man who was on punishment diet?—I cannot recollect it. I am not certain. I think I have, and in the County Cork Gaol.

855. You take a great interest, you told us, in all your duties of life?—Yes; I take an honest and dutiful interest.

856. In that case, did you inquire in the first place what punishment diet was?—Oh, I knew the punishment diet. I knew the prison regulations.

857. At that time did you consider whether that punishment diet was adequate to keep a man in ordinary health?—I don't think I did.

858. Which do you think a well-fed strong man or a weakly ill-fed man could better sustain himself on the prison dietary?—For the first few days a strong man may live better on any deprivation. A fat strong man may live better for the first few days.

859. I am not talking of a few days but a few months?—I think a weakly thin delicate man would live better.

860. An ill-fed man will do better than a well-fed man?—I think he will sustain physical punishment and low diet better. It will materially undermine a well-fed fat man.

861. That is an opinion you don't give from actual experience?—No; I can judge as a physiologist, having a fair knowledge of physiology.

862. Of course as a visiting justice, you are aware that prison discipline must be enforced?—Yes, I am aware of that.

863. Are you aware of any mode of coercing a refractory prisoner except by punishment?—No. I don't think either the statutes or prison bye-laws allow any except by prescribed punishment. A prisoner for infraction of the prison laws may be brought before a justice outside the prison altogether.

864. I think I understood you to say yesterday, you did not know Mr. Mandeville previously?—No, but by reputation. I knew his physique only by reputation.

865. You had no personal knowledge of Mr. Mandeville?—No personal knowledge.

866. You don't form in your own mind medical opinions of men you never saw?—No, not medical opinions; but I would form pictorial opinions as to their appearance.

867. Do you think that the ordinary prison dietary and the two hours' exercise allowed would have endangered the life of Mr. Mandeville for the two or three months for which he was sentenced?—I don't think it would, except so far as the deprivations to any man in good health from his usual domestic comforts and surroundings would injure a man.

868. Of course, Doctor, it is a very great change for a man who has been accustomed to the conveniences and all the other arrangements that we have in civilized and home society, to be put upon ordinary prison fare and prison service?—A tremendous change. It breaks some men's health and other men's minds.

869. You made no medical examination of Mr. Mandeville?—No, never.

870. This test that we have been speaking of, is not that a usual test?—Well, no, it is a test.

871. Is it an improper test?—Oh, no, it is not an improper test, but it is a suspicious, a vicious kind of test.

872. It not being an improper test, is it a good test?—I think not; a man might have a most depressing

Mr. *Murphy*—continued.

depressing lowering diarrhœa of a simple innocence-like character, without showing much physical results, or copious results, and that would be more mentally painful to a man than perhaps the copious form. For judging of the character, it is not a useful test.

873. It is a good test; is it not the best test?—Oh, no; a most fallacious test.

874. Is it desirable for a physician when dealing with a matter of that sort to know the character of the affection he is dealing with?—It is.

875. Apart from this diarrhœa, would the confinement of a man of John Mandeville's habits, who led an active life in prison, have a tendency to give him a flabby appearance?—It would, but not the marked bad symptoms I noticed in the appearance. The peculiar bluish lips and leaden face, the congested eye membrane, the shallow respiration, all these indicated to my skilled eye a devitalised state.

876. Would not a man's eyes have a congested appearance if he had not slept well the night before?—Yes, they would; but not the suffused and watery appearance I noticed.

877. I suppose you will agree with me that, if a gentleman has been accustomed to an easy bed all his life, and that he has suddenly to take to a plank bed, even with a mattress on it, that he is likely to suffer to some extent from sleeplessness?—Oh, yes.

878. Do you consider that diarrhœa is an affection of a dangerous kind?—No, not diarrhœa alone.

879. Of course, if it became dysenteric, it may be?—Yes.

880. And frequently it is simply an effort of nature to relieve the system?—Yes, it is sometimes a beneficial effort.

881. In your opinion, if a gentleman accustomed to live well, had for some reason or another to live upon the ordinary prison fare, might that cause such an alteration in his system as would amount to diarrhœa?—Yes, any change might do it.

882. You would not say that the affection caused by such a change of diet was of a dangerous character?—Not if it did not continue; if it continued, it would be dangerous.

883. Is it not a dangerous thing sometimes to check that affection rapidly?—Yes, to check it rapidly sometimes.

884. Is it not dangerous sometimes to let it run its course?—Yes, but I would like to watch it particularly in the conditions of Mr. Mandeville's case under such depressing conditions.

885. For the purpose of watching it to see whether it might be allowed to run its course or checked, is not the test we have been speaking of a proper test?—Yes, one of the proper tests; but what particularly irritated Mr. Mandeville was that, it implied an unbelief on the part of the Doctor, or, at all events, a suspicion that Mr. Mandeville was shamming. That is what I derived from Mr. Mandeville's expressions.

Mr. *Murphy*.] To the last part of that answer, I object going upon the depositions.

The *MacDermot*.] I will tell you why, to my humble judgment, it is a very good, and a suitable answer. When a doctor treats a patient, he has to take into consideration the condition, mental, as well as bodily, of the patient for the test that might be applied with ruder and rougher minds; if he finds it is one revolting to the patient, he says, it would not be a proper test to apply on that particular occasion on that particular patient.

Mr. *Murphy*.] I have put a general question to the Doctor, and he gave a clear specific and intelligible answer; and furthermore, I respectfully submit that it cannot be explained by this gentleman what was passing in the mind of Mr. Mandeville.

Mr. *Harrington*.] We must protest against it being said to a witness that he won't be allowed to explain.

Mr. *Murphy*.] Do you know, Mr. Harrington, when any substance of itself is read out, a witness cannot by taking up a specific answer to any question make it evidence. You know that this man's opinion of what was passing in another man's mind cannot be evidence.

886. *To Witness*.] Now this cell in which you found Mr. Mandeville, was that a well-lighted cell?—No, there was a small gas jet when I was there on a wintry day after six o'clock. It was insufficient, not well lighted.

887. You had no opportunity of judging as to the light of the cell in the day-time?—No.

888. Did you ever see a prison cell lighted with gas before?—Oh, yes, it was the usual prison gas-lighting; it was not well lit.

889. No. It was as well lighted as any prison cell you ever saw?—Yes; I should say it was regulation light.

890. And the cell was the ordinary prison cell, or was it better or worse?—I would say the ordinary prison cell, but a very insufficient cell for a man of Mr. Mandeville's size; not up to his breathing capacity.

891. How many cubic feet of air is necessary to contain a man of Mr. Mandeville's size?—The regulated size is 600; I should say he would require 10 or 12 hundred feet. I would say at least 800 cubic feet. I would put the cell down about 480 or 500 feet. I consider he had insufficient footage in the cell.

892. Did you notice the ventilation of this particular cell?—I won't say that I know much about the ventilation of it. I know about the cubic footage of it.

893. The cell was covered with matting?—Yes, a cane cell.

894. Did you observe whether he was supplied with a mattress or not?—I am not sure; I noticed a heating pipe running through the cell.

895. Did you feel them if they were heated?—I did; they were warm.

896. Did you ever treat a case of this acute inflammation of the throat?—I have treated many serious inflammations of the throat.

897. Did you ever see an opening made on the outside to give relief?—Do you mean tracheotomy?

Mr. *Murphy*—continued.

899. No?—I don't know.

900. Is it known to the medical and surgical profession?—It is; I have done it myself. It is making an opening in the cellular tissue.

901. Would you do it for inflammation?—No, not until inflammation extended to suppuration.

902. Would you have performed such an operation in this case of Mr. Mandeville?—I would not like to give an opinion without seeing the case.

903. You heard a description of this poor gentleman's illness given by Dr. M'Craith?—I did.

904. Would you have adopted the same course of treatment?—I would rather not answer.

905. Are you able to appreciate the condition of the patient from the description given by Dr. M'Craith?—I think I have formed a good idea.

906. I ask you, would you at the several stages which Dr. M'Craith described have adopted the same measures?—You know doctors differ.

907. Yes, and we know the result sometimes. I would like to have the benefit of your opinion?—We all view a particular case according to our own lights, and hence we differ.

908. Do you consider that that was proper and adequate treatment at the several stages?—I don't think it is a fair question.

> The Coroner ruled that it was a fair question.
>
> Dr. *Ronayne*.] We all differ. Perhaps if you asked different doctors they will give you different answers. I would not have adopted all the treatment of Dr. M'Craith. I would have adopted some, and I would not have adopted others.

909. Now, Doctor, I ask you to tell me the particulars of the treatment in which you agree?—I agree with the steaming, with the external warm fomentations in the first step, with the sweating medicine given; I also agree with the administration of the chlorate of potash and the muriatic tincture of iron.

910. At the particular time it was administered?—Yes.

911. In what other particulars do you agree with him; in none other?—I don't remember any.

912. Now, will you specify the particulars in which you disagree with the measures taken by Dr. M'Craith?—But this would be only my own opinion.

913. I would like to have the benefit of your opinion?—I don't know about the sweating mixture in the last stage as prescribed, nor I am not sure about the leeching or the exploring needle.

914. Now, Doctor, was there anything else in the treatment tried by Dr. M'Craith that you don't agree in; do you disapprove of any others of minor importance?—These are the only ones; but if I had been in consultation with Dr. M'Craith I might not disagree with them. He might give his reasons for using those measures, and I might agree with him.

915. What, in your opinion, would have been the effect of this sweating mixture at the latter stage of his illness?—Lowering.

916. Am I right in supposing that at that time you should have thought he should be kept up?—Judging from my lights, I think so.

917. What in your opinion was the effect of the leeching on a patient in that condition?—If there was an acute oedema I would leech; but the idea I formed was one, it struck me that the leeching and copious bleeding was weakening.

> The *MacDermot*.] There was no copious bleeding.
>
> Dr. *Ronayne*.] I was under the impression there was copious bleeding.

918. Did you conclude, from the evidence of Dr. M'Craith, that at that particular time, when the leeches were applied, there was no inflammatory mischief and acute oedema?—That would be very hard for me to answer without examining the patient. One touch of my own finger would satisfy me.

Mr. *Harrington*.

919. Did you conclude, from Dr. M'Craith's evidence, that at that time there was acute oedema?—I really cannot say; one touch of my own finger would tell me.

Mr. *Murphy*.

920. What led you to the conclusion that the application of those leeches was not a course that you would have adopted?

> The *MacDermot*.] He did not say it.

921. I ask you as to the particulars of the treatment adopted by Dr. M'Craith with which you disagreed, and you said the application of the leeches at the time was one. What answer do you give to this?

The *Coroner*.

922. Doctor, did you hear Dr. M'Craith mention anything about poisoning?—I did.

923. Would not it be necessary to apply sweating mixture?—I don't know.

Mr. *Murphy*.

924. Would this sweating mixture be applicable for blood poisoning?—I think the sweating mixture, as administered first by Dr. M'Craith, was a judicious measure.

925. But not afterwards?—I think not.

926. You heard the description of the last scene at which Dr. M'Craith was present; his description of the patient almost up to the last?—I did.

927. What would you say was the immediate cause of death?—I think heart failure and syncope.

928. Would asphyxia be likely?—Not by the appearance of the last moments. It was too sudden for asphyxia; asphyxia would lead on gradually. I am certain it was heart failure.

The *Coroner*.

929. Was it a sudden death?—It was.

Mr. *Murphy*.

930. Would a sudden discharge of an internal abscess cause it?—I think not.

931. You

Mr. *Murphy*—continued.

931. You heard the condition of the patient described on Saturday night?—Yes.

932. Would you, under similar circumstances, have left the patient upon that night?—I don't know. I could not answer that unless I saw him.

933. Now, from the description given here of the several stages of the illness of this poor gentleman, do you think that tracheotomy would have been a proper treatment at any stage?—I could not answer that without seeing him. It is only the breathing sound could tell me that.

934. You stated, in the course of your evidence, that you referred in your conversation with the Governor to certain matters that occurred at Kilkenny; are you clear about that?—I am quite clear; I either wrote it or said it.

935. You did not write it; it appeared?—I don't know.

936. Did you make more than one report?—Yes; I am quite clear of the circumstances of that statement; whether it was in words to the Governor, or in writing, I am not sure.

937. Did I understand you only made one report on the 15th November?—Only one on the 15th November.

938. Was not that the only occasion on which you made any remark on Mr. Mandeville?—The only occasion.

939. And if you made it in writing on that occasion, it must be in the report that was produced here yesterday?—Yes.

940. Well, it is not there?—Not in the paragraph I read.

941. Now can you take upon yourself to swear that you made use of that expression?—Certainly; I either wrote the words or spoke them.

942. You did not write them you know?—No, but I spoke them; I remember it most distinctly.

943. When I was asking you about your agreement or disagreement with Dr. M'Craith's evidence, you mentioned about not being sure about the use of the exploring needle. At the time it was used, what effect would that have upon a patient, as described?—I don't think much effect. I don't think it led up to any purpose. If such a thing had to be used, I would prefer using the knife, but Dr. M'Craith might have used this as an exploratory test to see if there was pus there.

944–5. If the gentleman used this exploring needle, and subsequently used hot water to keep open the wound, would you approve of it?—Yes, if there was pus discharged.

The *Coroner*.

946. Then you do agree with Dr. M'Craith?—To give exit to pus I prefer the knife; if exploring for pus I would use the needle.

Mr. *Murphy*.

947. If he used it for the purpose of giving relief by allowing a flow of this serous matter do you think it was adequate?—I don't think so. I think it necessary to add, that the character of the serous discharge spoken of, the whole course of this disease, the sudden collapse ——

Mr. *Harrington*.] Let us confine ourselves to the serous discharge.

Witness.] Were all at variance with what they would be under ordinary circumstances, and clearly indicated an impaired, injured, and prematurely broken-down constitution.

Re-examined by Mr. *Harrington*.

948. You were asked a good deal about your agreement or disagreement with Dr. M'Craith; do you approve of the treatment given by the prison doctor?

Mr. *Murphy* objected to the question, but the Coroner admitted it.

Witness.] No; for I believe Mr. Mandeville should have been removed to the infirmary.

949. Did you ever in your experience hear of bread and water prescribed for diarrhoea?—No; especially in the case of brown bread, which would be an excitant, and a very wrong thing to allow.

950. Now you were asked whether it might not be better sometimes to allow diarrhoea run its course. Do you think under any circumstances it ought to be allowed run its course on bread and water in a punishment cell?—No; I think it was inhuman; I think it was cruel.

951. Ought not the hospital have been prescribed for a man in Mr. Mandeville's condition?—I am of opinion, and I stated that opinion in writing, that the infirmary or hospital was essential.

Mr. *Murphy*.

952. If the patient were getting white bread instead of brown bread, he would not get this excitement?—No; but white bread and water is not fit treatment for diarrhoea, and no doctor would order or allow it.

Dr. Patrick J. Cremen, of Cork; Examined.

The *MacDermot*.

953. You come from Cork, Doctor, I think?—Yes.

954. You are a member of the Queen's University, Ireland, and member of the Royal College of Surgeons?—Yes.

955. How long have you been practising, Doctor?—For 20 years.

956. Do you hold any position of importance in Cork?—Yes; I am medical officer of Cork Union Hospital, and also attached, as physician, to the North Charitable Infirmary.

957. Do you recollect being summoned by telegram to come to Mitchelstown on Saturday, 7th July?—Yes.

958. You reached about three o'clock?—About three.

959. You saw Mr. Mandeville, the patient, in

The *MacDermot*—continued.

in consultation with Doctors M'Craith and O'Neill?—Yes.

960. Immediately on your arrival?—Yes.

961. At Mr. Mandeville's house, of course?—Yes.

962. Will you state shortly the condition in which you found the patient, and the symptoms?—I examined him very minutely, after first inquiring into the history of his case.

963. Now, give the result of that?—His pulse was 120 a minute.

963. What is normal?—Between 60 and 72 a minute. One hundred and twenty soft, that is indicative of debility. His temperature was 102·3°.

964. What is normal temperature?—98°.

965. What does that indicate?—A certain amount of fever present, or inflammation.

966. What was the character of the heart's action?—Rapid and feeble.

967. Have you anything else to say before we come to what he complained of?—I examined the urine, and found it to be high coloured, acid, and the specific gravity 1·025, scanty, and containing a considerable quantity of albumen. I examined his throat, which he complained of, and his mouth and surrounding part.

968. In what condition did you find them?—I found that the soft palate and the uvula were of a dusky colour, the uvula being œdematous.

969. Would you explain to the jury what you mean by œdematous?—It is the water getting into the palate, or the watery constituent of the blood.

970. Was the palate swollen?—Yes; the soft palate. The tonsils, as well as I could see, were also of the same dusky colour as the soft palate, but I had a difficulty in seeing the tonsils as well as I saw the palate, for there was a stiffness about the angle of jaw, and I could not open his mouth. The parotid gland was enormously enlarged at the right side, hard, stony hard; tongue dry and slightly swollen, not so much when I saw it. There was also a slight swelling in the submaxillary and sublingual gland. The tongue had been leeched by Doctors M'Craith and O'Neill previously, and when I arrived he said he was able to swallow better than before. The leech-bites were still bleeding.

971. Did his statement indicate that the application had been useful?—I should say so.

972. Any other symptoms, Doctor?—I think these are the principal symptoms.

973. What treatment was suggested?—Before I saw him, I said the leeches had been applied, and he had got some medicine and the steam and hot fomentations externally.

974. Now, Doctor, did you consider all that treatment you have been speaking of as judicious?—Well, as preparatory treatment it seemed to have acted well, so far. I must say about the leeches that they gave him great relief, and are recommended by some authorities in such cases; but in my own practice, as Dr. Ronayne said, I always prefer incisions, if possible. At the same time, I am fully certain that he derived benefit from the application of the leeches from what I saw.

975. Would this disease be properly described as œdematous laryngitis?—No. As regards the treatment to be adopted, I suggested that he should get about half an ounce of brandy about every two hours, supported with milk and beef tea, and a mixture of muriate tincture of iron and chlorate of potash, and one bottle of diaphoretic mixture containing ammonia; and the reason I selected this course, as regards the sweating mixture is, his kidneys were intensely congested, and in his state I judged that it would be quite safe to promote the action of his skin, and thus relieve the congestion of the kidneys by a drug that would not be lowering in character. We then consulted as to the future course of action, and I then gave it as my opinion that, from previous experience in such cases, he would not live until Monday. We discussed the probability. There is one point I was forgetting, the question of incisions rose to my mind at this time, to make incisions to relieve his tongue as the proper course to be adopted, if it could be done with safety. Taking into consideration the fact that he had been leeched immediately before I saw him, and bleeding profusely from these leeches, I thought it would not then be well to run the risk of depleting him further by incisions. There was one spot at the lower angle of the jaw, in front of the internal lateral ligament, where there seemed to be a tendency to matter forming. I suggested to Dr. M'Craith to make an incision into this at the earliest possible time, if the remedies that we used did not bring about suppuration. I omitted to mention that, besides inhaling the steam of hot water, that I suggested that his mouth should be bathed frequently with hot water in the event of the disease extending to the windpipe. I suggested that it should be opened at once, or that laryngotomy should be performed, and I told Mr. Mandeville's friends, on the intimation of the slightest change to send at once for a doctor, and pointed out to them what would be the unfavourable symptoms possible to arise. I gave directions, as I was extremely anxious about his case, that I should be telegraphed to next morning as to his condition. That is all I have to say about him.

976. The place or spot you describe as having a tendency to pus, that was the spot where the probing-needle was applied by Dr. M'Craith?—I do not know I indicated to Dr. M'Craith the proper spot to use the probing-needle.

977. You said that you thought that he would not survive Monday?—No.

978. You did not consider that any human power would restore him to health?—No.

979. In fact, you thought at that time that he was dying?—I did.

980. Now, Doctor, it is proved in this case that this gentleman was in prison from the 31st October to the 24th December, that he had all the usual comforts of life before he went to prison. It was proved that while he was in prison he was several times undergoing punishment, on one occasion punishment for three days together on bread and water, and that during that time he was suffering from diarrhœa. It was also proved that he could not eat, nor did eat, the prison food for a period of twenty hours. They said, in presence of the Governor, that

The *MacDermot*—continued.

that he had been for a considerable time without food. I ought to have said that before he went to prison he was described as a jocose man, with a good complexion, and never had a necessity to receive any medicine beyond a cough mixture or a pill. It was stated that this change occurred in prison, that his breathing was short and shallow, by Dr. Moorhead. That his lips became bluish, and that his face became flabby and pasty. That there was tremor in both his hands, that he complained while in prison of sore throat, that he stated before the Governor, at half-past three o'clock, he had twelve attacks of it. He complained of feeling cold up to his knees, and of rheumatism. Now, all this was proved by various witnesses. It was proved when he came out of prison, for a month this strong man was unable to carry his great coat without inconvenience, or his boots without inconvenience. Before he went in he wrote a good hand, but for three months he was unable to write after coming out. That he complained of this sore throat a few days before he died. Now, Doctor, I want to ask you whether you consider that prison treatment I have described, will it lead you to the conclusion that he became a subject more susceptible of disease and less able to resist it?—I should say that the succession of conditions involved in the course of his imprisonment, and to a great extent the change in the normal condition of life, had a lowering effect on his system, which predisposed him to the class of disease which he suffered from when I saw him.

981. Would you say it also rendered him less able to resist it?—Certainly, when the constitution is lowered he would be naturally unable to resist disease so well.

982. Now, I want to ask you whether, to a person suffering from diarrhœa, what is called punishment diet (which means bread and water) for three days, or the hospital was the proper place?—I think it would answer all purposes to state in broad terms what I have said with regard to that question. I have always a horror of criticising the treatment of any man, because I do not know the conditions at the present time. It is a thing I do not like.

Cross-examined by Mr. *Murphy*.

983. What was the disease from which Mr. Mandeville died?—Diffused cellular inflammation of the throat and mouth.

984. Was there considerable swelling under the jaw?—No, the parotid glands were of a stony hardness, though considerable swelling did not exist or nothing would prevent me having made an incision.

985. Did you observe any blueness of his nails or lips?—No, he had no blueness of his nails or lips when I saw him, he was of a florid colour.

986. Were you in a position to judge, from your examination, whether that disease of the kidneys was long-standing or recent?—I judged that, from the high specific gravity of the urine, it was an acute affection and not a secondary disease.

987. Can you tell us the frequency of his respiration?—I think about 28 or 30

Mr. *Murphy*—continued.

988. Was that normal?—Oh, it was over normal; not very much.

989. At the time that you saw him, about 2.30 on Saturday, had the disease attained considerable development then?—Yes, it developed very quickly.

990. And was it in an advanced stage?—Well, it developed very quickly. It was not in an advanced stage. It was the glands that were particularly involved. There was very little subcutaneous diffusion about at all. It was particularly in the glands.

991. You said that you thought the remedies applied by the other physicians were good preparatory remedies?—Yes.

992. Did you consider that they were adequate to the condition in which the patient was when you saw him?—Up to that time they were, and the best proof of that was that they afforded him considerable relief.

993. Even though remedies may afford patients relief, are not there some further remedies that might have afforded greater relief?—Different medical men will have different opinions.

994. Your remark makes me think that something else could have been done?—I explained in my examination about the leeches.

995. Did you observe any inflammation?—Very little, except at the angle of the jaw where I described in my direct examination. That was the only spot; there seemed to be some diffusion.

996. Did you see where Dr. M'Craith applied these leeches?—I saw that he applied them at the angle of the jaw externally, and he applied, I think, two to the tip of the tongue, and a couple at the side of the neck, about eight altogether.

997. Would you have adopted that treatment?—I would not have adopted the same plan of treatment.

998. What was it suggested to you the propriety of having resort to laryngotomy?—The probability that the upper portion of the windpipe is covered over by a lid, and if this receives the watery portion of the blood it will interfere with respiration, and therefore it becomes necessary to have respiration carried on, and you cannot have respiration carried on except by opening the windpipe and inserting a tube until you can relieve the patient by other means.

999. Was there any lividity?—No. I never saw Mr. Mandeville before, but he was not livid.

1000. This was of course an inflammatory affection?—Yes, a low inflammatory affection.

1001. Is it a fact that men of stout habit don't bear up against that disease so well as men of a sparer habit?—A strong healthy man, stout or otherwise, would bear up against it, but men whose constitutions are lowered by any cause, such as blood disease or profusion, exposure, bad organic disease of some of the viscera, bad hygienic surroundings, all these causes will predispose to the disease.

1002. This particular affection from which Mr. Mandeville died; might not a man who never had been subjected to any of these matters that you have suggested, and who suddenly got a severe

Mr. *Murphy*—continued.

a severe attack, succumb to it rapidly?—Any cases that I saw of it were in broken-down constitutions.

1003. You never saw a case of diffused cellular inflammation except in a man of broken-down constitution?—No, except the result of a poison wound; that is the only exception, and then that has different forms of affection, termed septic inflammation, and it would not be cellular diffused inflammation.

1004. Do you mean to say that a man whose constitution was not broken down, and had his full strength and vigour, might not be subject to diffused cellular inflammation, and succumb to it?—It is quite possible.

1005. Do you consider that a man who had any local predisposition to throat affection could with impunity have taken part in meetings in the open air during the months of December and January, and up to the summer?—I would say it was very imprudent of him.

1006. And would the chances be that that delicacy would develop into a serious disease?—Not into the disease or affection he was suffering from; but other throat affections would be aggravated by it considerably.

1007. Could this diffused cellular inflammation arise by reason of a man having got a severe wetting?—Yes, if he was predisposed to it by debilitating causes.

1008. If these leeches had not been applied before you came, would you have used the knife?—I possibly would have made an incision into the spot I mentioned at the internal angle of the jaw.

1009. When you suggested to Dr. M'Craith the possible prudence of making this incision, did you convey to him what it was to be made with?—Oh, yes.

1010. What?—The knife; but I must say, in explanation, Dr. M'Craith explained satisfactorily why he did not use the knife on the occasion. The swelling of the parotid gland having increased, there was considerable difficulty in opening the jaw.

1011. This particular place that you indicated that the knife should be applied, that was not the palate?—It was in front of the palate I indicated the place. It is opposite the internal lateral ligament.

1012. Why would an external incision be improper under the circumstances?—Because in an external incision there was nothing to incise; it was in the parotid gland that the particular inflammation and hardness was. It would be different if the inflammation was in the submaxillary gland. This was a case of stony hardness of the parotid gland, and there was nothing to incise.

1013. Dr. M'Craith told us that there was this swelling under the jaw?—It may have occurred afterwards, but not when I was there. He seemed to me as being a very full man about the neck.

1014. All this swelling that you have described was at the right side?—At the right side.

1015. Was there any at the left side?—No; except in the palate and uvula, and diffused inflammation of both tonsils, as well as I could see. I saw the uvula and palate, and they were all a dusky colour.

1016. What was the meaning of putting the leeches at the left side?—I don't think they were put to the left side.

1017. Do you know Doctor Ahearne?—Yes.

1018. Are you aware whether or not he saw Mr. Mandeville?—I heard he saw him after I saw him. I heard that a few days afterwards.

1019. Did you hear that from Doctor Ahearne himself?

The *MacDermot*.] I object to these questions.

Mr. *Murphy*.

1020. Had you a conversation with Doctor Ahearne with reference to this case?—Yes.

1021. Do you think that a post-mortem examination would have been of any assistance in ascertaining the cause of death?—I am afraid that from the septic nature of the disease, the decomposition having set in, as it does rapidly, in such cases, that it would not throw much light on it.

FIFTH DAY.

Saturday, 21st July 1888.

Dr. O'NEILL, of Mitchelstown; Examined.

The *MacDermot*, Q.C.

1022. WHAT are your qualifications?—I am an M.D. of the University of Edinburgh.

1023. Do you hold any public appointment?—Physician to the workhouse here.

1024. In Mitchelstown?—Yes, sir.

1025. How long have you been practising as doctor?—Some 30 years or more.

1026. Were you acquainted with the late Mr. Mandeville before he was sent to prison?—I was.

1027. From the time he came to Mitchelstown, I suppose?—Yes.

1028. Did you ever attend him as a medical man?—Never.

1029. You say you were acquainted with him; were you intimately acquainted with him?—Yes.

1030. Judging from his appearance, and such opportunities as you had of judging, did he seem to be a healthy man?—Very.

1031. A strong man?—Very.

1032. Did his temperament appear to be a man of strong or weak nerve?—Strong.

1033. Was his temperament gloomy or joyous?—Joyous.

1034. Was his complexion ruddy, or was it flabby and pasty-looking?—Ruddy and healthy.

1035. Did he ever complain to you of any illness?—Never.

1036. Had you any opportunity of knowing whether he was a man of sober or intemperate habits?—I had.

1037. Well, was he of sober or temperate habits?—Temperate.

1038. I suppose, Doctor, you did not see him during the time he was in prison?—No.

1039. Did you see him when he was discharged from prison?—Yes.

1040. How soon?—A few days after.

1041. Did you continue to see him frequently from the time of his discharge until the time he died?—I did.

1042. During that period you saw him frequently, I suppose?—Yes.

1043. Did he seem to you to have preserved all this appearance of health which you have already described?—He did not.

1044. Did he seem to you to have preserved or lost weight; did he seem to have preserved or lost the joyous expression of countenance?—To have lost.

1045. Did his nerves appear to you to have remained strong or to have grown weak and tremulous?—Tremulous.

1046. Did his complexion seem to have lost any of its ruddy hue?—It did.

The *MacDermot*, Q.C.—continued.

1047. Had his face grown flabby?—Yes.

1048. How did his eyes appear to you?—His eyes appeared defective; he was wearing glasses when I saw him.

1049. Before he went to prison did his eyes appear defective?—No.

1050. Were you called in professionally to attend him; on what date were you called in?—On the 7th.

1051. Are you sure it was not the 6th?—Yes, Saturday the 7th.

1052. You accompanied Dr. M'Craith to his house?—Yes.

1053. Will you state now about what hour?—About eight o'clock in the morning was my first time.

Mr. Murphy.

1054. The notes you are reading from, when were they written?—They were written every time I went out.

The *MacDermot*.

1055. Looking on your notes, would you just state in what condition you found him?—On viewing him I considered his case a hopeless one.

1056. State what symptoms you saw?—There was intense swelling of the right side of the glands. The glands were very hard and painful.

The *Coroner*.

1057. What gland?—The parotid.

1058. Then the submaxillary glands were also swollen?—The submaxillary glands were also affected; in like manner the tonsils were enlarged, and the aperture to the pharynx.

The *MacDermot*.

1059. What was the colour?—Purplish.

1060. Was there any swelling of the skin?—No, or at least very little indeed.

1061. Was the tongue to any extent swollen?—Slightly.

1062. You say you considered the case hopeless?—I did, sir.

1063. Did you state so much to your colleague, Dr. M'Craith?—I hinted as much.

1064. What treatment was used?—We applied two leeches to the angle of the jaw on the right side.

1065. Did the place where they were applied bleed much?—Freely.

1066. Did they seem to give relief?—Decidedly.

1067. Did you apply both of the leeches to that place?—Quite near each other.

1068. What other treatment did you prescribe?—Stupes

The *Mac Dermot*—continued.

—Stupes and fomentations and inhalations of steam.

1069. I suppose you considered all that proper treatment?—I could think no other better.

1070. You sent for more leeches?—Yes, about half-an-hour after they were applied. There were four applied to the right side and two under the tongue.

1071. Is it over the parotid gland?—Yes, and down to the chin.

1072. Where did you put the other two?—Under the tongue.

1073. Would that be where the sublingual gland was?—Yes.

1074. Did they bleed freely?—Yes, and the bleeding was encouraged more by hot sponging.

1075. Had that the effect of giving relief?—It had.

1076. Do you know while you were there was any salts given?—There was a saline mixture given for purgative purposes.

1077. Do you know whether gargle was used also?—Yes, I also applied nitrate of potash and alum to the tongue to reduce the inflammatory action.

1078. Was a sweating mixture administered?—Yes.

1079. That was for the purpose of producing sweating?—Yes.

1080. Did you consider all that treatment good?—Yes.

1081. What was recommended to be given for strengthening?—Champagne, brandy, new milk from the cow, and chicken broth.

1082. Was there any preparation of iron?—Not at that time.

1083. All this was done before Dr. Cremen arrived?—Yes.

1084. Dr. Cremen arrived about half-past three?—Yes.

1085. You returned there about half-past three?—A little before it.

1086. You, Dr. Cremen, and Dr. M'Craith had a consultation?—Yes.

1087. Up to that time did you approve of the treatment administered?—Yes.

1088. Did Dr. Cremen approve of the previous treatment?—He did.

1089. What was the treatment pursued when Dr. Cremen arrived?—He ordered a mixture of chlorate of potash and perchloride of iron.

1090. What else?—He ordered nothing more in the way of medicines, but directed to continue the treatment as heretofore.

1091. Did he say anything about using the knife?—He did.

1092. What did he say?—If it was required; if there was any threatening symptoms of impending suffocation it would be well to use it.

1093. Did he say anything about cutting or scarifying for any collection of pus that might be at the right side of the jaw?—Yes, he said it would be well to do it.

1094. Is that the place where you had put the leeches?—Yes.

1095. Did he say anything about performing a more serious operation?—He talked about tracheotomy and laryngotomy.

1096. After Dr. Cremen left was the exploring needle used?—Yes.

The *Mac Dermot*—continued.

1097. By Dr. M'Craith?—Yes.

1098. Where?—At the angle of the jaw.

1099. Is that the locality or place where Dr. Cremen had spoken of scarifying?—Yes.

1100. What was the effect of that?—A quantity of matter came away. Sanguino-purulent matter.

1101. Is that the same as a sanious discharge?—The very same.

1102. What is the nature of that discharge?—It is a mixture of blood and pus.

1103. Did that come in a small quantity, or a large quantity?—In a fair quantity.

1104. Did it give relief?—Apparently so.

1105. Was that done on your visit on Sunday morning?—Yes, the early visit.

1106. Would an external incision be of any use?—No.

1107. You came there a second time on Sunday?—At two o'clock.

1108. Were you there when the patient died?—I was. He died in my hands; my hands held his head on the chair.

1109. About what hour did he die?—Half-past two, exactly.

1110. Of what, in your opinion, did he die?—Failure of the heart's action, and blood poisoning.

1111. What did that arise from?—Blood poisoning.

1112. Is that what was called by Dr. Cremen diffused cellular inflammation?—Yes.

1113. Was there any presence of suffocation?—None whatever.

1114. You have been in court during the hearing of this trial?—I was.

1115. You said you knew the patient during his life. While in prison his eyes became congested, his breathing rapid and shallow, and laboured, his lips black, his countenance flabby and pasty, a nervous tremor in both hands, sore throat, diarrhoea, rheumatism. Assuming that all these things occurred to a person, would you be able to form a medical opinion as to whether these things render him more susceptible of disease and less able to resist it?—I would.

1116. Now, Doctor, would you consider keeping a patient on punishment diet, as bread and water, suffering from diarrhoea, proper or improper treatment?—Very improper, I would say, indeed.

1117. Which do you consider, the present prison cell or the hospital, the proper place for such a patient?—The hospital.

1118. Do you consider a punishment cell opposite a draughty door a fit place for a person complaining of a sore throat?—No.

1119. When a question was asked by my friend, Mr. Murphy, of Dr. Cremen yesterday, he gave an answer, and I want to see whether you agree in that answer. He said this was a low inflammatory affection which no man may get but a man whose conditions are lowered by bad hygienic circumstances by morbid conditions of the blood by privations, by exposure, by organic disease. All these causes lead to that; do you agree with him?—I do.

1120. You knew the patient before he went in, and you knew him after he came out, and you have heard what I have read to you; would you

say

The *MacDermot*—continued.

say as a medical man whether in your opinion this disease from which he died is attributable to his treatment while in prison?—I would say so.

Cross-examined by Mr. *Stephen Ronan*, Q.C.

1121. Doctor, you were first called in professionally to attend Mr. Mandeville on Saturday the 7th in the morning?—Yes.

1122. Where was he then, Doctor?—He was lying in bed.

1123. Dr. M'Craith was with you at the time?—Yes, sir.

1124. Did you make a careful diagnosis of the case then?—Yes.

1125. And you discovered immediately that the case was hopeless. Have you a note in your book of the symptoms that you observed on that occasion?—I have.

1126. Would you read it out to me?—I saw him for the first time on Saturday morning at seven o'clock with Dr. M'Craith.

1127–8. Tell me the result of your diagnosis on Saturday morning, as you have no note of it?—His pulse was 120, and weak respiration about 30 and rather laborious, great swelling on right side of face, difficult and painful deglutition or difficulty in swallowing, extreme restlessness and anxious to get out of bed. Temperature, 102·2.

1129. Do you remember, Doctor, which of you took the temperature?—Dr. M'Craith.

1130. From these symptoms, what was the irresistible cause of death you saw?—Failure of the heart's action.

Here the witness referred to his book, and Mr. Ronan demanded that the book be handed to him. The book was accordingly handed to Mr. Ronan.

Mr. *Ronan*.

The CORONER.] Doctor, point out the entry made on Saturday morning, 7th instant.

1131. Tell me, sir, when was that entry made?—Upon my oath it was made on the Saturday morning.

1132. The entry is under the date Monday, 9th July 1888, and here is the entry: "I saw him for the first time in his fatal illness on Saturday morning the 7th at eight o'clock with Dr. M'Craith. On your oath, if you made that entry on *Saturday morning*, how did you know it was fatal?—By his appearance.

1133. "I saw him for the first time in his fatal illness on Saturday morning, the 7th instant, in company with Dr. M'Craith. I considered his case hopeless then. We took leeches with us, all we had, and applied them and sent immediately for half-a-dozen to Fermoy and had them applied in about two hours. Fomentations and inhalations of steam, alum, and nitrate of potash put on the dorsum of the tongue. A saline aperient was given. Met Dr. Cremen about 1.30. He had but slender hopes of his recovery. He ordered him mixture, chlorate of potash and perchloride of iron. He was ordered brandy and new milk frequently, alternate with chicken broth. Saw him again same, same evening, he was much worse. Next morning saw him at eight o'clock; he was then sinking fast. At half-past two o'clock he breathed his last; my hand supported his head." Now, Dr. O'Neill, on your oath, was the whole of that entry written at one time?—It was not; it was in detached pieces.

1134. How much was the first portion. "I saw him for the first time in his fatal illness on Saturday morning at eight o'clock in company with Dr M'Craith; I considered his case hopeless then." On your oath, was that written on Saturday morning?—It was, on my oath.

The *Coroner*.

1135. When was the first portion written?—That which was written on *Saturday* morning.

1136. Up to what word?—*Witness* reading: "We took two leeches with us, all we had, and applied them, and sent immediately for half-a-dozen others to Fermoy, and had these applied in about two hours with fomentations, inhalations of steam, alum, chlorate of potash over the dorsum of the tongue." That much was written that day; it was after I came home that night I wrote the other things.

1137. All the occurrences of Saturday were written on Saturday night?—On Saturday evening.

1138. At your own house?—At my own house.

Mr. *Ronan*.

1139. What is the last word of Saturday?—"And had them applied in about two hours." I think that is the last I wrote on Saturday evening. That is the last.

1140. Doctor, is this your current book for the present year?—No, sir.

1141. Where is your current book for the present year?—It is at home.

1141. You keep a record of your visits to your patients?—No.

1142. What is in the current book?—Oh, lots of things that I could not tell you about; I would not expose them. I have no book at all this year; my patients are gone.

1143. On your solemn oath, sir, what did you mean by saying your book for the current year was at home?—The current year. I don't exactly understand you. Well, I will swear to you now that I have no book.

The *MacDermot*.] You asked him was that your book for the current year, he said not.

1144. Is this the first year you gave up keeping a book?—No; some years I kept no book. Latterly I did not think it worth while to keep a book; patients were so few and visits so far between.

1145. Mr. *Ronan* (*handing Witness his book*.) Now, would you read that for me?—"It is scarcely necessary to advise caution in the use of the leech in this region."

1146. Was that after you had seen Dr. Cremen?—Yes.

1147. On your oath is that on the page before you wrote this?—That entry was made after I had seen Dr. Cremen.

1148. On your oath is that on the page before this thing you say was written on Saturday. Was the account of the interview with Dr. Cremen written

Mr. Ronan—continued.

written on the Sunday?—It was written on Sunday evening.

1149. Dr. Cremen did not see you on Sunday; was not that entry written on Sunday?—It was.

1150. What o'clock was it on Saturday when you saw Dr. Cremen?—Half-past three.

1151. And when you were making your note on Saturday evening why did you leave out all about Dr. Cremen; in Saturday night's note?—I don't know.

1152. On your oath was not the whole of that written after the man's death?—It was not.

1153. Do you mean to say you wrote his illness was fatal and the man still alive?—I wrote that on Saturday evening.

1154. Now this exploring needle I want to ask you about; did you use that for the purpose of diagnosis?—For the purpose of evacuating matter, not for diagnosis.

1155. That was corresponding to the scarification which Dr. Cremen recommended? Something similar.

1156. Did you ever hear before of an exploring needle being used for an operation?—I often opened pus with an exploring needle myself.

1157. But when scarification is prescribed, did you ever hear of it being used?—Not usually.

1158. Did you ever hear of scarification being done with an exploring needle?—I did not. How could scarification be done with an exploring needle.

1159. When Mr. Mandeville returned here after his imprisonment you noticed a great change in his appearance?—Indeed I did.

1160. Wasted?—Yes.

1161. Shrunk?—Yes.

1162. Pale?—Yes.

1163. Loss of weight?—Yes.

1164. That was obvious to any one who knew him before?—Judging from his physiognomy.

1165. Now tell me, wasting and shrinking, could you form any estimate for the jury as to how much weight he lost while he was in prison?—I would say he lost over two stone.

1166. Do you stick to that?—To the best of my belief, and judging from his appearance.

1167. Your opinion on that, I presume, is about of as much value as on other matters?—That very same.

1168. Was Mr. Mandeville an abstemious man?—As far as I knew him, he was.

1169. He was a man of strong will and firm nerves?—Yes.

1170. Did you ever hear of a man of strong will, firm nerves, and abstemious, taking the pledge against whiskey?—I did.

1171. What was the cause?—To keep away from temptation.

1172. A man of strong will, steady nerves, and abstemious, taking the pledge against whiskey alone; tell me the names of the other men who did it?—Many men took it that I don't know. I cannot enumerate them. (*Laughter in Court.*)

1173. What you told me, Doctor, was that you have known many a man of strong will, abstemious habits, and steady nerves, who took the pledge against whiskey alone?—I knew many a man to take the pledge against everything.

Mr. Ronan—continued.

1174. Did you ever know any man in your life?—I won't say I ever saw one.

Mr. *Harrington.*

1175. You merely said whiskey, not whiskey alone?

Mr. *Ronan.*

1176. In the whole course of your experience could you say you ever heard of a man of strong will, abstemious habits, and steady nerves, taking a pledge against whiskey alone?—I am not prepared to swear that.

1177. Can you say you did?—I don't think I can.

1178. You were a very intimate friend of Mr. Mandeville's; can you give us any explanation why he took this extraordinary pledge against whiskey?—I cannot.

1179. On your oath, in your heart, do you believe that he knew he was taking too much of it?—I don't believe that.

1180. Can you suggest any other motive?—I cannot.

1181. Did you know that he had taken any pledge before against whiskey also?—No.

1182. Did you ever hear?—I don't know.

1183. Did you think it was because he used to take too little of it he took the pledge?—I cannot say.

1184. On your oath do you think he took the pledge because he took too little of it?—It was not.

1185. Was it because he took the right quantity?—I don't know.

Mr. *Harrington* objected to these questions as being ridiculous.

The *Coroner*.] The question is, does he believe why he took the pledge?

Mr. *Harrington*.] Yes, and he says no.

Mr. *Ronan.*

1186. Mr. Mandeville was a man of splendid physique and constitution when he went into gaol?—He was.

1187. So that if any man was fit to bear prison treatment, he was?—He was a good subject going in.

1188. Was his own impression, when he came out, so far as you know, that his constitution had been shattered?—No; he said nothing at all about it to me; he is a very reticent man.

1189. As far as you could gather, what was his impression?—I could not tell you.

1190. He gave you nothing that led you to think that he believed his constitution was shaken?—No.

1191. Saw him frequently?—Not very frequently.

1192. Did you hear, sir, on your oath, that after he came out he said they had not taken a feather out of him?—Never.

1193. Do you read the newspapers?—Occasionally, not every day.

Mr. *Harrington.*

1194. The English "Times" I am sure?—No, I read the "Sportsman," "Bell's Life," and so forth, and the "Star," occasionally.

1195. Do

Mr. Harrington—continued.

1194. Do you read a Cork daily paper?—No.

Mr. Ronan.

1195. Could you give me any idea of the number of speeches Mr. Mandeville made after coming out of gaol?—I could not.

1196. You heard he made some?—Yes, if they were speeches.

1197. How else would you describe them?—He might have been talking.

1198. What part of the treatment was for the septic condition?—Potash and iron.

1199. What part of the treatment was for the blood poisoning?—The septic case and it are synonymous.

1200. Was there any lividity in his lips?—There was blueness.

1201. Or the nails?—There was.

1202. Was there on the general surface of the body?—No; I did not remark it.

1203. Are you speaking of the time immediately before death or after death?—Before death.

1204. How long before?—The first day I saw him he had it.

1205. Did that continue until death?—It did, I think.

1206. I want you to be sure?—I am certain it never left him.

1207. When did you last see the surface of his body before death?—I saw it the day he died.

1208. What time?—In the morning and during the forenoon up to half-past two o'clock, the day he died.

Mr. Ronan—continued.

1209. You saw the entire surface of his body?—Not the entire surface; his breast, and hands, and arms.

1210. Was he dressed, doctor?—Covered with sheets and blankets.

1211. Did you take off the clothes to examine the body?—Not except the parts exposed.

Re-examined by The MacDermot.

1212. You said Mr. Mandeville had strong nerves and will, and abstemious habits; do you think that a man with good nerves and a fair amount of will and abstemious habits won't sometimes take a little too much?—Many a man does it.

1213. And if a man does find that he takes too much sometimes is it wrong for him to take the pledge?—Not at all.

1214. Did you ever see him drunk?—On my oath I never did.

1215. Did you ever dine in his company?—I did, once or twice.

1216. You already stated that you met him a few times, and that he was very reticent, that he said nothing about his constitution being shattered; do you think Mr. Mandeville was a man who, if he suffered loss of constitution in prison, would go about telling people that his constitution was shattered?—No.

1217. Do you think he would be too proud to do it; do you think that he would be more likely to boast that not a feather had been knocked out of him than to complain?—I do.

DANIEL GOULDING, Ex-warder of Tullamore Gaol; Examined.

Mr. Harrington.

1218. I BELIEVE you were a warder in Tullamore Prison when Mr. Mandeville was imprisoned in Tullamore?—Yes.

1219. You remember the time of his going to prison?—I was told, but I did not see him that day; I did not see him till about three days after his arrival.

1220. Had you ever seen him before?—No.

1221. Did it strike you what was his appearance?—Yes.

1222. As being remarkable?—Yes.

1223. As being a big, strong man?—Being a very big, able man, strong and healthy.

1224. Where was he at the time you saw him?—At exercise.

1225. Was there any other prisoner with him at exercise?—Mr. O'Brien.

1226. Were you in the yard with him?—I saw him from a window.

1227. Was he in your charge any time?—Never, unless on a Sunday, when other officers would be present.

1228. At that time Mr. O'Brien and he were both in their own clothes?—Yes.

1229. Was any other prisoner exercising with them?—No.

1230. Do you recollect having seen Mr. Mandeville brought before the governor on any occasion?—Yes; but I did not recollect the day after his imprisonment.

Mr. Harrington—continued.

1231. What charge was brought against him?—Refusing to wear prison clothes.

1232. Can you recollect what reply he made?—He was reported by Warder Mooney for refusing to wear prison clothes. I was present. He was asked by the governor what he had got to say. He said, "I have nothing to say but that I won't wear prison clothes." The governor said he was handed up to him as a convicted criminal, and "I must punish you." Mr. Mandeville said he was not a convicted criminal; he was a political prisoner, and thought himself as such, and would not wear the prison garb. "Very well, I must punish you," said the governor; "48 hours' bread and water."

1233. Do you know where that punishment was undergone?—In his cell.

1234. You know how much bread is allowed during the 48 hours?—Sixteen ounces of bread each day, divided into three parts; the coarse brown bread, six for breakfast, six for dinner, and four for supper.

1235. What drink had he with that?—Water, it is supposed to be. I did not see him receive this, but that is the usual bread-and-water allowance.

1236. Can you tell me in what quantity water is given to a prisoner?—There is plenty of water.

1237. I believe, with some prisoners, it is customary

Mr. Harrington—continued.

customary to make changes in his cell?—Yes, everything is taken out of his cell with the exception of his stool, cell-pot, prayer-book, beads, and drinking quart.

1238. What is taken away?—The plank bed, all the clothes, the mattress, and the rules and regulations. The walls are left bare and naked.

1239. Were you brought into contact with Mr. Mandeville during the time he was in prison?—Yes.

1240. Can you tell me how long he was in prison before that occurred; can you tell me the date?—The 21st of November.

1241. Is that the occasion on which he was stripped of his clothes?—Yes.

1242. Will you tell how you were brought into contact with him on that evening; were you present when he was stripped of his clothes?—I went off duty at 6.30 that evening. About 7.30 Warder Houlehan informed me the governor wanted me. I went to the prison, and the governor opened the door, and he desired me to go for Warder Wilson. I did so, and found him in bed. I told the governor that Warder Wilson was in his bed. He desired me to go back and tell him to come up. While I was away for Warder Wilson, the warder who came for me also went for Warder Mooney.

1243. What hour was this?—Surely, I would say about eight o'clock p.m. We were marched in by the governor himself, Warder Wilson, Mooney, Bagnall, and the chief warder, George Bartley. They were marched in and formed in line on the parade ground. The governor informed us that he had instructions to strip Mandeville, and that he expected us to do our duty. "It is very hard," said he, "but it must be done. Lead on men," and he proceeded up the stairs, along the centre landing, until we came to Mr. Mandeville's cell.

Coroner.

1244. What hour was that?—About eight o'clock. The light is put out at eight o'clock, and it was not lighting at the time. Chief warder Bartley opened the door from the outside.

Mr. *Harrington.*

1245. How is the cell fastened?—By a bolted lock. The governor said, "Light the gas."

1246. Was the cell dark when you entered?—It was dark. The chief warder lit the gas.

1247. Could you see Mr. Mandeville then?—Yes, he was lying on the bed asleep. He had his cell stool propping his pillow.

1248. What is in the pillow?—Fibre.

1249. Are you aware how many pounds of fibre in the mattress?—Seven pounds. He did not wake up when we entered the cell.

1250. Did any of the men approach him?—Yes, the chief warder. The chief warder went over to him and he caught the stool in his right hand and he pulls it away, at the same time saying, "Get up out of that." Whilst getting up he leaned on his right elbow, then rubbed his eyes, and asked what was up. The governor informed him that he should take off the clothes.

Coroner.

1251. Was Mr. Mandeville in his ordinary clothes?—He was in his own clothes, and in bed.

Counsel.

1252. Well?—Mr. Mandeville said he would not. "If you do not give them up," said the governor, "we must take them from you by force. I have instructions to do so." He said that he would not without a struggle. "Very well," said the governor, "men, do your duty." The chief warder, Wilson, McCulla, Bagnall, and Mooney——

Coroner.

1253. What about yourself?—[*Witness.*] I was looking on. They seized him while he was sitting down on his plank bed. They caught hold of his coat, opened it; they were pulling it off his shoulder, and they succeeded in getting it off after a struggle. Mr. Mandeville said he did not wish to strike them, that they were too numerous. They opened his waistcoat, and forced that off him. He had a knitted gansey over his shirt; that was pulled off. They pulled off the trousers then; Warder Wilson opened the buttons.

Mr. Harrington.

1254. Do you know whether they were holding his hands?—Yes, they were holding his hands. Then they caught him by the shoulders and pulled off his shirt. He said, "For decency sake, leave me my shirt; I won't give up my shirt without a struggle." Warder Wilson placed a sheet around his loins; after doing so he lay down. Warder Mooney when coming to the cell had the clothes with him, and he left them in the cell. The governor told Mandeville that they were nice clean clothes, and to put them on. He said he would not, that he would remain naked. His own clothes were gathered up by Mooney. We left the cell, and the door was locked and the light put out.

1255. Where was McCulla?—He was inside; McCulla was the warder on duty.

1256. I believe the warders keep a book?—Yes, there is a book for the warders to enter any complaints.

1257. Do you know how often Mr. Mandeville was on bread and water whilst in gaol?—I am not quite sure.

1258. About how often?—I think about nine periods.

1259. And these periods would be 24 and 48 hours, and so forth?—I do not know.

1260. Were you aware that he was a portion of the time in the punishment cell?—Yes.

1261. Do you know whether it is in the same condition as when Mr. Mandeville was confined in it?—No, it was improved since.

1262. I believe it has been floored since you left?—Yes, boarded.

1263. Did you see Mr. Mandeville about the time he left?—I saw him the night before he left.

1264. Did you observe any change in him?—Yes, then and during his imprisonment. His face was thin, a dark circle round his eyes, his lips of a bluish colour, his clothes seemed too big for him.

1265. Had

Mr. *Harrington*—continued.

1265. Had he his own clothes on?—Yes, he had his own clothes on at that time, and on the whole he was a different man from the first day I saw himself and Mr. William O'Brien.

1266. When a prisoner is punished for a breach of the rules, not doing work, and so on, that is always done on the report of a warder?—Yes.

1267. Did it come to your knowledge that Mr. Mandeville was punished without any such report?——

Mr. *Ronan* objected.

Coroner.

1268. Are you aware that Mr. Mandeville has not been punished without his being reported?—I am aware that Mr. Mandeville has been punished without his name being entered in this book. There may be another book besides one.

Cross-examined by Mr. *Ronan*.

1269. When Mr. Mandeville was wakened he had one hand under his jaw?—Yes.

1269. What was he doing with the other hand?—I cannot say.

1270. After he awoke and stood up where was his other hand?—Ask the question straight, and I will answer.

1271. What did you tell us before about his hands?—I said when the stool was pulled from under his head, after that he got up on his right elbow.

1272. When they were taking the clothes off him, what was Mr. Goulding doing with his right hand and his left?—Both in his pockets.

1273. The other warders were engaged, but never did one of Mr. Goulding's hands leave his pockets?—Never, while I was in the cell.

1274. That is because he had an objection to take part in this nefarious business?—I won't answer you.

1275. You must!—I had an objection to take off the clothes.

1276. And therefore it was because you had an objection to take part in this, that you kept your hands in your pockets?—Yes.

1277. Did you go to the cell determined to keep your hands in your pockets?—Yes.

1278. Why did you not refuse to go?—Simply because there would be no one to tell the story.

1279. Oh, your object in going up there was to be a witness of what took place?—Yes.

1280. And you believe the governor, chief warder, and all your colleagues there would give a false account of what happened?—They would give a true account to their authorities, but they would not give it to the public.

1281. If you were not there, no one else would give a true account to the public?—Yes.

1282. And you were the one man who would give a true account to the public?—Well, I had no other means of knowing it. I had my own opinion.

1283. Was it your opinion that you alone would give a true account to the public?—I did not form any opinion at the time.

1284. Did you not tell me that the reason you went up there was that there would be no one to tell the truth?—I went up there to see that the man was not killed on the spot.

Mr. *Ronan*—continued.

1285. Did you anticipate that he might be killed on the spot?—I went to see, fearing he might be killed by the shock.

1286. Was there a scrape of a pin on any man's hand after that struggle?—No.

1287. Was there a scrape of a nail?—No.

1288. Was there the slightest hurt to anybody?—To Mr. Mandeville's feelings, as there would be to mine.

1289. Was there a single article of his clothing torn?—I did not examine them.

1290. What do you believe?—I cannot say yes or no; they might be, or they might not.

1291. But you described minutely every portion of the act, how each article of clothing was taken off. Can you say now that a single article was torn?—I cannot say it was.

1292. Was there any injury done except the injury to his feelings?—No.

1293. How long were you in Tullamore?—About 16 months.

1294. Had you ever to deal with refractory prisoners, and do you believe in dealing with refractory prisoners their clothes can be taken off without being torn?—I do not know.

1295. What do you believe?—I have no belief as to whether a man's clothes could be taken off without tearing them.

1296. What weight did you say was Mr. Mandeville's mattress?—Seven pounds.

1297. There is no doubt about that?—No.

1298. When did you see his mattress?—I had a couple of occasions of seeing it.

1299. Is there only one kind of mattress used in the gaol?—There are two.

1300. What is the weight of the other one?—Fourteen pounds.

1301. Had not Mr. Mandeville a mattress with 24 lbs. in it?—To my own knowledge, no.

1302. How often were you in his cell altogether?—About four or five times.

1303. Tell again all that was taken out of the cell?—The plank bed, the mattress, the bedding, and the rules.

1304. His first punishment was 48 hours?—Yes.

1305. On your oath, have you conveyed to the jury the truth about what takes place as to that cell for 48 hours?—Yes.

1306. On your oath, is not the bedding given back every night?—Yes.

1307. You were greatly shocked at the scene that you went up to witness for the public good?—Yes, it reminded me of the Jews stripping Our Lord.

1308. And of course, when you make such an appalling comparison as that, it entered very deep into your feelings. When did you first communicate it to the public?—I won't answer.

1309. You must?—I won't answer.

Coroner.] You are bound to answer.

Witness.] Immediately after I came out that night.

Counsel.

1310. Who did you tell?—I told my wife, and I told a reporter for the "Freeman."

1311. What is his name?—I do not know.

1312. Did you tell him that night?—Yes.

1313. When first did you tell the solicitor who

Counsel—continued.

who is conducting this case; when did you first tell your evidence?—I never told Mr. Mandeville.

1314. Who did you give your evidence to?—To Mr. Mandeville's clerk.

1315. How did they find out that you knew all about it?—By letter (*hands letter to Counsel*).

1316. You got something before that?—(*No answer*).

1317. Have you been dismissed for making false reports, and telling lies?—(*No answer*).

Coroner.

1318. Have you been dismissed from Tullamore?—Yes.

1319. For what?—For a statement got up by the governor, that he visited me when on night duty one night at 12.30, and he said I did not peg the clock. I was dismissed for saying that I was in number four and pegging the clock at 12.30, and for being in my stocking soles.

Mr. Ronan.

1320. Were you dismissed for telling a lie to the governor?—I cannot say.

1321. Were you charged with telling a lie to the governor?—He charged me with it.

1322. And on that charge you were dismissed?—I have no doubt but that is the charge I was dismissed on.

1323. When were you dismissed?—On the 10th July.

1324. And this letter is dated the 11th?—Yes.

1325. Did you write to anybody the day you were dismissed?—No.

1326. Nor had no message sent to anybody?—I won't answer.

1327. Why do you decline to answer?—On the grounds that I had many persons to write to or send a message to.

1328. Did you send a message to anybody on the 10th?—I did.

1329. Is that the message you decline to tell me about?—I decline to answer on the subject.

1330. Had that message anything to say to this case?—No.

1331. Did you send any message about Mr. Mandeville on that day?—No.

1332. Did you send any message to Mr. Mandeville?

The *MacDermot* objected, unless the message was in writing.

Mr. Ronan.

1333. Did you send any letter to anybody about Mr. Mandeville?—At what period?

1334. At any time?—No.

1335. And why did you ask me "At what period"?—To know what you mean; you are asking me such crooked questions; upon my soul I do not know what you mean at all.

1336. You sent a verbal message about Mr. Mandeville to some one?—No.

1337. And why, when I asked you, did you decline to answer; what did you decline to answer?—That I sent a verbal message.

Mr. Ronan—continued.

1338. Why did you decline to answer?—I do not see what it has to do with the case.

1339. You got this letter the day after you were dismissed?—Yes.

1340. Were you surprised at getting this letter?—I was not surprised at anything.

1341. How did Mr. Mandeville know here in Mitchelstown on the 11th July that you were dismissed the previous day?—I do not know whether he knew I was dismissed or not.

1342. Were you served with a subpœna; were you given a little money to come down here?—No.

1343. Are you in any employment now?—No.

1344. You got no money to come down here?—No.

1345. Where are you stopping here?—At a friend's.

1346. Who is the friend?—Maurice Connor's.

1347. Did you know him before you came here?—No; but I knew his wife.

1348. Did you pay for your ticket out of your own money?—Yes.

1349. Were you talking to any one in Tullamore about what evidence you would give here?—Yes.

1350. To whom?—To several parties.

1351. What parties?—I was telling Mr. Meenahan I would come here.

1352. Were you telling him or any one what your evidence would be?—I did not tell any gentleman what my evidence would be, unless that legal gentleman.

1353. You saw Mr. Mandeville leaving prison?—Yes.

1354. He was emaciated, worn, wasted, pale?—Not pale, but thin.

1355. Blue marks on his eyes?—They appeared to me to be more black.

1356. You noticed that when he went in he was a fine man, healthy, and so on?—Yes.

1357. Were you here to-day?—Not all day.

1358. Can you give me your estimate how much weight Mr. Mandeville lost?—I cannot say; I would say he lost three stone.

1359. How far is your house from the gaol?—Nearly opposite.

1360. Do you know how Mr. Mandeville found out your address?—I suppose Mr. Mandeville, the deceased, told him, as Mr. Mandeville, the deceased, asked me where I was from in prison.

1361. Can you suggest any reason why Mr. Mandeville should write a letter to his brother about you?—He did not tell me the reason for taking my address.

1362. Were you showing any letter written by Mr. Mandeville to anybody else?—No.

1363. It was on the 22nd November you saw this stripping scene?—Yes.

1364. I suppose you looked on the people who did it as being as bad as the people who stripped Our Lord?—It reminded me of the scene. It reminded me of the Jews.

1365. And for over six months you remained in their employment until you were turned out?—I was turned out for no charge.

1366. Did you swear you were a while ago?—No.

Mr. *Ronan*—continued.

1367. Why did you remain on in the gaol until you were turned out? Are you married? —Yes.

Mr. *Harrington.*

1368. I believe all the warders live in Charleville-row, where you live?—Nearly all.

1369. Did you know of any bit of meat being thrown to Mr. Mandeville?—No.

Mr. *Ronan.*

1370. Did you tell any one what had happened to Mr. Mandeville?—I told the "Freeman" correspondent.

Mr. *Ronan*—continued.

1371. Where did you see that correspondent? —In Tullamore.

1372. How did you know he was correspondent?—He told me so.

1373. Did he give you any money for the information?—No.

1374. Did you give him the same statement as you gave here to-day?—No, I did not tell exactly all.

1375. Did you tell the substance of it?—I did.

1376. From that time, till after your dismissal, did you tell any one?—I did.

1377. Can you recollect to whom you told it? —No.

SIXTH DAY.

Monday, 23rd July 1888.

Mr. Pierce Joyce, Mervilla, Corbally; Examined.

Mr. *Murphy*, Q.C.

1378. What is your occupation, Mr. Joyce?—Inspector of Prisons in Ireland under the Prisons Board.

1379. How many inspectors are there?—Two in Ireland.

1380. Who is the other?—Captain Hill.

1381. Is the country divided into districts between you and Captain Hill?—Yes.

1382. Which is your district?—It comprises the south-west and part of the east.

1383. Is Tullamore within your district?—No, but I may qualify that; it has recently been added to my district.

1384. Do you remember, in November 1887, whether your colleague was away?—He was ill.

1385. During the illness of one, how is the work done?—By the other.

1386. Did you visit Tullamore Prison?—I did.

1387. What is the date of your visit?—The 11th November.

1388. Can you tell us when you visit a prison what is your duty with regard to the prison and prisoners?—I see that the prison is clean and orderly, and that the rules in respect to prisoners are carried out.

1389. Do you inspect the whole prison?—Not on every occasion.

1390. Upon that occasion did you see Mr. John Mandeville?—I did.

1391. Where did you see him?—I saw him in his cell.

1392. How would you describe that cell?—A good cell.

1393. Was it commodious for a prison cell?—Yes.

1394. Covered with matting?—It was.

1395. Had it all the conveniences that are allowed in the prison rules?—Yes.

1396. When you go to the prison, do you see the prisoners alone?—Sometimes alone, and sometimes in presence of the prison officials.

1397. On this occasion did you see Mr. John Mandeville alone?—I did; and also in the presence of the governor.

1398. Was any notice given to the officials of the prison of the time of your visit?—No, none whatever.

1399. And was the interview between you and Mr. Mandeville in the presence of the governor?—I interviewed him with the governor.

Mr. *Murphy*, Q.C.—continued.

1400. You remember what passed between you and Mr. Mandeville when the governor was present?—I do.

1401. What passed between you?—I asked Mr. Mandeville if he had any complaints to make, and he replied that he had none. The governor then left the cell, as well as I remember, for the purpose of seeing what the thermometer outside in the passage registered. I then said to Mr. Mandeville that he was making his imprisonment worse than it was intended to be by not complying with the prison rules, and I asked him if he did not think it would be better to conform to the prison regulations, and make his imprisonment easier. He smiled slightly, and said he was all right.

1402. How long are you connected with the prison system in Ireland?—About 10 years.

1403. And you have considerable experience, I suppose, in the working of prisons?—Yes.

1404. And it is necessary for the discipline of the prison that every prisoner should conform to the prison rules?—Yes.

1405. Apart from a disciplinary point of view, what is the effect of allowing a prisoner to disregard or disobey the prison regulations?

Question objected to by The MacDermot, and allowed.

Witness.] It would cause the greatest confusion and disorder.

1406. In your experience as a prison inspector, do you know prison officials ever to have experienced any difficulties before in respect to prisoners wearing prison clothes?—Not that I heard.

1407. Outside the matter of discipline, is there any reason why the wearing of these prison clothes should be enforced?—For sanitary purposes.

1408. Are you aware of the ordinary dietary allowed in prisons?—Yes.

1409. I believe it varies according to the period for which a prisoner is incarcerated?—It does, and varies according to the days of the week.

1410. From your experience, can you say the dietary allowed to persons upon their first entry, such as Mr. Mandeville's was, has been found sufficient for a man of his physique?—I believe it is.

1411. Was

Cross-examined by *The MacDermot.*

1411. Was that your first visit to Tullamore Prison?—I was there once or twice before.

1412. How long before were you in it?—About three years.

1413. You went there on the 11th November?—Yes.

1414. Were you aware when you were going there that Mr. O'Brien and Mr. Mandeville were there?—I was.

1415. Had your going there any special reference to them?—None whatever.

1416. Before you went there were these two gentlemen mentioned to you as being there?—No.

1417. Did you receive any special instructions going there?—I received instructions to visit Tullamore Prison.

1418. On what date?—I do not know what date.

1419. Were they written instructions?—They were.

1420. Have you them here?—No. I am not certain whether they were written instructions or not.

1421. What hour of the day did you go to the prison?—About 11 o'clock in the morning.

1422. Did you then see the governor?—I did.

1423. The doctor?—I did.

1424. Which was the first cell you visited?—I cannot say.

1425. Did you visit Mr. O'Brien's cell?—Mr. O'Brien was in hospital.

1426. Did you visit him?—I did.

1427. Whether did you see him or Mr. Mandeville first?—I cannot say.

1428. Have you any recollection?—I really cannot say.

1429. Are they the two prisoners you visited first?—I am sure they were not.

1430. Can you give me the name of the first cell or the first prisoner you visited?—I cannot. As well as I remember, I went to the centre of the prison, and then visited the cells in line.

1431. Now, you visited Mr. Mandeville's cell in company with the governor?—Yes.

1432. At the time he was wearing his own clothes?—He was.

1433. Before you reached the prison in Tullamore did you know he had declined to wear prison clothes?—I may have seen it in the papers.

1434. Did you otherwise know it?—No.

1435. Were you informed before you went there that Mr. Mandeville had refused to put on prison clothes?—No, except by the papers.

1436. Were you informed that he refused to associate with criminals?—No.

1437. What hour were you at Mr. Mandeville's cell?—I cannot possibly say.

1438. Can you give me an approximation?—Some time between 11 and one o'clock.

1439. Before you entered his cell, had you been made aware otherwise than by the papers that he had been refusing to comply with the prison rules?—I was.

The MacDermot—continued.

1440. Were you also aware that Mr. O'Brien had declined to comply with the prison rules?—I was.

1441. Had your attention been drawn to the written report of Dr. Ronayne before you entered his cell?—No.

1442. Is it the duty of the Inspector of Prisons to read the reports of visiting justices?—No.

1443. Do you mean to tell me that it is not your duty to ascertain everything that will throw light on the condition of the prison?—Yes.

1444. Did you read Dr. Moorhead's report?—As well as I remember, I did.

1445. Have you told the whole conversation that occurred between you and Mr. Mandeville?—I have.

1446. Did you ask him whether he had been suffering from embarrassed breathing?—No.

1447. Did you go back afterwards and ask him whether he had been suffering from embarrassed breathing or whether he had been suffering from sore throat?—No.

1448. Did you ask him whether he had had a change of linen from the time he came to Tullamore?—No.

1449. I think you will agree with me that Mr. O'Brien and Mr. Mandeville were of a class different from the ordinary prisoners?—Yes.

1450. Will you agree with me that the food and nourishment required for the support of a man who had been accustomed to the comforts of life would be different from that of a person accustomed to humble fare?—The privation would be greater.

1451. And the physical loss more felt?—I think it would; it would entirely depend upon a man's former habits.

1452. Do you not think a man's former habits included the food he was in the habit of nourishing himself with?—It would.

1453. Do you not think that a change from that food is more telling than a change from meagre food?—Of course it would.

1454. You said the disregard of prison rules by a prisoner would lead to confusion; I suppose I must be right in saying, to allow prisoners to disobey the rules would lead to greater confusion?—It would.

1455. Was Mr. O'Brien allowed to disregard them?—He did.

1456. Was he allowed to do so?—I do not think he got special permission.

1457. Without permission he never wore the prison clothes?—No.

1458. Without permission he never cleansed his cell?—No.

1459. Without permission he never associated with criminals?—No; I have nothing to do with that at all.

1460. Was that on account of his condition and respectability?—No.

1461. Why was he not compelled?—On account of his health.

Capt. W. J. Stopford, *of the Home Office, London*; Examined.

Mr. *Ronan*.

1462. I believe you have been 22 years in the English prison service?—I have.

1463. And you are at present a Commissioner of English Prisons?—I am.

1464. You are also, I believe, a Director of the English Convict Prisons?—I am.

1465. Can you tell me some of the offices you have held in the prison service?—I have been Deputy Governor of Chatham Convict Prison, Governor of Dartmoor Prison, Governor of Portsmouth Convict Prison, and Inspector of Military Prisons.

1466. I believe you visited Ireland twice at the request of the Government for the purpose of inspecting and reporting on the Irish prisons?—I did.

1467. The first time, at the request of Lord Spencer, to report on the state of Irish prisons, and how far the recommendations of the Commission had been carried out?—Yes.

1468. Did you examine into the regulations of the Irish prisons with a view to comparing them with the English?—I did.

1469. As to the regulations as to dress, is there any difference between the English and the Irish rules?—There is not. The Irish rule, No. 88, provides that a convicted prisoner shall wear a prison dress and shall be compelled to wear it.

1470. In your vast experience of English prison life, has that rule been invariably enforced?—Yes.

1471. Do you know the practice in Ireland that every convicted prisoner is compelled to keep his own cell clean; is it the same in English prisons?—Yes.

1472. And is it enforced?—It is.

1473. Do you know in Irish prisons the practice as to time and manner of prisoners taking exercise together?—No.

1474. What is the English rule?—The exercise is distributed throughout the day according to the recommendation of the medical officer and as may be found convenient.

1475. Is it essential in your opinion for the proper administration of a prison that those rules should be carried out?—It is.

1476. There are numerous instances in England of convicted prisoners coming from the class of persons who are in affluent circumstances?—Yes.

1477. Is there any special class for such persons?—That depends on how they have been sentenced.

1478. If they are not first-class misdemeanants there is no special class?—No.

1479. And they are treated in precisely the same manner as persons in the humblest rank, and made to obey the rules?—Yes.

1480. Taking as a whole the Irish system and the English, apart from the question of diet, is there any substantial difference between them?—They are practically the same.

1481. Now about the question of diet, is there a difference?—There is.

1482. Tell the Coroner and jury what it is?—In the diet at first the difference is considerable.

Mr. *Ronan*—continued.

The English prisoner gets no stirabout diet at all; no milk at all. In addition to the diet of English prisoners the Irish prisoners get two pints of milk per day, new milk. The remainder are practically about the same.

1483. What is the meaning of what is properly known as "skilly"?—Gruel.

1484. What is the composition of that gruel?—Meal boiled in water.

1485. What quantity?—I cannot tell the quantity.

1486. Is there any difference in giving prisoners cocoa in Ireland and in England; what is the rule?—Cocoa is one of the regular diets in England; cocoa for breakfast, and gruel for supper.

1487. Does he get that at first?—Not till he has passed the first stage.

1488. On the whole, is the English or the Irish diet better?—The Irish is the best in the points that I have explained to you.

1489. And the ordinary food of the Irish prison is better?—In that respect.

1490. Is there any respect in which the English prison has the advantage?—No.

1491. During your experience have you had men convicted of Fenian conspiracy and people of that class under you?—I have.

1492. I believe, among others, you had Michael Davitt?—He was in Dartmoor when I was director of the prison.

1493. Did he ever object to conform to the rules?—He gave no trouble at all.

1494. Had you ever any trouble with those Fenian prisoners on the subject of prison clothes?—None.

1495. You proceeded to Tullamore; I think you gave me the date of your visit; I think it was about the middle of November; I think it was on the day the rule of clothes was brought in?—No.

1496. Was any information given to the Tullamore prison that you were going?—I believe the Governor was told to admit me, but I gave none.

1497. You had no authority to see the prisoners themselves?—No.

1498. When you went there what did you inspect; the food?—I did.

1499. What was the result of your inspection?—It was good.

1500 Did you go round the corridors of the prison with the Governor?—I did.

1501. You had a conversation with him?—I had.

1502. Did you make other investigation than that necessary for you to make a report, from the Governor?—I did.

1503. What was the general result of your examination and investigation?—I saw that the prison rules were carried out.

1504. You made a personal examination of the food?—I did.

1505. And you made a personal examination of the general cleanness and condition of the prison?—I did.

Mr. *Ronan*—continued.

1506. You did not enter the cells where the prisoners were confined?—No; I had no authority.

1507. In what you saw and heard was there anything to find fault with?—No, I saw nothing to find fault with.

1508. Did you learn anything to find fault with?—No.

1509. You have nothing whatever to do with the Irish Government?—No.

1510. You are a thoroughly English official?—Yes.

1511. Although you are nearly an Irishman?—My father was.

Cross-examined by Mr. *Harrington*.

1512. Do you mean to convey by your evidence that there was no comparison between the diet Mr. Mandeville received in prison and the diet of the Fenian prisoners?—No; I do not know what diet Mr. Mandeville was on.

1513. Can you tell me the scale of diet allowed to the Fenian prisoners in Dartmoor in your time?—No, I do not remember.

1514. Are you still in connection with the English prisons?—I am.

1515. Can you now tell us what scale of dietary is in any of the convict prisons?—Not without referring to the dietary.

1516. And that interesting report you made for the Government was a report made, I suppose, made by comparing the English book with the Irish book?—Comparing the Irish scale with the English scale.

1517. Do you not think that could be done in England?—But I had to visit the prison as well.

1518. Was it from the Governor you ascertained at Tullamore that the rules were carried out?—It was.

1519. Did you ever find a governor of an English prison who told you he was not carrying out the rules?—No.

1520. When did you make this comparison with the English scale?—In November last.

1521. Now I ask you, are you in a position at present to make that comparison?—I am.

1522. What is the diet for Class II.?—I cannot give the diet without referring to the dietary scale.

1523. Are you aware how long the milk I refer to is supplied to prisoners in Ireland?—Since the holding of the Royal Commission.

1524. Now, Captain, I ask you, is it your oath that a pint of milk is supplied to prisoners of Mr. Mandeville's class?—I do not know what he got.

1525. Are two pints of milk given to other convicted prisoners in Ireland?—I believe so.

1526. From whom did you learn that?—From the diet scale.

1527. Did you ask the Governor in Tullamore?—No.

1528. And you do not know whether he carried out that rule?—I cannot say.

1529. Now, you were asked whether Mr Davitt had ever given any trouble as to prison dress; did you ever see Mr. Davitt in anything other than prison dress?—No.

Mr. *Harrington*—continued.

1530. Do you know anything of Mr. Davitt's treatment during his imprisonment in England?—I do not know.

1531. Do you know anything as to whether the late Home Secretary gave any directions regarding him?—I never heard.

1532. You never learned from the newspapers?—I never heard the subject before.

1533. Do you know of your own personal knowledge whether Mr. Davitt had given any trouble about the prison dress?—I do not know of my own knowledge. I believe he did not; I never heard he did.

1534. Do you know of your own knowledge whether Mr. Davitt ever cleaned his cell?—I do not.

1535. Do you know of your own knowledge whether he refused to associate with criminals?—I do not know.

1536. In all your 23 years' experience, did you ever find a man in an English prison and wearing prison garb, prison dress, and treated as a convicted criminal for having made a speech?—Never.

1537. Did you ever meet any clergymen in prison during your time; did you meet any imprisoned for clerical offences?—No.

1538. For what offences were they in prison?—Civil offences.

1539. You did not see the Rev. Mr. Fox?—No.

1540. Can you tell me what offences were these respectable official persons convicted of?—Several offences; fraud, embezzlement.

1541. When prisoners refuse to comply with prison rules, what would you do with them?—They are generally reported.

1542. What did you do with them?—I heard the charge, and if it was proved against them, they were punished.

1543. What was the nature of that punishment?—No more than three days' bread and water.

1544. Did that entail the loss of exercise?—Yes, necessarily.

1545. How long should a prisoner be after punishment before you could repeat the punishment?—Twenty-four hours.

1546. Have you in your experience removed a prisoner off punishment when you thought him ill?—Yes, I have.

1547. Now, as to the matter of comparison with the English system; as a matter of fact, the English prisoner is not detained so long in his cell as the Irish prisoner?—I think he is.

1548. Is he not brought out to prayers in the morning?—He is; but the Irish prisoners get two hours' exercise, and the English one.

1549. On your oath is that statement accurate?—It is.

1550. Is it true as to short-sentence prisoners?—It is.

1551. Only one?—One.

1552. I ask you whether it is from the scale or from your knowledge of carrying out the rules you give that answer?—It is from the result of my inquiry.

1553. Did you ever carry out that rule yourself with regard to short-term prisoners?—I never had an opportunity of carrying it out.

1554. Can you say whether the prisoners you refer to are engaged in the open air or not?—They are engaged in their cells, and no exercise

Mr. *Harrington*—continued.

is given to prisoners who are engaged in the open air.

1555. And now you pledge yourself that no exercise is given to short-term prisoners who are engaged in the open air?—No, it is not mentioned by the rule.

1556. Do you know it of your own knowledge?—I do; I know it as Commissioner of Prisons.

1557. How often do you visit prisons as Commissioner?—About once a year, or thereabouts.

1558. How many prisons did you visit in Ireland in November?—Four; Kilmainham, Richmond, Wexford, and Tullamore.

1559. Did you meet any prisoner in Kilmainham?—No.

1560. Or in any of the others?—No.

1561. Did you meet the prison doctor in Kilmainham?—No.

1562. Did you see there any book of reports by visiting justices?—No.

1563. Did the governor show you in Tullamore any book of reports by visiting justices?—No, he did not.

1564. Did you see the cells in Tullamore?—I did.

1565. Can you say in what part of the prison you saw the cells?—In the main part.

1566. Were they flagged?—I think they were.

1567. Did you meet any other official in Tullamore with whom you might have an opportunity of examining except the governor?—The storekeeper.

1568. The governor was apprised of your going to visit the prison?—I think he was.

Mr. *Ronan*.

1569. The Commissioners of Prisons, of which you are one, are the supreme authority in England?—No, the Secretary of State.

1570. Prisoners kept in penal servitude are not under your charge?—No.

1571. Are you also Director of Convict Prisons?—I have said so.

1572. That is an independent post?—Yes.

1573. Are the Commissioners of Convict Prisons under the supreme authority for the direction of convict prisons?—Yes.

1574. The comparison you made of diet was between the English local prison and the Irish local prison?—Yes.

1575. And these are the official scales of diet (*hands witness scale*)?—Yes.

1576. You were asked about punishments; the provision of the rules as regards punishment is substantially identical with those of the Irish?—I think so.

1577. Have you a copy of the English prison rules?—I have not.

1578. You said you had certain clergymen in prison under your control; was there any distinction made between those prisoners?—No.

1579. If a prisoner is sentenced to imprisonment in England for having broken the rules, have the authorities any power to make any difference regarding his treatment?—They have no power to do so.

1580. You were asked by Mr. Harrington if you ever had a man under your control in prison for making a speech. In your experience of English life and society did you ever know of a case of a gentleman inciting ignorant peasants to resist the law?—No.

The MacDermot.

There was Mr. Cunninghame Graham in prison for having broken the law in Trafalgar-square?

Mr. *Ronan*.

1581. No exception was made in his case?—No.

Mr. *Harrington*.

1582. It was the same Government that prosecuted and imprisoned Mr. Graham, you are aware?—I suppose so.

1583. Have you any doubt?—I do not know.

1584. Do you mean in the evidence you gave here to convey that you have never known prison rules to be relaxed?—Yes, on the recommendation of the doctor.

Mr. *Ronan*.

1585. Does the Home Secretary ever interfere as to a prisoner's discharge or as to his treatment in prison?—No, I do not recollect a case.

Mr. *Harrington*.

1586. Do you remember the imprisonment of Colonel Baker?—I do.

1587. Do you believe he was treated as an ordinary prisoner?—He was convicted as a first-class misdemeanant.

1588. And he was convicted of a criminal assault on a lady, I believe?—I believe he was.

1589. You remember the imprisonment of Mr. Stead of the "Pall Mall Gazette"?—I do.

1590. Can you tell me what class of Irish diet you compare with English diet?—I compare them all.

1591. You compare Class II. with Class II.?—I do.

1592. On your oath is the standard of Class II. in England and Ireland the same?—Yes.

1593. Are the items for classification the same?—They are. Class II. in Ireland is for men with hard labour, it is also for men without hard labour, and for women and for boys under 16 years of age.

1594. In all prisons with hard labour or without hard labour, women and children under 16 years of age are all supported on Class II. diet?—Yes.

1595. Can you tell how prisoners are classed in England?—For the first month they are on the 1st Class diet; after the first month they go to Class II.; after the second month they go to Class III.

1596. When do they get Class IV.?—After those three months.

1597. Is there Class V.?—No, Class IV. is the highest, and they get it during the remainder of their sentence.

1598. Is not Class IV for untried prisoners?—It is, and for convicted prisoners as well.

1599. Do you see a head there for Class IV. (*producing diet rules*)?—Yes.

1600. Who gets Class IV.?—Men with hard labour, men without hard labour, women and children under 16 years of age.

1601. Now do these observations you have made apply to English and Irish prisons alike? They do.

Mr. *Murphy.*

1602. I believe you are now member of the Local Government Board?—Yes.

1603. Previous to that, you were one of the Commissioners on the Prisons Board?—I was medical member of the Prisons Board for a year before that.

1604. Up to what time did you continue to be on the Prisons Board?—Up to the 17th of March last.

1605. Of course you are a physician?—I am fellow of the College of Physicians and member of the College of Surgeons.

1606. In your capacity as medical member of the Prisons Board, did you in November last visit Tullamore Prison?—I did, on the 19th of November.

1607. Did you see Mr. Mandeville?—I did.

1608. Where did you see him?—In his cell.

1609. Was the medical officer present with you?—He was, and the governor.

1610. You afterwards saw him alone?—Yes.

1611. Will you tell us in your own language what passed between you and Mr. Mandeville, at the first interview, when the governor and doctor were present; and, secondly, when you called by yourself?—I had seen a report with reference to Mr. Mandeville's health; in fact, I had some of them with me; and I had with me also some letters that the medical officer had written to the Prisons Board on the subject. I therefore took particular notice of the late Mr. Mandeville. I went into his cell, and I was agreeably surprised by his appearance. He appeared to me to be in vigorous health. I had some conversation with him, and while speaking I observed his respiration; then I asked him to permit me to examine him. I told him that I was a medical man, and, in fact, a medical member of the Board; but I must say, said I, there does not appear to be much the matter with you. I can compliment you upon having a very fine figure. Have you anything to complain of as to your health? While I was speaking to him I put my hand on his pulse, which was full, regular, and strong. I asked him to take a deep breath. He did so; and I smiled, and said, "I do not think I shall want this," unscrewing my stethoscope and putting it into my pocket. In answer to my question whether he had anything to complain of respecting his health, he said he had suffered from diarrhoea, but that he was then well in that respect. He complained of his throat. I examined it, and could find nothing wrong. I said to him, I can find nothing wrong. Then he said, "If you allow me to put your finger on the spot, I think I can show it to you." He guided my finger to the right side of his throat, and I examined it by touch. I could detect no hardness or swelling. The medical officer of the prison then remarked that Mr. Mandeville had complained of his sight. I took him over close to the window and examined his eyes. As far as superficial examination could detect anything, I observed nothing wrong. I then asked the governor and the medical officer of the prison, in the presence of Mr. Mandeville, to leave the cell. I closed the door, and had a little private conversation with Mr. Mandeville.

Mr. *Murphy*—continued.

1612. Now, before you go from that, Dr. MacCabe, did you observe a pasty, flabby look about him?—Certainly not.

1613. Had he bluish lips?—No.

1614. Had he suffused eyes, and was his breathing rapid and shallow?—No.

1615. Did he exhibit any symptoms of heart failure?—Well, I did not examine his heart, for the reasons I will explain. I thought it would be absurd. I explained to him I do not want this stethoscope, and put it in my pocket.

1616. Would not the pulse indicate the state of the heart; if there was any heart failure, the pulse would not be strong and regular?—Certainly not.

1617. Was there any indication of the want of proper oxidation?—No.

1618. Proceed with the narrative between you and Mr. Mandeville, after the governor and doctor went away?—It was confined to an effort on my part to induce Mr. Mandeville to comply with the regulations. I used every argument I could think of.

1619. Will you tell exactly what you can remember about it?—Well, I said to him that the regulations were made in the interest of all prisoners; that it was a customary thing that all persons going in there should wear the prison dress. I used every argument I could to induce him to do this.

1620. What was his response?—He said it would be a sort of admission of criminality. I said, I do not look at it at all in that light; you are simply accepting the conditions which are incidental to imprisonment. I pointed out to him that if I were to question all the prisoners in the prison, that there would be a very small proportion would admit that they were guilty at all, and, if they were to be exempted from wearing prison dress because they did not consider themselves guilty, there would be no order or discipline in the prison. We had a cheerful conversation on his side, as well as on mine; and he said, "But he says you must remember mine is a political offence." I think I reminded him of Mr. Johnson of Ballykilbeg.

> *The Mac Dermot* objected to this evidence, and Mr. Ronan said, in the absence of the medical officer of the prison, this was the best evidence that could be offered. On these grounds he pressed it, and if not taken, he would ask the Coroner to take a note of it.

Examination resumed by Mr. *Murphy.*

1621. Did you examine other prisoners in Tullamore Gaol that day?—I did.

1622. Did you examine Mr. Wm. O'Brien?—I did, very carefully.

1623. Did you on your return to Dublin indicate to your Board the result of your examination of those two gentlemen?—Yes; in writing. I laid

Mr. Murphy—continued.

I laid a formal memorandum before my Board on the health of the prisoners who were confined under the Criminal Law and Procedure Act.

1624. What did you represent in reference to Mr. Mandeville, in your opinion as to whether Mr. Mandeville was fit to be subjected to prison discipline and dietary. In regard to prison dietary, I believe you are an expert?—Well, I had a great deal to do with it, a great deal of labour in connection with it.

1625. Were you one of a committee of three physicians who fixed the prison dietary in Ireland?—Yes; I was one of a committee of three persons who fixed the prison dietary as it stands with the exception of the modifications since made on the recommendations of a Royal Commission.

1626. Your colleagues on that committee were?—Dr. Robert M'Donnell, a very leading surgeon, and Dr. Grimshaw, the present Registrar General, and Hospital Physician, of very wide experience also in Dublin.

1627. Had you yourself had occasion prior to this of considering this matter of dietary?—I had occasion, in connection with workhouses under the Local Government Board.

1628. Did you yourself work out the nutritive value of prison fare?—Yes; we worked out the nutritive value by a tabular form and ascertained the nutritive value.

1629. In your opinion, was it then fixed by you fully sufficient for the maintenance of a man?—We believed so.

1630. Do you say it was full and adequate for a man of Mr. Mandeville's physique?—Yes.

1631. Subsequent to 1883 and 1884 was there an addition made to the dietary which you previously fixed?—Yes; Class I., which existed for the first seven days, was restricted in its operation to three days. Class II. was immensely improved on the recommendation of the Royal Commission by the addition of two pints of new milk daily to that diet. Classes III. and IV. remained unaltered.

1632. Any person sentenced to imprisonment for two months, upon what class does he commence?—He would at once commence upon Class II. for the first month, and for the remainder upon Class III.

1633. To a man living on Class II. diet, such a man as Mr. Mandeville, would the infliction of three days' punishment on bread and water injure his health?—I do not think it would do him the slightest harm.

1634. If three days would not do him harm, I assume that if three days would not do him any, that two days would not injure him?—No.

1635. Do you know as a matter of fact how long from the 2nd November to the 24th December Mr. Mandeville spent in punishment?

Question objected to by *The MacDermot*.

Mr. Murphy.

1636. Assuming that he spent eight days in punishment during that period, do you think it would injure his health, not altogether, of course, but at different periods?—In my judgment it would not, because I have seen many prisoners put on strong punishment without any injury to health.

1637. Do you know the cubic contents of the cell in which Mr. Mandeville was confined?—I never measured them.

1638. Assuming that it contained 774 cubic feet, would that be a sufficient allowance of air for a man of Mr. Mandeville's health?—More than sufficient.

1639. Under your Board what allowance do you require for your houses?—We advise, under the Local Government Board, the adoption of a standard of 400 for healthy adults, 500 for aged and infirm who occupy the same ward day and night, and 600 in ordinary hospital wards.

1640. In your opinion, is that sufficient?—It is found quite sufficient.

1641. As to the matter of prison clothing, is that a matter to which you attach any importance as a matter of discipline or hygiene?—I attach great importance to the observance of that rule upon grounds of public health. I do say because of the immense number who are annually committed to our prisons a very large proportion come from town districts, where infectious diseases may prevail. If we did not insist on the adoption of prison clothing by prisoners on admission, I believe our prisons would never be free from fever. During the past twelve months we had over 4,000 commitments to local prisons in Ireland. I mention that to show how impossible it would be with such a large number of these commitments coming from towns to keep out disease, if we did not insist on the adoption of prison clothes.

1642. Has the insistence of these rules a beneficial influence on that preservation of health in the local prisons?—I believe so.

1643. You stated also that you examined Mr. O'Brien. Did you form any opinion as to whether this enforcement of prison clothing should be enforced in the case of Mr. O'Brien?—I formed the opinion that it should not be enforced, on medical grounds; on the grounds of his health.

Cross-examined by *The MacDermot*.

1644. I think I understood you to say, Dr. M'Cabe, that you and Mr. Mandeville parted on friendly terms. Did you do so?—I did.

1645. The impression was rather favourable?—It was.

1646. You think he got too much air for health?—I do not understand that.

1647. Is it not true that you stated on your oath that he got too much air?—No.

1648. Did you not say this: "Assuming that he got 774 cubic feet of air, it was more than enough"?—It is more than enough.

1649. Well, now, you thought he got more than enough of air, more than sufficient to maintain his health. Do you think he got more than sufficient food?—No.

1650. Did you not say that you considered your dietary more than sufficient for any man?—Yes, to maintain a man's health.

1651. Do you not know that on the recommendation of the Royal Commission, they got milk?—Yes.

1652. Then

The MacDermot—continued.

1652. Then did Mr. Mandeville get better treatment than you thought necessary to maintain his health?—Yes.

1653. You came down to Tullamore as a member of the Prisons Board?—Yes.

1654. How long had you been a member of the Prisons Board?—About a year.

1655. Did you come down for the purpose of inspecting Mr. O'Brien and Mr. Mandeville?—That was my object.

1656. Sent down by the Government?—No.

1657. Sent down by whom?—As a member of the Board, on my own responsibility.

1658. I ask you, were you sent down by the Executive Government?—I was not.

1659. Did you receive a communication from any Member of the Executive Government with regard to coming down?—I did not.

1660. Or from the Prisons Board?—I am a member of the Prisons Board.

1661. You are a medical member; did you receive any communications from any other members of the Board?—I did not.

1662. Who is the head of the Prisons Board?—The chairman is the Honourable Charles Bourke.

1663. Was the Honourable Charles Bourke aware of your coming down?—I do not know.

1664. Another member of the Board is Mr. O'Brien; was he aware of your coming down?—I do not think he was.

1665. Did you know before you went down that Mr. O'Brien had declined to wear prison clothes?—Yes.

1666. And Mr. Mandeville?—Well, I am not sure about Mr. Mandeville, but I am sure about Mr. O'Brien.

1667. Were you aware that Mr. O'Brien and Mr. Mandeville had refused to clean their prison cells?—I think I knew Mr. Mandeville was not doing that; but I do not remember about Mr. O'Brien.

1668. Did you know that Mr. O'Brien and Mr. Mandeville had declined to associate with criminals?—Yes.

1669. You said you attached great importance to prisoners wearing prison clothes. You are aware that first-class misdemeanants do not wear them, even to prevent infection?—Yes.

1670. And debtors also wear their own clothes, and untried prisoners?—Yes.

1671. Do you think Mr. Mandeville's clothes would carry infection?—Oh, no, not for a moment.

1672. Were you in the smallest way influenced by that notion of infection with regard to his wearing his own clothes?—No.

1673. Do you not think, if the danger of fever be the cause of it, it ought to be applied to untried prisoners?—I think so.

1674. In your opinion, then, you would think it prudent to require them to take off their own clothes?—No; how could you require them under the present state of the law?

1675. How long is it since you have been practising as a physician; when had you last a patient?—You must remember I am prevented by statute; a medical commissioner cannot practise.

1676. When did you last treat a patient?—I do not practise.

1677. When did you last get the opportunity of treating a patient?—Not since I became connected with the Local Government Board.

1678. How long is that?—That was in '76.

1679. Where did you practise before '76?—I practised for 11 years as medical superintendent of a county asylum.

1680. Where did you last practise in '76?—I said that in '76 I was in charge of the County Asylum for Waterford county and city; I was at the head of that asylum.

1681. And had you private patients in the city of Waterford?—Yes.

1682. A lot?—I had some.

1683. Apart from public employment, did you ever make 500 *l.* a year by your practice?—No.

1684. Did you ever make 400 *l.*?—I think about that; I entered the public service very young.

1685. When you came to Tullamore, Mr. Mandeville told you he had sore throat?—Yes.

1686. Where was the place he put your finger?—Towards the windpipe.

1687. Do you think he was shamming on that occasion?—Oh, no; I am sure he was not.

1688. He was not shamming about the diarrhœa either?—No.

1689. Was he shamming when he said his eyes were weak?—No.

1690. And although he complained of his eyes being weak, and of his sore throat, you came to the conclusion there was nothing wrong with him?—Nothing that I could see.

1691. You were aware that Dr. Ronayne and Dr. Moorhead had given it as their opinion that he was ailing?—Well, they did not examine him, I believe.

1692. Dr. Moorhead said his breathing was laboured; you could not see that?—No.

1693. Dr. Ronayne swore it was shallow and rapid; you could not see that?—No.

1694. Dr. Moorhead said there was blue on the face; you did not perceive that?—No.

1695. Do you remember Dr. Ronayne stating that four days before you were there his countenance was flabby; did you see anything of that?—No.

1696. He said it was pasty; you saw nothing of that?—No.

1697. He was healthy-looking?—I said so.

1698. Did he seem to you fit for punishment?—I do not think it would have injured him.

1699. Was he fit for it?—I think he was fit for it.

1700. You consider he was fit to be left without exercise for 72 hours?—I think it would not have injured him.

1701. I ask, was he fit for it?—If by that you mean that he could go there without injuring his health, I think so.

1702. You would consider confinement in a punishment cell on punishment diet, bread and water, fit treatment for a man suffering from diarrhœa; for a patient of yours?—I would not consider a patient suffering from diarrhœa ought to be punished on bread and water.

The MacDermot—continued.

1703. Do you not think that a man in a punishment cell, and attacked with diarrhœa, ought to be removed forthwith to hospital?—No, I do not; I think he ought to be treated in his own cell first.

1704. What change would you make?—I would first take him off brown bread.

1705. Dr. MacCabe, I ask you, supposing you had a patient like Mr. John Mandeville, and supposing he was suffering from diarrhœa, what food would you give him?—Really it would depend upon circumstances. I should know the character of the diarrhœa.

1706. Supposing it was ordinary diarrhœa, what food would you give him?—I would put him on white bread, and I should probably order him rice pudding.

1707. Supposing he was a private patient outside the prison, what food would you order him if he was suffering from ordinary diarrhœa?—I should order him white bread and milk, and rice pudding.

1708. What medicine would you give him?—I could not say without examining him. If you take up a medical book you will see the treatment is very variable. I cannot lay down one general rule.

1709. Do you not think a comfortable warm room would be necessary for a person in diarrhœa?—Yes.

1710. Having regard to that answer, do you think you would send a patient of yours into a flagged cell, with a fibre matting, and no fire?—Decidedly not, if suffering from diarrhœa.

1711. Would not you consider that to spend 72 hours on punishment in diarrhœa would be inhuman, barbarous treatment of a patient?—If he were known to be suffering from it I think it would be improper.

1712. I think you said he complained of weakness of sight?—I did not.

1713. Who told you?—The doctor.

1714. And did not you go to the window and examine him?—I did.

1715. It has been proved by other witnesses that he had a nervous tremor in his hand. In your opinion, as a medical gentleman, where there was tremor in his hand, would it be a symptom of nervous attack?—That would indicate an attack on the nervous system.

1716. Would weakness of the sight be also a symptom of nervous affection?—It is sometimes.

1717. And I suppose, if there were both tremor in the hand and weakness in the sight, the tremor in the hand would tend to show that the weakness of the sight was from the same cause?—Probably.

1718. Do you think, Dr. MacCabe, that a number of men going to the bedside of a sleeping man, drawing the pillow from under his head, arousing him from his sleep, and proceeding to drag off his clothes, would be calculated to affect his nervous system?—I think it would give him a great shock.

1719. Do you think that it would be barbarous, inhuman treatment?—I think, under the circumstances you describe, it would be unbecoming and improper treatment.

1720. Would it not, in your opinion, be inhuman treatment?—No.

1721. No matter with what deliberation it was done?—I would not call it inhuman.

1722. Would you consider the removal of his clothes, including his shirt, in the way I describe, would amount to indecency?—I would not call it indecency, but I would call it a very regrettable necessity.

1723. Do you think it was right and justifiable?—Right.

1724. You approve of it on behalf of your Board?—I do, and accept the responsibility, and would do it under similar circumstances.

1725. Under similar circumstances, even though it would give a shock that would cause a man's life?—No, certainly not.

1726. You have already told me it was calculated to give a very great shock?—Yes.

1727. Supposing a man was not asleep, you would consider it quite right to do it yourself if you were a governor of a prison?—That is no part of the duty of the Governor. The Governor was present to see that no unnecessary violence was done.

1728. And to see that all necessary violence was used?—To see the law obeyed.

1729. I ask you, Dr. MacCabe, was it not part of the duty of the Governor to see that all necessary violence was used?—All necessary compulsion.

1730. You won't say violence?—No, for violence is not the proper word to use.

1731. To the extent of taking off the shirt?—Yes.

1732. If that would be calculated to produce any injury to his health, ought it to have been done?—If it were calculated to produce serious injury it ought not to have been done.

1733. If it were calculated to affect his nervous system, ought it to have been done?—If, in my judgment, it were calculated to affect his nervous system, I would not allow it to be done, as I did not allow it to be done in Mr. O'Brien's case.

1734. Do you think that remaining partially naked for 24 hours is calculated to damage health?—Calculated to give him a bad cold, and would injure his throat.

1735. Do you think physical force should be used to compel prisoners to obey the rules?—I think it is a deplorable necessity.

1736. Does that apply to convicted prisoners of all classes?—Yes.

1737. Male and female?—Yes.

1738. Do you think that if a delicate lady was convicted of making a speech, and had an aversion to associating with bad characters that were convicted, should she be compelled to associate with them?—I would refer that to the Prison Board.

1739. I mean a sensitive lady; would you compel her to comply with the prison rules by physical force, or would you refer the case to the Board?—I would bring that before the Board.

1740. Now, in the case of Mr. O'Brien and Mr. Mandeville, did you not think it desirable to relax the prison rules about herding with criminals and doing menial work; do you not think there is a great distinction between men convicted like Mr. O'Brien and Mr. Mandeville and ordinary criminals?—I think there is a great distinction.

The MacDermot—continued.

1741. Do you not think the cleaning of a cell or the wearing of the clothes of criminals would be an absolute horror to such men?—I think it would be disagreeable.

1742. Now, you stated that you had taken a great deal of trouble in connection with the dietary on the Royal Commission?—I did.

1743. Did you ever spend any time on it; did you ever spend any time using your own dietary?—Yes; I have lived more poorly. When I was a medical student in London I often lived on worse diet.

1744. You never saw Mr. Mandeville except on that occasion?—No.

Mr. *Murphy*.

1745. Dr. MacCabe, you were asked as to whether a man in Mr. Mandeville's position ought to be subjected to the same treatment as persons convicted of immoral crimes. Do you consider the man who incites to crime, or the person who acts on his incitement, the more morally guilty?—The man who incites.

1746. If a man gets a chill or cold from remaining naked for 24 hours, while he has clothes available to put on, to whom does the responsibility for that cold attach?—I think to the man himself.

Mr. Murphy—continued.

1747. You were in court yesterday when that man Goulding gave his evidence as to the manner in which the clothes were taken off Mr. Mandeville?—Yes.

1748. Dealing with a man such as you say Mr. Mandeville was, who had not a weak heart, would you think the treatment, even as described by Mr. Goulding, would have a serious effect on his nerves?—I do not think it would have a serious effect, but I think it would cause a great shock. The waking up would cause the shock, but I do not think the rest of the proceedings would be calculated to do so.

The MacDermot.

1749. Now, you were asked a hypothetical question by Mr. Murphy, whether those who incite, or those who are incited, are the more guilty. Now, I put you another hypothetical question, whether are those who compel the gaol officials to apply the rules in a barbarous fashion and inhuman manner, or the warders who carry them out, the more guilty?—To the best of my honest belief, nothing of the sort ever happened in this country.

SEVENTH DAY.

Tuesday, 24th July 1888.

Dr. MacCabe, called in; and further Examined.

The MacDermot.

1750. Where are the head-quarters of your Prison Board?—In the Castle.

1751. How is it you came down without anybody directing you to come down; did anybody suggest to you to come down?—Yes; Mr. Bourke.

1752. At the Castle?—Yes.

1753. Was Sir West Ridgeway aware that you were going down?—Well, I don't know. If you let me explain. I was particularly anxious to correct my evidence at one important point; it was this: I stated in answer to counsel that I had received no instructions from the Chief Secretary to visit Tullamore. I further said that I had no communication with any member of my own Board as to my intended visit. At the time I said so I spoke to the best of my belief, because I had had neither written directions from nor personal communication with the Chief Secretary on the subject. On thinking over my evidence last night I remember that Mr. Bourke in conversation told me it was the desire of the Chief Secretary that I should visit Tullamore. I was anxious, sir, to make that correction.

Mr. William Webb, of Cork, called in; and Examined.

Mr. Ronan.

1754. What office do you hold in the prison?—Assistant Clerk.

1755. Is the entry of Mr. Mandeville's weight there in your handwriting (*producing a register from the prison*)?—Yes.

1756. Did you weigh him yourself on that day?—Yes.

1757. He was weighed on the 1st November; does that entry truly show the weight as shown by the weight the scales made him?—Yes.

1758. Were you present in February last when these weights were tested?—Yes, sir.

The Coroner.

1759. By the constabulary?—Yes.

Mr. Ronan.

1760. Were they found correct?—No.

1761. According to the correction, what would be the true weight of Mr. Mandeville?—Two hundred and thirty-three pounds.

[The Witness was not cross-examined.

Major Richard Roberts, called in; and Examined.

Mr. Ronan.

1762. Major Roberts, you have been Governor of Cork Gaol for how long?—About 13 years.

The Coroner.

1763. You are still?—Yes.

Mr. Ronan.

1764. You have scales and weights which are used for weighing prisoners?—Certainly.

1765. From the time you were appointed until the February of the present year had they been tested?—They had not.

1766. They are large iron weights. It is an ordinary scale?—Yes.

1767. Were they found correct?—No.

1768. When did you receive Mr. Mandeville?—31st October last.

1769. Refer to the register. That is the register (*produced*)?—Yes.

1770. Read the entry?—"John Mandeville; age, 38; height, 5 feet 11 inches; hair turning grey; eyes blue; complexion fresh; scar on corner of right ear; weight, 226 lbs.; where born, Carrick-on-Suir."

1771. When was he transmitted to Tullamore?—On the 2nd November.

Cross-examined by Mr. Harrington.

1772. Mr. Mandeville was not long in your charge?—No.

1773. What was he like when he entered prison?—He was a strong healthy-looking man.

1774. Well, there is a portion of Mrs. Mandeville's evidence I wish to ask you about. Were you aware that Mr. Mandeville was ordered flannels by the doctor of the prison?—Yes, he was ordered flannels. He was not then in prison clothes.

1775. Is it true that there is a rule of the Prisons Board that no prisoner must be removed from one prison to another without a doctor's certificate of fitness for removal?—There is.

1776. Was that rule violated in Mr. Mandeville's case?—Not carried out.

1777. Don't

Mr. Harrington—continued.

1777. Don't you think it was violated?—I suppose it was.

1778. If a prisoner was guilty of it, it would be violation?—Yes, it was not carried out. The doctor had not signed the certificate.

1779. Was the doctor asked to sign the certificate?—He was not.

1780. So that the doctor is not responsible?—Yes.

1781. Now, who is responsible for that violation of the rule?—Well, I suppose I was.

1782. Do you think you were responsible for that violation of the rule?—There was no time to get a doctor to sign it.

1783. Exactly, that is just what we want to come at. At what hour did you get the order for Mr. Mandeville and Mr. O'Brien's removal?—It was after 10 o'clock at night.

1784. Was it near 12 at night?—About 11; between 10 and 11.

1785. Who gave that order?—It came from the Castle.

1786. You know there are a great many departments in the Castle?—It came from the Prisons Board Department.

1787. At what hour were you ordered to have Mr. Mandeville in readiness for transference from the gaol?—At 5.15 in the morning.

1788. Do you remember whether any question arose about wearing prison clothes while Mr. Mandeville was in Cork?—Yes; I asked him would he wear the prison dress, and he protested against wearing it.

1789. You did not then put him on bread and water?—No, because he was leaving next day.

1790. You did not order him bread and water?—No.

1791. Did you seek advice or instructions from the Prisons Board on the question?—I had my instructions.

1792. Did you seek any advice from the Prisons Board?—I did.

Mr. Ronan.] I object to any communication between an officer of a department and the authorities of that department.

Coroner.] Even though they affected the prisoner?

Mr. Ronan.] Yes.

Coroner.] They are not State circulars.

Mr. Harrington.

1793. (*To Witness.*) Did you receive instructions?—I received a reply.

1794. What was the reply?

Mr. Ronan.] Now, I object on the ground that a confidential communication between a department of State and their officers is a communication privileged on the ground of public policy.

The MacDermot.] We press the question.

Coroner.] I allow it.

Mr. Ronan.] When it affects the inquiry in this court there is no privilege.

Coroner.] This is a matter affecting the treatment of prisoners in prison. It was in respect to one of the matters that he was

Mr. Harrington.

1795. The question has been asked, and the Coroner has ruled. (*To Witness.*) Was it in writing?—I think it was; it was a telegram.

Mr. Ronan.] This is not a superior court, and certiorari only lies to inferior courts.

Mr. Ronan (*looking over the correspondence between Major Roberts and the Prisons Board*).] The first of these documents I decline to produce, as it is an Order of the Lords Justices, representing the Lord Lieutenant.

Mr. Ronan (*to The MacDermot*).] Do you insist upon that?

Coroner.] The first was by telegram, and that must be produced.

Mr. Ronan.] Major Roberts has handed me four documents. The first is an official article marked "Secret and confidential," and the second also "Secret and confidential." The third is an Order of the Lords Justices. The other two documents are private and confidential.

Coroner.] That is not telling me what they are.

Mr. Ronan.] I won't tell you. Representing the Prisons Board here, I tell Major Roberts to decline to produce these documents. I advise Major Roberts to decline to give any information as to their contents.

Mr. Harrington.

1796. (*To Witness.*) Have you the letters here?—I have the letters in court.

1797. Are these letters marked private and confidential?—Yes.

1798. Are they arising from communications with the Prisons Board?—They are.

1799. Do any of them affect Mr. Mandeville?

Mr. Ronan.] Don't answer that question.

Mr. Harrington.

1800. Now, do any of these documents marked private and confidential refer to Mr. Mandeville's treatment in prison?

Mr. Ronan.] I object to the question.

The Coroner.] The objection must come from the witness.

Mr. Ronan.] I object, as I am the counsel for the head of the department.

Mr. Harrington.] We don't know who you are counsel for.

The MacDermot.] I say the rule of privilege is that the witness must claim it for himself. The head of department must claim it for himself.

Mr. Ronan.] I am counsel here for the Prisons Board, and claim privilege for these documents.

Mr. Harrington.] It is a question affecting the treatment of Mr. Mandeville.

Coroner.] It is incumbent on me to prevent any compulsion on the part of any

Mr. Harrington—continued.

Mr. *Ronan*.] Do you allow the question?

Coroner.] I rule the question is admissible.

Mr. Harrington (to the *Coroner*).] I ask you, Mr. Coroner, to make Mr. Ronan sit down until the question is asked, and then let him object.

Mr. *Harrington*.

1801. (To Major *Roberts*.) Do you refuse to answer that question?—Yes.

1802. Do you refuse to produce the documents?—Yes.

The MacDermot (to the *Coroner*).] Do you rule that he should produce them?

Coroner.] Yes.

The MacDermot.] Taking on myself the responsibility of it, I am satisfied with you having taken it down upon your notes, and that they ought to be produced, and the witness declined to produce them at the instance of counsel for the Prisons Board.

Mr. *Ronan*.] That is, you don't ask the Coroner to enforce the order.

The MacDermot.] No; it is a situation I hope you will get into often.

Mr. *Murphy*.] We accept the situation.

Mr. *Harrington*.

1803. (To *Witness*.) Was not there a telegram?—There was; that was private and confidential.

1804. And you decline to produce it?—I do.

1805. Had Mr. Mandeville's clothes been taken from him during his time in custody in Cork Gaol?—Yes.

1806. At what time were they taken from him?—About half-past nine on the evening of the 1st November.

1807. Were prison clothes then given to him?—They were placed in his cell.

1808. Was he transferred from your prison in prison clothes?—No.

1809. Did he before his transfer in the morning get back his own clothes?—He did.

1810. Who gave them back to him?—The Deputy Governor.

1811. Were you aware of it?—I ordered it.

1812. Is that the first instance in your life as prison governor in which you had sent from your gaol to another a convicted prisoner in his own clothes?—I think so.

1813. So that, though the clothes were taken from him at half-past nine at night, they were restored at what time in the morning?—About four or half-past four o'clock.

1814. Were they restored without any demand on his part for them?—They were.

1815. Were you amongst those who went into Mr. O'Brien's cell in the morning?—No.

1816. Where did you see Mr. O'Brien on his removal?—On his way to the gate.

Mr. *Harrington*—continued.

1817. Did he say anything about all this mystery?—I did not hear anything about it. I remember saying good morning.

1818. He did not ask you where he was going?—I am certain he did not.

1819. Do you think he knew?—I don't think he did.

1820. Would you think it strange being called up at two o'clock in the morning, and hurried out of gaol?—He did not ask me anything; he might have asked somebody else.

1821. Did the police come of their own authority into the gaol to test the weights, or were they sent for?—They were sent for.

1822. Then you cast doubts upon the justness of the weights?—I think so.

1823. Are you aware that before that there was a discussion in Parliament as to Mr. O'Brien's weight in Cork Gaol?—Yes.

1824. Before that suspicion was introduced?—Yes.

1825. Were you aware that Mr. O'Brien and Mr. Balfour had differed in views and statements as to Mr. O'Brien's weight?—I think I saw it on the paper.

1826. Have you any doubt you saw it before the scales were doubted in Cork?—In or about the same time.

1827. Were you directed, Major, to have them tested?—Yes.

1828. And for the first time in twelve years you got instructions to have these weights tested?—Quite so.

Re-examined by Mr. *Ronan*.

1829. Mr. Harrington asked you a question in reference to Mrs. Mandeville's evidence. Mr. Mandeville stated that some flannels he had on him were taken off?—No flannels he had were taken from him.

1830. Were flannels given to him?—They were handed into the cell, but he did not put them on.

1831. Was he prevented from taking them with him?—No.

1832. But the complaint was that his teeth were chattering from the want of them, as they were taken from him?—There was no question of flannels at all.

Mr. Harrington cross-examined the *Witness*.

1833. At his removal, if he asked to have the prison flannels, would he be allowed to take them?—Yes; I would take the responsibility of letting him have them.

1834. Did you see him in the morning?—I met him on the way down.

1835. Will you undertake to swear that when he got his own clothes, the prison flannels as well as the other prison clothes were not taken out of his cell?—I cannot swear that.

1836. Is not it likely they would have removed the flannels?—They might, or might have left them to the middle of the day.

Mr. *Ronan*.

1837. Did you ever hear he was refused the flannels?—No.

1838. I understand

The *Coroner*.

1838. I understand you would have undertook the responsibility of giving the flannels if he asked you?—Yes.

Mr. *Harrington*.] We only wish he had not left Major Roberts's charge while he was in gaol.

Mr. *Ronan*.

1839. Did you see him before he left?—Yes.

Mr. *Ronan*—continued.

1840. Was the subject of these flannels mentioned in your presence?—Certainly not.

Mr. *Harrington*.

1841. Will you undertake to swear he was not refused by anyone else?—I am almost certain he was not.

1842. Will you swear that that statement is untrue?—I cannot do that.

GEORGE BARTLEY, Chief Warder, Tullamore Prison, called in; and Examined.

Mr. *Murphy*.

1843. YOU are Chief Warder of Tullamore Prison?—Yes.

1844. You remember the 3rd November; Mr. Mandeville was received on transference from Cork Prison?—Yes.

1845. What was his appearance on that occasion?—He was a fine healthy-looking man.

1846. Upon his reception where was he sent to?—To his cell.

1847. Was he seen by the doctor?—He was.

1848. How soon after his reception?—A few minutes, as the doctor was in the prison at the time.

1849. This cell in which he was placed, you know the dimensions of it?—I do.

1850. What were the dimensions?—Fourteen feet long by seven feet four inches wide by nine feet two inches in height.

1851. The cell is arched; that is not the height to the crown of the arch?—Yes.

1852. How much to the spring of the arch?—Six feet.

1853. What size is the window of this cell?—It is 3 feet by 16 inches; that is, the smallest portion.

The *Coroner*.

1854. The admission of light was 3 feet by 16 inches?—Yes.

Mr. *Murphy*.

1854. What was the furniture given to Mr. Mandeville in that cell?—A plank bed and mattress, one pair of sheets, two single blankets and one quilt and pillow, and pillow cover, one form and table; the table is a fixture, there is a washbasin, towel, comb, quart tin, one cell chamber. That is all, with the exception of the cards. There is also a Bible.

1855. This mattress that you speak of, how many classes of mattress have you in the prison?—Four or five.

1856. What class of mattress was this that Mr. Mandeville had?—It was 24 lbs. weight, there was 20 lbs. of fibre in it, and ticking 4 lbs.

1857. Had Mr. Mandeville the use of that mattress during the whole time he was in prison?—Yes.

1858. Had he it in the punishment cell when he was there?—Yes.

1859. After Mr. Mandeville's reception to Tullamore, did you weigh him?—I did on Monday the 7th November; he was five days there.

1860. Had you any conversation with Mr. Mandeville with reference to his weight?—Yes, after I weighed him.

1861. Did you weigh him?—Yes; he was [illegible] lbs.

1862. What is the character of the scales you have at Tullamore?—It is a table scale with ordinary weights.

1863. How long has it been in the prison?—About two years.

1864. Apparently new?—Yes; it is in good order.

1865. You said you weighed him; you had some conversation with him about his weight?—Yes; he said he was nearly 11 stone when he was admitted to Cork Gaol.

1866. Did you then communicate with the Governor?—I did immediately after.

The MacDermot.] I won't have that conversation. I object to it.

Mr. *Murphy*.

1867. Did you communicate the result to the Governor?—Yes.

1868. That was on the 7th. Previous to that day did you require Mr. Mandeville to put on the prison garb?—Yes, sir.

1869. When?—On the Saturday he was asked before that.

1870. On the day of his admission he was asked in your presence to put on the prison garb?—Yes, they were brought to his cell, but he refused.

1871. What was the next occasion that he was asked?—On Saturday.

1872. What day of the week did he go in?—On Wednesday.

1873. On the Saturday, then, he was asked by you?—By the Governor in my presence.

1874. Did he refuse then?—Yes.

1875. Was he ordered any punishment?—Yes.

1876. What was it?—Twenty-four hours.

1877. That was on Saturday the 5th November. He went through his 24 hours?—Yes.

1878. That was 24 hours' bread and water in his own cell?—Yes.

1879. What was the next occasion on which he was required to comply with some of the rules, and he declined?—A few days afterwards.

Mr. *Murphy*.] I produce the punishment book kept under the prison rules. The entry is the 5th November, No. 114

The MacDermot.] Just give the dates of the punishment.

Mr. Murphy—continued.

Mr. Murphy.] John Mandeville, probationer; offence, refusing to put on prison dress. Hours sentenced to bread and water and his cell, 24 hours. Next is the 14th November. John Mandeville, probationer, refusing to dress in prison clothes, sentenced to bread and water for three days. The sentence was inflicted by the Governor, but there is a note by the Governor. Discontinued by medical officer on third day.

The MacDermot.] I object to anything except the awarding of the punishment.

Mr. Murphy.] Twenty-eighth November, refusing to clean out his cell, bread and water for 24 hours; 8th December John Mandeville, refusing to clean his cell, bread and water for 48 hours; 20th December, refusing to clean his cell; and the penalty on that occasion was awarded by Mr. Smith, R.M.; to be confined in a punishment cell for two days.

Mr. Murphy.

1880. [To Witness.] Did not Mr. Mandeville undergo all this punishment?—Yes, sir.

1881. You remember when he was sentenced on 14th November, that he was sentenced to three days' bread and water?—One day of the three was remitted; two days he served.

1882. Were you present on each occasion that those punishments were awarded?—I was.

1883. Was Mr. Mandeville informed of the charge that was brought against him?—Yes.

1884. What did he say to them?—He said he objected to them.

The Coroner.

1885. To do them?—Yes, sir.

Mr. Murphy.

1886. Now, except in respect to these particular matters of discipline to wear the prison clothes or clean his cell, did Mr. Mandeville give any trouble?—None whatever, except that

Mr. Murphy—continued.

1898. And when he went out?—Yes.

1899. Was there much difference in his appearance?—No, except he was paler. In his body I did not remark much difference.

1900. You are in the habit of weighing prisoners from time to time in that prison?—Yes, I have to weigh all prisoners on extra or change of diet.

1901. So far as you could judge from appearance, was there any change in Mr. Mandeville between the 8th December and the day he was discharged?—I could not discern any change.

1902. Could he have lost two stone weight or three stone weight without its having been visible in his appearance?—Certainly not.

1903. Mr. Goulding, who was a warder in your prison, swore he looked three stone lighter going out than going in?—I could not discern any difference in the fitting of his clothes; he got the same clothing out that he had in.

1904. Did you notice any change in his appearance, in his apparent weight, from the time he came in until the time he left?—None.

1905. Could you, by looking at him, know whether he had altered two or three pounds in his weight?—No, I could not.

1906. Do you remember the 22nd November?—Yes.

1907. That was the occasion on which the clothes were taken away from Mr. Mandeville?—Yes.

1908. Were you with the Governor and other warders when they went to Mr. Mandeville's cell?—Yes.

1909. What time was it?—Eight o'clock.

The Coroner.

1910. In the evening?—Yes, sir.

Mr. Murphy.

1911. Was the gas in the prison lighting, or had it been cut off?—It was lighting, sir.

1912. Was it lighting in Mr. Mandeville's cell when you went there?—It was; it was not shut off in the cells at that hour.

Mr. *Murphy*—continued.

1923. And the doors are iron?—They are.

1924. You yourself unlocked the door?—Yes, and opened the door.

1925. When you went in where was Mr. Mandeville?—He was lying in his bed.

1926. Describe exactly the position he was in?—As I opened the door he raised himself upon his elbow in the bed; he appeared to have been sleeping; he looked towards the door as I entered; he asked what was the matter. I did not make any reply, but lifted the cell form which was under the side of the mattress to raise his head. I lifted it, and his own private shoes, and turned round and left them outside the door on the landing.

1927. Did his head drop down when you did that?—Oh, no, he was sitting up then. He was standing on his feet on his bed when I came back.

1928. I believe this bed is a low thing?—Yes, the plank is only seven inches from the floor, and the mattress on the top of that. Two warders were around him when I returned in, and the governor asked him would he change his clothing. He said he would not. The governor said if he would not he would have to remove them by force. He protested still, and said he would not take them off himself; then the warders surrounded him and took his coat off first.

1929. Describe how they took his coat off?—They took a hold of his arms, and drew the sleeves down.

1930. Did he resist?—No, he protested, but did not show any forcible resistance.

1931. What was the next garment?—His vest, and then, I believe, his guernsey, which was outside his white shirt, and then his shirt. When they were taking off his shirt, the governor told Warder Wilson to get a sheet and put it round him. The trousers was the last thing.

1932. Did he make any resistance to any of the several garments being taken off him?—Slightly, not much; I believe he did resist slightly in each of them.

1933. Were any of his clothes torn?—No.

1934. During the time that the clothes were being removed, was there a suit of prison clothes in the cell?—Yes, they were brought in at first.

1935. Did he see them there?—Yes, they were left down on the table.

1936. Having removed the clothes, did you, the governor, and the warders retire?—Yes, leaving the prison dress there.

1937. Was the gas still left lighting?—Yes, it wanted 20 or 25 minutes of the time it should be turned off.

1938. You left it lighting when you came out of the cell. How long were you in the cell altogether?—About five minutes.

1939. Now, you remember the next morning, the 23rd, at six o'clock, did you go to the cell, to Mr. Mandeville?—Yes.

1940. What time was that?—A few minutes before seven o'clock.

1941. Where was Mr. Mandeville, then?—He was in bed.

1942. Did you speak to him?—I did. I asked him was he all right, and he said yes.

1943. You left him there, then?—Yes.

Mr. *Murphy*—continued.

1944. How soon after that did you see him again?—After breakfast hour.

1945. What time is breakfast?—Half-past nine.

1946. You saw him again after breakfast?—Yes, he was in bed still.

1947. Had you any conversation with him then?—No.

1948. Later on in the day did you go to his cell?—Yes.

1949. About what time?—About five o'clock in the evening.

1950. In what condition was he then?—He was walking about in his cell with a quilt outside, and either a sheet or a blanket inside.

1951. During all this time was there a suit of prison clothing lying on the table in the cell?—Yes, sir, from the night before.

1952. Had you any conversation with him at nine o'clock?—I had; I asked him would he not put on the clothes, and I advised him to put them on. He still protested against it, and said he would not put them on. I then told him if he would not put them on we would be compelled to take away his bed clothing. He told me, except the bed clothing was removed, he would not put them on. I told him that we would then remove them, and did so.

1953. Were you by yourself?—No, sir.

1954. Tell us how it came that the bed-clothing was removed; after you told him that, you left the cell?—No; the governor came in while I was speaking to him.

1955. Did you tell the governor what occurred between you and Mr. Mandeville?—He was listening to the latter part of the conversation. I then had the clothes that were lying on the mattress, not including whatever portion he had on him, removed out of the cell. I then went away.

1956. What about the clothes he had on him?—I believe he handed them out to the warders, but I did not see him.

1957. How soon after that time did you see him again?—In half an hour or thereabouts.

1958. How was he dressed then?—He was dressed in prison clothing.

1959. You came back in half an hour?—I think it was a little more. I was around checking the prisoners.

1960. What was done then with the bedding and bed-clothes?—They were put in again into his cell before lock up.

1961. Lock up is at six o'clock?—Yes.

1962. How long was the bedding and bed-clothes out of the cell altogether?—Not an hour, sir.

1963. From that time out did Mr. Mandeville regularly wear the prison clothes?—Yes.

1964. What sort of bread was given to Mr. Mandeville during his imprisonment in Tullamore?—Brown bread, up to the 15th.

1965. From the 15th to the 24th, when he was discharged, what sort of bread did he get?—White bread, instead of brown.

1966. Was that under the doctor's directions?—Yes, sir.

1967. Did he get that white bread, whether he was on punishment or whether he was not?—He got it at all times; it was all the same.

Mr. *Murphy*—continued.

1968. The white bread that is supplied, is it supplied by a baker in Tullamore?—Yes; it is the ordinary white bread that is sold to anybody else.

1969. Is the brown bread also supplied the same way, or is it made in the prison?—It is made in the town. It is a contract.

1970. Do you remember Mr. Mandeville at any time complaining of diarrhoea?—Yes.

The MacDermot.

1971. Was it to you he complained?—No.

Mr. *Murphy.*

1972. Did you ever hear he complained?—I did to the doctor once.

1973. Do you remember any special arrangement having been made for Mr. Mandeville's convenience?

The MacDermot objected.

Witness.] Yes.

Mr. *Murphy.*

1974. Was it availed of by Mr. Mandeville?—It was.

1975. Where was this convenience placed?—In the next cell to where he was.

1976. That cell was not occupied by any person?—No.

1977. Do you remember the time he was sent into the punishment cell?—I do.

1978. That was on the 20th of December?—Yes.

1979. Will you give us the dimensions and a description of that punishment cell; have you measured it?—Yes; it is 12 feet long, 6 feet 3 inches wide, and 9 feet 10 inches high; that is the archway.

1980. What height is the spring of the arch?—It reaches to about 6 feet 6 inches.

1981. How many feet of hot water pipe is there?—Thirty-one or 32 feet of four-inch pipe.

1982. There is an iron door to it?—Yes.

1983. In stone jambs?—Yes.

1984. How does the door fit in respect to these jambs?—It fits as close to the stone jambs as a door could possibly do.

1985. Was it so fitting when Mr. Mandeville occupied it?—Yes, it has never been interfered with since.

1986. Now, in the same wall is there a ventilation shaft?—Yes.

1987. Is that the inlet?—Yes.

1988. At what height from the ground is that inlet?—It is 6 feet 8 inches from the floor.

1989. That is, from the bottom of the ventilator to the ground is 5 feet 8 inches. Now, the outlet ventilating shaft, where is it?—It is in the wall right opposite, the same height as the inlet.

1990. Now, the plank bed in that punishment cell, how is it situated?—It runs along the wall opposite the door.

1991. Which is the head of the bed?—The head of the bed is opposite the door.

1992. What is the length of the bed?—Six feet six inches.

1993. Now, these ventilating shafts, the inlet and the exit, are they over the head or the foot of the bed?—The foot of the bed.

1994. In giving the length of the cell, is that measured from the door to the plank bed?—It is.

Mr. *Murphy*—continued.

1995. With regard to the light, how is it conducted into the cell?—There is a small window a distance of between 7 and 8 feet from the floor.

1996. In which wall is it placed?—In the same wall as the door.

1997. How does the door open?—It opens out into the yard.

1998. Around this yard are there high walls?—About 12 feet high.

1999. What is at the back of this punishment cell?—A large room.

2000. Have you ever been in that punishment cell when the door was closed to?—I was.

2001. Have you tried to read there?—I have not.

2002. When Mr. Mandeville refused to remove those matters from his cell, had you to make other arrangements to get them removed?—We had.

2003. By prisoners or by warders?—By prisoners.

2004. The warders of the prison, some are married and some unmarried, I suppose?—Yes, most of them are married.

2005. Married men live outside the prison?—Yes, sir.

2006. Where do they take their meals?—Outside in their own houses.

2007. The unmarried men reside within the precincts of the prison?—Yes, they have a mess-room over the front gate.

2008. Do you remember at any time medicine being supplied to him by the doctor?

The MacDermot.

2009. By your own knowledge?—I brought it to him.

Mr. *Murphy.*

2010. Were you present with the doctor prior to bringing the medicine?—No.

2011. Did you give it to him?—No, sir. He would not take it.

2012. Can you give us the date of bringing that medicine?—Yes, it was on the 14th December.

2013. Do the warders ever dine on the corridors outside the cells?—No, sir, it would not be a proper place for them. The night-guard brings in some tea, or whatever he likes for his supper, but that is all.

Cross-examined by *The MacDermot.*

2014. You are one of the prison officers, I believe?—Yes, sir.

2015. Are you a married man?—Yes, sir.

2016. How long have you been in that prison?—Eight years.

2017. What is your salary?—£.76 a-year.

2018. Have you rations inside?—No.

2019. Have you lodgings?—I have quarters.

2020. Have you gas?—Yes.

2021. Coal?—Yes.

2022. No food of any kind?—No, sir.

2023. Of course you get your uniform?—Yes, sir.

2024. You had never seen Mr. Mandeville until he came there on that occasion?—No, sir.

2025. I think you said he was a fine able-looking man?—Yes, sir.

2026. Healthy?—Yes, sir.

2027. Did

The Mac Dermot—continued.

2027. Did you approve of all the treatment he received from the time he went there until he left it?—I could not tell, sir; I could not understand what you mean.

2028. Do you approve of the treatment he received?—As far as the officers were concerned; as far as I am concerned.

2029. Do you approve of the treatment he received from the beginning to the end?—According to the rules.

2030. Do you approve of them as a humane man?—According to the rules, I do.

2031. I am not speaking of the rules of the prison. Do you, as a humane man, approve of the treatment he received from the beginning to the end?—I cannot answer you that.

2032. I ask you, as a humane man, did you approve of the treatment he received from the beginning to the end?—That is a question I cannot answer.

2033. Why cannot you say yes or no?—I never did anything except what was strictly according to the prison rules.

2034. As a humane man, did you approve of the treatment he received from the beginning to the end?—I don't know of anything.

2035. Answer my question, yes or no?—I could not disapprove of it.

2036. Did you approve of it?—I am bound to approve of it. (Applause in Court.)

2037. Well, I pity you. You gave the dimensions of that cell; you spoke of the mattress. How long has that mattress been in store?—I cannot tell you.

2038. How long was it in store before you gave it out?—I think it was new, to the best of my opinion. I got it made myself within the last six months.

2039. On your oath, sir, is Mr. Mandeville out of prison more than six months?—I mean six months before Mr. Mandeville got it.

2040. Who made it for you?—One of the prisoners; I don't know which; I had several of the prisoners working.

2041. Can you name any of the prisoners who made that mattress?—I could not. I had several prisoners working.

2042. What is the thickness of one of these mattresses?—Between three and four inches.

2043. And you spread this on the plank bed?—Yes.

2044. You thought it was good enough for John Mandeville?—I lay on it myself.

2045. What is the ordinary weight of a prison mattress?—Seven, fourteen, or twenty lbs., and the larger ones for hospital use.

2046. What is the size for a convicted prisoner?—Fourteen pounds for any classed prisoner.

2047. What are the seven pounds for?—Old men over 60, and boys, and for men on probation class.

2048. What is the weight for hospital?—About 30 lbs. The first sizes are supposed to be made with seven lbs.; the second, 14 lbs.; the third, about 20 lbs., weighs about 24, and there is a larger size for hospital beds, about 30. There is no scale laid down.

2049. John Mandeville was a large man?—He was.

2050. Some of these mattresses are larger than others?—Yes.

2051. In superficial surface?—Yes.

2052. Does not that help to explain whether it was wider?—Of course it does.

2053. His cell you gave the dimensions of, was that the first cell he went to on his arrival?—Yes.

2054. Now, with regard to the weighing, where do you weigh a prisoner?—At the guard-room of the entrance gate.

2055. You take the prisoner out to weigh him?—If we weigh a prisoner in the class we have to bring him out.

2056. Do you weigh many prisoners?—All the prisoners put on extra diet or change of diet.

2057. Except those, do you weigh any prisoners?—Yes; if I was in the guard-room I would weigh a prisoner going out, or prisoners on extra diet.

2058. Do you weigh them when you are going to lessen the diet, as well as when you are going to increase it?—No, sir.

2059. It is only when you are going to increase it?—Yes, sir.

2060. Then it is only in case of extra diet you weigh them?—Yes, sir, and change of diet.

2061. What do you mean by change of diet?—A man may get a change of diet, but not a larger quantity of it.

2062. There is in it a case of a change of diet, or a variety of it?—Yes, sir.

2063. Why did you weigh him on the 8th December, when he was at that time on 48 hours' punishment diet?—He was coming off it.

2064. Did not he get 48 hours on the 8th?—The doctor remitted a day.

2065. The day was discontinued on the 18th November. I am talking now of the 8th December. You weighed him on the 8th December; on the 8th December he got 48 hours for refusing to clean his cell. Why did you weigh him on the 8th?—That had nothing to do with my weighing at all.

2066. Had increase of diet anything to do with it?—No.

2067. You say he is only weighed on account of every change of diet or increase of diet. What was the increase of diet that made you weigh him then; don't you say you never weigh except on a change or increase of diet?—Yes.

2068. Why do you swear that you never weighed except when there was an increase or change of diet. Tell me, are you in the habit of weighing prisoners?—Except on change or increase of diet I only weigh them according to the doctor's order.

2069. How often do you weigh them?—According to the doctor's orders put down in the book.

2070. Do you ever weigh them except by order of the doctor?—We weigh any prisoner on extra diet.

2071. Do you get a special order for weighing any prisoner on extra diet?—Yes.

2072. Do you get any other special order?—Prisoners on change of diet and extra diet, and that is all, except the doctor directed.

2073. When you weighed John Mandeville on the 8th December was it because he was on change of diet or extra diet?—No, but it was by the doctor's orders.

The MacDermot—continued.

2074. Who was present?—No one to my knowledge.

2075. Was not he on punishment at the time?—I believe he was.

2076. Is not it part of the punishment for a prisoner to remain in the cell for the 24 hours?—If in the punishment cell.

2077. Were you violating the rule confining him to his cell, by bringing him to weigh him?—No.

2078. Will you tell me the name of a person whom you took within the last 12 months during a period of punishment diet to weigh him?—I don't know a person who for the last 12 months was at the same time on change of diet and on punishment diet. I never remember one on white bread and punishment.

2079. The change you speak of took place on the 16th November?—Yes.

2080. When did you weigh him next?—I only weighed him three times altogether.

2081. Why did not you weigh him after the 8th December?—I had no orders.

2082. Was not he on the change of diet?—He was, but the doctor sometimes puts them on for a month.

2083. For what length of time was the extra diet ordered?—Twenty-four days. The doctor did not repeat that order, and I consequently weighed him after.

2084. You say that he lost no weight all this time?—No.

2085. Will you swear that?—I will swear that; that was the correct weight then.

2086. After referring to your entry, will you undertake to swear that this weight remained unchanged from November?—Yes.

2087. He grew pale?—Paler than when he came in.

2088. Were you here when Mrs. Mandeville was examined?—No.

2089. Were you here when the doctor was examined?—No.

2090. Would it be true to say when he left prison he was thinner and paler than when he came in?—It would be.

2091. Would it be true that he had a blueness about his lips?—I could not say.

2092. That did not strike you?—No.

2093. Would it be true to say he was flabby-looking in the face?—I could not say.

2094. Would it be true to say that he was shrunken in figure?—He did not appear to me to be.

2095. Will you undertake to swear he was not?—I will not.

2096. Did he complain of weakness of sight while he was there?—He complained of small print in the Bible.

2097. Did he complain of weakness of sight?—Not that I am aware of, but that the print was too small for his eyes.

2098. Did he say that he could not read it?—Something to that effect.

2099. Did he complain of sore throat?—I never heard him complain.

2100. Were you aware that Dr. Ridley prescribed for his sore throat?—I saw it on the book.

The MacDermot—continued.

2101. Did you know he was more than once suffering from diarrhœa?—I think I heard of him twice.

2102. Now, with regard to this arrangement that was made for him during the night, as you talked of a while ago. How was that managed during the night it was placed in a different room?—It was placed sometimes in his own cell.

2103. You lock up at eight and open at seven?—Yes.

2104. I suppose no warder would have a key to open the door?—Certainly not after lockup.

2105. Up to the 23rd November he was allowed to wear his own clothes?—Up to the 23rd November.

2106. Up to that date he did not cleanse his own cell?—No.

2107. Up to that date he had not associated with criminals?—I think not.

2108. What time did Mr. O'Brien go to hospital?—I think on the 7th.

2109. Did Mr. Mandeville not exercise from the 7th down to the 23rd?—He did, sir, by himself.

2110. Not with other prisoners; did he exercise with other prisoners?—He did, sir, after, up to the time he went out.

2111. Do you swear that?—I do.

2112. With whom?—With a number of prisoners under the Crimes Act.

2113. Now these were what are called the Tory prisoners?—Yes.

2114. He never exercised with any man in for stealing?—No, he never was asked.

2115. What hour did you leave the prison on the night of the stand, before you went to Mr. Mandeville's cell?—I went to my quarters in the prison after lockup.

2116. What time elapsed before you were summoned to proceed to Mr. Mandeville's room?—I left there about half-past seven.

2117. You were in Mr. Mandeville's room about eight?—About eight.

2118. So far as you know he had received no warning, and nothing was said to him during the day that an attempt would be made to carry off his clothes that night?—I think not.

2119. Up to that date you have already stated he had given no trouble?—Not except refusing to wear the clothes.

2120. He was quiet and gentlemanly?—Yes.

2121. I think you left out the name of one of the warders who was with you, Bagnall?—He was not there for duty.

2122. You unlocked the door?—I did.

2123. Do you think it was your unlocking the door awakened Mr. Mandeville?—I think so.

2124. Will you swear you did not get into the room before he awoke?—He was turned up leaning on his elbow.

2125. On your oath, was not his head on the pillow when you got into the cell?—It was not.

2126. Who was first in?—I was.

2127. He was lying calmly on his bed?—He was turning round towards me when I went in.

2128. He seemed to be asleep when you went in?—He did; he jumped up when he heard the bolt of the door drawn.

2129. When

The MacDermot—continued.

2129. When you opened the door you saw the light in the cell still lighting?—I am perfectly sure.

2130. When the door was opened did any other light come in?—No, there is no light near the cell.

2131. Was there light outside when you entered?—There was a light in the bottom of the hall, we were on the second landing. There was no light on the corridor.

2132. Have you given an accurate and true account of what occurred?—To the best of my knowledge I have.

2133. Did Mr. Mandeville say then he was a defenceless man?—I did not hear him say it.

2134. Do you swear he did not?—I don't.

2135. Did he say it was shameful treatment?—I did not hear him say anything to that effect.

2136. Did you hear anything to the effect that you were too many for him?—I think not.

2137. Now would not it be true to say that he said this was shameful treatment for a defenceless man who is in your power?—I never heard him.

2138. Did he say anything except protesting?—I heard him say that he was informed that to force his clothes off in this manner was an assault.

2139. An assault on him?—Yes.

2140. Did he say that it was an assault on a defenceless man?—No.

2141. Did he say it was an assault on one man by a number of men?—Not to my knowledge.

2142. What did you take out of the room?—I took the form that was under the end of the mattress.

2143. What else did you take away?—His own private boots.

2144. Why did you put the stool outside the door?—Because it was in the way.

2145. Were you preparing for a battle?—No

2146. Why did you put out the stool?—To put it out of the way. It was in the way.

2147. Did you put anything else belonging to him outside?—No.

2148. Why did you put his boots outside?—Because they were his private clothes.

2149. How many men took a hold of his hands?—I could not say.

2150. Did you take a hold of him?—I did; I took a hold of his right hand and drew off his coat.

2151. Before the warder placed the sheet round his loins did he exclaim against the indecency of taking his shirt?—I think not.

2152. Did you feel ashamed of that transaction at that time?—No, sir.

2153. Did you dislike it?—I did not like it.

2154. Did you think it bad treatment?—I don't know. I did my best to get him to do it. I advised him several times to put on the clothes and conform to the rules, and we would do the best we could for him.

2155. And not having conformed to your advice you thought he deserved it all?—I thought nothing of the kind.

2156. Did you shrink from treating a gentleman in that way?—I did not, sir.

2157. Now, after you had left him there you told him next day you would take away the bed-clothes?—I told him what we would be compelled to do.

The MacDermot—continued.

2158. Did you think you were made the bearer of truth or falsehood?—I think it was intended to do so.

2159. You took them away afterwards?—Yes.

2160. You took away the mattress?—Yes, sir, and the blankets.

2161. Assuming that it was sworn to by the doctor who saw him that day that it was a sheet and a quilt he had on him, would you contradict it?—No.

2162. If he did not put on the prison clothes did not that mean that it was to pass the night without mattress or blankets?—I don't think he would.

2163. You think it was not intended to be real?—No; at that time it was not in contemplation, so far as I know.

2164. Did not you tell him that you would deprive him of the bed-clothes?—Not at that time; but if he would persist we would have to do it.

2165. Not that night?—Perhaps next day.

2166. It would come, at all events?—Yes, I should think it would have to come.

2167. Now this occurred on the 22nd or 23rd November?—Yes

2168. Did you then think of compelling him to cleanse his own cell?—He had been asked all along.

2169. Did you then think of beginning to compel him?—We could not compel him.

2170. Was not the three days' sentence of bread and water passed on him a dreadful punishment?—It is to some.

2171. Was not it to Mr. Mandeville a dreadful punishment?—I should say so.

2172. Was not that sentence put on him to compel him to clean his own cell?—It was for not doing it.

2173. The day that was taken off the three days' sentence, was not that after Dr. Moorhead and Dr. Rowayne stated, one that it might cause a malignant fever, and the other that it might destroy his health?—I don't know.

2174. Did not you see Dr. Rowayne there on the 15th?—No; he may have been there.

2175. Did not you see the books?—I don't read their books.

2176. You put him on fresh punishment on the 25th November?—I could not say.

2177. You cannot remember what he was punished for next time?—It was for not cleaning his cell.

2178. After a sentence of three days on the 14th November, on the 25th he got 24 hours more for the same thing?—Yes.

2179. Was not he on the 8th December sentenced to two days more for not cleaning his cell?—Yes.

2180. Was not he on the 20th December sent to the punishment cell for the same thing?—Yes, I think so. They were all for the same offence, I think.

2181. With regard to that punishment cell you were talking of, after this, on the 20th December when he was there, was there any means taken to keep the draught from coming in by the door?—There was no means taken until Mr. Mandeville complained there was a draught.

The MacDermot—continued.

2192. What happened then?—There was a bag put round the bottom of the door.

2193. Was the draught coming in?—I don't know, I did not feel it.

2194. Did you believe him?—I did not disbelieve him.

2195. Did you do anything to improve that cell since Mr. Mandeville left it?—It was floored with boarding some two or three months since.

2196. Was there anything else done to it?—No, sir.

2197. What is the size of this little window?—It has a pane of 18 inches long by six and a-half inches wide.

2198. Is it in the top of the room?—It is near the ceiling.

2199. I suppose there is a good deal of iron in it?—There are two small shutters.

2190. You consider the light good?—It is.

2191. If the sight was good a Bible with ordinary sized type could be read?—Yes.

2192. Is not it the chaplain gave that Bible?—It was.

2193. Was not it intended to be read in that cell?—Yes.

2194. And expected that he could read it. Don't you think the fact that he was not able to read a Bible intended to be read in that cell was a feebleness of sight?—I don't know.

2195. Is it a condition of the Prisons' Board system to have diet that cannot be eaten, Bibles that cannot be read, and cells that cannot be slept in. You said, as a reason for weighing this man on the 8th December, that the period for which the doctor ordered extra diet according to rule had expired. Will you show me the entry that entitled him to extra diet?—There is no order put on that.

2196. Show me where the order is?—It is the 21st November.

2197. Did not you swear the reason why you weighed him on the 8th December was because the order made on the book had expired?—Yes.

2198. Did not you say the order was made for 24 days on the 21st November?—Yes.

Mr. *Ronan.*

(*Reading from the prison book.*) "John Mandeville, confined in 130 ward; white bread in lieu of brown; brown disagrees with him; when put on, November 15th; period for which extra diet is put on, 24 days."

Mr. *Murphy.*

2199. In whose handwriting is that book?—Dr. Ridley's.

The MacDermot.

2200. I want you to explain about three different mattresses. When an ordinary full-grown man not 60 years of age goes into prison does he get any mattress on his plank bed for the first month?—No.

2201-2. An old man over 60, or boy under 16 years, does he get a mattress?—He gets a unstamped mattress.

2203. That rule is modified under the order of the medical officer, and any mattress may be given under the directions of the medical officer?—Yes.

2204. Was this mattress given to Mr. Mandeville by the order of the doctor?—Yes, sir.

Dr. M'Craith was then called by Mr. *Ronan*, as he said he wished to ask him one or two questions.

Mr. *Harrington.*] He is gone to the Hellespont. I understand he sailed to-day for Smyrna.

Mr. *Ronan.*] It is a fine joke of the doctor whose food treatment of Mr. Mandeville has been impeached.

Service of the summons having been proved by Constable Drudy, Mr. *Ronan* applied for a warrant.

The *Coroner.*] I will give you a warrant in the morning.

Alexander M'Cull, Warder in Tullamore Gaol; Examined.

Mr. *Ronan.*

2205. You were a warder in Tullamore Gaol during the time Mr. Mandeville was confined there?—Yes.

2206. I believe you were specially looking after him for most of the time?—Yes.

2207. Except in the matter of using the prison clothes, refusing to clean his cell and refusing to exercise with the other convicts, did he give any trouble?—No, sir.

2208. An easy-going, quiet gentleman?—Yes.

2209. Were you one of those who accompanied the chief warder and the governor the night Mr. Mandeville's clothes were removed?—Yes.

2210. About what o'clock was it when you reached his cell?—About eight, or a little before it.

2211. Who went in first?—It was the chief warder.

2212. When the door was opened was the gas lighting inside?—It was.

Mr. *Ronan*—continued.

2213. There is no mistake about that?—Not in the least.

2214. Did you see the clothes taken off him and taken out?—I did.

2215. About how long did the whole thing take?—I should say about five minutes.

2216. Was anybody hurt?—No.

2217. Any of the clothes torn that you saw?—No.

2218. Did you all get away from the place some time before the hour for putting out the lights in the prison?—Yes.

2219. Were you present on the occasion that Mr. Mandeville's bed-clothes were taken out of the cell?—I was not.

2220. Did you see Mr. Mandeville when he was leaving the prison at the end of his imprisonment?—I did.

2221. Was there much change in his appearance when leaving from what he was coming in?—I could not detect any.

2222. Was

Mr. *Ronan*—continued.

2222. Was his face paler?—I could not see that.

2223. Did you see him with his own clothes on him coming away?—No, not with his own clothes on him.

2224. Used you clean out the cell?—Yes. I was in charge of a prisoner who did it.

2225. You were responsible for it?—Yes.

2226. Was that done by some other prisoner every day?—Yes, with the exception of one day.

2227. Where did Mr. Mandeville take exercise?—In the exercise yard beside the wing.

2228. Would he exercise with other prisoners who were in under the Crimes Act?—Yes.

2229. Were they formed into a class of first committals?—Yes.

2230. What would you say of the treatment of Mr. Mandeville, did he get the full benefit of the prison rules?—Yes, as far as I saw.

2231. Except the forcing of him to wear the prison clothes and trying to force him to clean his cell, did you see any barbarity or inhumanity practised towards him?—Certainly not.

Cross-examined by Mr. *Harrington*.

2232. How long are you in the prison service?—Over three years.

2233. I suppose the chief warder ought to know a good deal about the rules of the prison; was Chief Warder Bartley right in saying that the gas in November is put out at half-past eight?—Yes.

2234. Is it the same all the year round?—There is some alteration in the summer months.

2235. The alteration takes place, I think, about the 1st of April?—Yes, I think so.

2236. Is there a different hour for rising and retiring in summer and winter?—There is.

2237. In summer what is the hour at which the gas should be put out; what is the hour at which the bell rings for the prisoners to go to bed?—At eight o'clock the whole year round.

2238. Does he get up at the same hour the whole year through?—No, he does not.

2239. But he goes to bed at the same hour the whole year through?—Yes.

2240. The difference is only in the morning?—Yes.

2241. You were never in any other gaol but Tullamore?—No.

2242. At what hour is the gas put out in the gaol?—At half-past eight.

2243. Will you swear that is the same the whole year through?—Yes, except changes on Sundays.

2244. Did you ever hear of anyone reported in the prison for leaving the gas-light to half-past eight?—Never.

2245. No warder was lately punished in Tullamore for leaving the gas burning in any particular cell until half-past eight?—No.

2246. You don't remember hearing of a warder being reported then?—I am certain there was not, to my knowledge.

2247. Was there anything about leaving the gas lighting in Mr. Byrne's cell a little after the hour?—I heard nothing of it.

2248. Were you the warder in charge of Mr. Mandeville all the time he was in?—Yes; except when I was out after a night guard.

Mr. *Harrington*—continued.

2249. If you were on night guard you slept the next day?—Part of it.

2250. Who had to report him for any breach of rules?—Me, when I was on duty.

2251. Now, can you tell me how long Mr. Mandeville was confined from exercise while you were in charge of him?—I don't know.

2252. Was he 20 days?—I believe he was not.

2253. Give us the number of days to the best of your belief; would you say he was 20?—I kept no record of the times from exercise.

2254. Is there no record of it kept in the gaol?—None, to my knowledge.

2255. We heard something of a first-committal class; when did you hear of that class first?—I don't know.

2256. A special class for first committals?—Not until then.

2257. You never before heard in the gaol of a class of first committals?—Not that I remember.

2258. From the time that class of first committals was formed did Mr. Mandeville ever refuse to exercise with them?—Not that I remember.

2259. Have you any doubt that if the class of first committals had been formed the first day he had been asked to exercise, he would exercise with them?—I would not give a decided answer.

2260. What is your opinion?—I don't know.

2261. Did he refuse when it was formed?—Not that I can remember.

2262. When Mr. Mandeville was asked to exercise with prisoners had this class of first committals been formed?—Not that I am aware of.

2263. Are you aware that Mr. Mandeville was punished repeatedly on bread and water for refusing to exercise with other prisoners?—I am not.

2264. Was he punished for refusing to exercise?—He never was.

2265. Could you tell me at what time that class was first formed?—I don't know.

2266. Was Mr. Mandeville in gaol before it was formed?—I could not fix a date for it.

2267. Try to fix a date?—I think he was about three weeks in gaol.

2268. The prisoners that were ultimately in the class with him were principally the Tang prisoners?—Yes, and others besides.

2269. Were the others not under the Crimes Act?—There was one that was not.

2270. Who was he?—He was a little boy.

2271. What was he in for?—I don't mind.

2272. Will you swear he was not in under the Crimes Act?—Yes.

2273. Were the Tang prisoners in the gaol before Mr. Mandeville arrived; you will remember that, surely?—I cannot, clearly.

2274. Have you any doubt that the Tang prisoners were in gaol a long time before Mr. Mandeville arrived there?—I don't remember.

2275. Are any of them in gaol still?—No.

2276. Are you aware that some of them were in for four months?—I don't know.

Mr. *Ronan* objected to time being occupied with this sort of question.

2277. Had you charge of any of the Tang prisoners?—Yes.

Mr. *Harrington*—continued.

2278. Were any of them in before Mr. Mandeville retched?—I cannot remember.

2279. When a prisoner is brought from his cell to be weighed who brings him to be weighed generally?—There is no one properly appointed for that. Sometimes I take one myself, and sometimes the chief warder takes him himself.

2280. If the chief warder sends for a prisoner to be weighed would he take him without communicating with you?—No.

2281. Did you ever get intimation from the chief warder or any other warder to have Mr. Mandeville up to have him weighed?—Not that I remember of.

2282. Did you know Warder Wilson?—I did.

2283. Was he with you on the night you went to the cell?—He was.

2284. Did you ever hear him say how he had taken the clothes off a prisoner before?—Never.

2285. Did you never hear him say how he had thrown a prisoner into the bath, clothes and all?—No.

2286. You are quite sure of that?—Yes.

2287. Did you ever hear it was done?—I think I saw something about it in the papers.

2288. Where was it done?—I don't know.

2289. You are sure it was not in Warder Wilson's journal you saw it?—I am.

Constable EUGENE D. M'CARTHY; Examined.

Mr. *Murphy*.

2290. WHERE are you quartered, constable?—In Fermoy.

2291. Did you know the late John Mandeville's appearance before he went to Tullamore?—I did.

2292. Were you at Mitchelstown on the 31st October last year?—I was.

2293. When next after that did you see him, and where?—The next occasion was at the meeting at Fermoy on April 22nd.

2294. What kind of a day was it?—It was a very wild day.

2295. Where was the meeting held?—In the old market place.

2296. Did you hear Mr. Mandeville make a speech there?—I did not.

2297. What did you see him do?—I saw him standing in the waggonette that was on the square.

2298. Were speeches being delivered at the time?—Yes.

2299. From the waggonette in which he was standing?—Yes.

Mr. *Murphy*—continued.

2300. Was his head covered?—I did not notice.

2301. When next after that did you see him, and where?—I saw him on the second of this month. There were illuminations in the town of Fermoy that night in consequence of Mr. O'Brien's case being sent back to the magistrates.

2302. Was that on a Monday?—It was.

2303. What time of the day did you see him in Fermoy?—It was about half-past ten o'clock at night. He passed up the Barrack Hill immediately after the bands and a number of townspeople.

2304. Was there a great crowd of people following those bands?—There were.

2305. Who was with him?—Mr. Manning and Mr. Coleman, the proprietor of the Temperance Hotel.

2306. Was there anybody there from this side of the country with him?—No.

(The Witness was not cross-examined.)

EIGHTH DAY.

Wednesday, 25th July 1888.

Captain FETHERSTONHAUGH; Examined.

Mr. *Murphy*.

2307. YOU are governor of Tullamore Prison?—Yes.

2308. How long have you held that position?—Over 20 years.

2309. Do you remember the 2nd of November last?—I do.

2310. You received into your custody Mr. John Mandeville?—Yes.

2311. Was he then dressed in his own clothing?—He was.

Mr. *Murphy*—continued.

2312. What time of the day did he arrive at your prison?—About ten o'clock in the morning.

2313. Was Dr. Ridley with you when Mr. Mandeville arrived?—He was.

2314. Did Dr. Ridley examine Mr. Mandeville or give any directions with regard to his clothes?

Question objected to by *The MacDermot*, and allowed.

2315. Were

Mr. *Murphy*—continued.

2315. Were you present when Dr. Ridley examined Mr. Mandeville?—I was not.

2316. Did he examine him?—He did.

2317. Subsequently to the examination, had you any conversation with Dr. Ridley?—I had.

2318. Did you take any steps on that date to remove Mr. Mandeville's clothes?—No.

2319. Does the prison doctor keep a book?—He does.

2320. Is that one of the official books of the prison?—It is.

(*Here the witness identified the prison journal kept by the doctor.*)

2321. Is this journal kept by Dr. Ridley?—Yes.

2322. Is this book, No. 8, a continuation of the prison journal?—It is.

2323. Now, you said you did not remove his clothes the day he came in?—Yes.

2324. Was he sent to his cell?—He was.

2325. What sort of cell was it; was it lightsome or not?—Very good, one of the best cells in the prison.

2326. Now, did you see Mr. Mandeville between the first and the 5th November?—I did.

2327. Had you any conversation with Mr. Mandeville before the 5th November with reference to his donning the prison garb?—I had.

2328. What was the first day you spoke to him on the subject?—On the 3rd.

2329. You remember what passed between you then?—I asked him to put on the prison clothes and he said he would not.

2330. Did you see him on the 4th November?—I did not.

2331. On the 5th did you go to his cell, or did he come to you?—I went to his cell.

2332. Who was with you?—The chief warder.

2333. What passed between you and Mr. Mandeville and the chief ward on that occasion?—The chief warder reported him for not wearing prison dress.

2334. Was that in the presence of Mr. Mandeville?—It was.

2335. Did Mr. Mandeville say anything with reference to the charge?—He said he would not wear them.

2336. Did you on that occasion sentence him to 24 hours bread and water. This is the punishment book (*producing book*)?—Yes.

2337. This is your entry?—Yes.

2338. Was that punishment carried out in his own cell?—It was.

2339. Did you see him between the 5th November and the 14th?—Every day.

2340. Had you any conversation with him during that time about his putting on prison clothes?—I had several times.

2341. What did you say to him?—I advised him to put them on; I told him the consequences of not putting them on, and I said to him, it would be my duty to punish him.

2342. On the 14th November, did you go to his cell, or was he brought to you?—He was brought to me.

2343. Where to?—Down to the hall.

2344. By whom?—By warder M'Calla.

2345. Was Mooney there?—He was.

2346. Did he, in the presence of Mr. Mandeville, make any charge?—He did.

2347. Is he the reception warder who has charge of the prison clothes?—Yes.

2348. What was the charge he made against Mr. Mandeville?—That he would not wear the prison clothes.

2349. Was that charge made in the presence of Mr. Mandeville?—It was.

2350. Did he say anything to the charge?—He said he would not put on the prison clothes.

2351. Did you say anything?—I did; I asked him to put them on. He said he would not; then I said, it was my duty to punish him.

2352. Did you punish him?—I sentenced him to three days bread-and-water in his own cell.

2353. This entry (*pointing out entry*) is authenticated by your signature?—Yes.

2354. Is this entry in your handwriting?—It is.

2355. After he had done two day's punishment, was the rest of the sentence remitted?—It was under the direction of the medical officer.

2356. Having put him through those two days on bread-and-water, do you remember the 22nd of November?—I do.

2357. Do you remember the evening of that day going with any persons to Mr. Mandeville's cell?—I do.

2358. Who were with you?—The chief warder Hartley, and warder M'Calla.

2359. What time did you go there?—Just at 8 o'clock.

2360. What time is the gas in the prison turned out?—At half-past eight.

2361. Is there a grating in the door through which you could look?—There is.

2362. When you came to the door, was the gas in that cell lighting, or was it put out?—It was lighting.

2363. Are you clear and distinct about that?—Clear and distinct.

2364. Who opened the door?—The chief warder.

2365. Were you with him at the time?—I was.

2366. Who went in first?—The chief warder.

2367. Did you follow him?—I did.

2368. Did you go before or after the other warders?—One other, I think, went in before me.

2369. When you went in, where was Mr. Mandeville?—He was on the plank bed.

2370. Do you recollect what position he was in?—He was leaning up with one hand under him.

2371. Was his head on the pillow?—No.

2372. What way was his face turned?—Towards the door.

2373. Did you say anything to him, or did the chief warder say anything to him with reference to his clothes?—Yes, he asked what we were about to do, and I asked him to put on the prison dress.

2374. Was there a suit in the cell at the time?—Yes.

2375. Was that suit ever used before?—No, it was quite a new suit out of the store.

2376. Had you done anything to secure that it

Mr. *Murphy*—continued.

it was dry, and all that?—Oh, yes; I had it properly aired.

2377. You asked Mr. Mandeville to put on the clothes?—Yes.

2378. Did you say anything to him about them being aired?—I told him that they were perfectly new clothes, and that they had been aired several times to have them ready any time he would put them on.

2379. Now go on and tell us in your own language what occurred under your own observation:—As soon as the chief warder took out the stool, which was under the mattress on the plank bed, Mr. Mandeville stood up, and I having asked him to take off the clothes, and his having refused, I directed the officers to remove them, and they did, taking hold of his hands, unbuttoning his coat, drawing it off, drawing off his waistcoat, and a sort of knitted garment.

2380. Did he make any real resistance to this?—Certainly not, but he protested against my giving this order at all, and told me I was acting illegally.

2381. Did they succeed in getting all the clothes off him?—Yes.

2382. Did you leave him in the cell and leave this suit of prison clothes with him?—Yes.

2383. Did you go to see him next day, the 23rd?—I did.

2384. What was the hour you saw him on the 23rd?—Well, I saw him several times on that day.

2385. Where was he when you saw him?—In his cell.

2386. When you left his cell after removing his clothes did the gas remain lighting?—It did.

2387. How long were you in the cell altogether?—About five or six minutes.

2388. You were served with a writ by Mr. Mandeville, and you duly appeared?—Yes.

2389. And that action was never brought to trial?—No.

2390. Did you ever hear any more about the action after that?—No.

2391. When you saw Mr. Mandeville on the 23rd November was he in his cell?—He was.

2392. And how was he dressed?—He had a quilt round his shoulders and a sheet for an under garment.

2393. Were the prison clothes lying on the table?—They were.

2394. Did you say anything to him or did he say anything to you?—I advised him to put them on.

2395. Did you also go into the cell with Dr. Moorhead?—I did.

2396. Was he in the same condition then?—He was.

2397. Did anything occur in Dr. Moorhead's presence that you wish to state?—Nothing occurred except that he gave a description to Dr. Moorhead of what had occurred the night before.

2398. Did he tell Dr. Moorhead that the gas was out when you came into the cell?—He did not.

2399. What did he tell Dr. Moorhead?—He said that the clothes were taken off.

2400. Did he give the same account of the transaction that you have given here to-day?—I think so.

2401. After Dr. Moorhead going away did you go in again to Mr. Mandeville?—I went in about five o'clock.

2402. Was he still dressed in this way?—He was.

2403. Who was with you?—The chief Warder and Warder Mooney.

2404. Did they go with you?—They did.

2405. Now what passed in reference to these clothes?—I asked him again to put on the prison clothes, and he said he would not. I said then that I would take out the bed and bedding, and they were taken out.

2406. What was taken out?—The mattress and the blanket that were on the bed. The quilt and sheet were left with him.

2407. Were you present when Mr. Mandeville parted with these clothes?—No, I was not in the cell.

2408. What time did you see Mr. Mandeville again?—Before locking up, six o'clock.

2409. Was he in prison dress?—He was.

2410. In a prison cell occupied by prisoners by whom are they cleaned every morning?—By themselves.

2411. You remember the 29th November?—I do.

2412. Was Mr. Mandeville brought before you on that day?—He was.

2413. By whom?—By Warder M'Culla.

2414. Where was he brought?—Down in the hall.

2415. Was there any charge stated against him by M'Culla?—Yes, that he would not clean his cell.

2416. Did Mr. Mandeville get an opportunity of saying anything that he had to say?—Yes, he said he would not do it.

2417. Did you then pronounce sentence on him of 24 hours' bread-and-water in his own cell?—Yes.

2418. Is this entry here authenticated by your own signature?—It is.

2419. Between that and the 8th December, did you see Mr. Mandeville every day?—Yes.

2420. Had you any talk with him about the cleaning of his cell?—Often.

2421. What did you say to him?—I advised him to conform to the prison rules, as I did advise many other prisoners before him.

2422. Was Mr. Mandeville again brought before you on the 9th December, and was that in the hall also?—It was.

2423. On the same charge?—Yes.

2424. You then pronounced a sentence of 48 hours?—Yes.

2425. And this is your entry (*pointing out entry*)?—Yes.

2426. When did he come off that 48 hours?—After two full days.

2427. Between the 9th December and the 20th did you see Mr. Mandeville every day?—I did, and advised him every day.

2428. Do you remember on the 20th December his

Mr. *Murphy*—continued.

his being brought up again, who was he brought before on that day?—The resident magistrate, Mr. Smith, on a charge of refusing to clean his cell by Warder M'Cabe.

2429. Did Mr. Smith take evidence on oath?—He did.

2430. Had Mr. Mandeville anything to say?—He admitted the charge.

2431. He then was sentenced to two days punishment cell?—Yes.

2432. Did you see Mr. Mandeville into the cell yourself?—I did.

2433. Did he make any complaint to you as to the condition of the cell?—No, not to me.

2434. Was he given a mattress?—He was.

2435. Was it the same mattress that he had been using in his own cell?—It was.

2436. What class of mattress was it?—It was what is called 24 lbs.

2437. And was that removed to the punishment cell when he went there?—It was.

2438. Do you know whether there were bags put in the door to stop the draft or anything like that?—I do; it was done by my directions.

2439. What was the temperature of this cell?—It was 58 the morning after he being put into it.

2440. Was it heated by hot water pipes?—It was.

2441. And are they always kept working?—Yes. I inspected the fire myself, and saw that it was properly kept up, and the officers had particular orders before to keep the fire up.

2442. What sort of bread was Mr. Mandeville getting while in prison?—He was getting brown bread first.

2443. Do you know when a change was made?—The 15th or 16th.

2444. From the time the change was made, did he get white bread every day?—He did.

2445. Is this entry in Dr. Ridley's writing (producing diet book)?—It is.

2446. It is the duty of the medical doctor to make an entry in that book of any changes made?—It is.

2447. Is that book regularly kept as one of the prison books?—It is.

2448. Whose handwriting is it in?—It is in the handwriting of Dr. Ridley, except the figures.

2449. Is this submitted to you?—I examine them periodically.

2450. It is your duty to carry out the directions given in it?—It is.

2451. Were the directions given in respect to Mr. Mandeville observed?—Strictly.

2452. You had plenty of opportunities of observing Mr. Mandeville's appearance and condition when he came in, and all the time while in your custody?—I had.

2453. Now going back to your recollection of Mr. Mandeville's appearance, did he appear to have wasted or diminished in size until he left you on the 24th of December?—No.

2454. Were you present when he was weighed?—No.

2455. Have you had other prisoners in your custody for these so-called political offences?—I had.

2456. Have they conformed to the rules?—Yes, Mr. Doughty did.

2457. Did he clean out his cell?—Yes.

2458. And did his work?—Yes, I had no difficulty with him.

2459. Mr. Goulding, who was examined here, was a warder in your prison for some time?—Yes.

2460. When were his services dispensed with?—On the 9th of July.

2461. That was a considerable time after Mr. O'Brien and Mr. Mandeville had left?—A long time after.

2462. What was the charge against him?—Making a false statement.

2463. Was that on a sworn inquiry, where he was heard?—Yes, before Mr. Joyce, the inspector.

Cross-examined by *The MacDermot*.

2464. Captain Fetherstonhaugh, did Mr. Mandeville impress you as favourably as he impressed Dr. MacCabe?—He was a very fine-looking man.

2465. Did he appear to you to be inoffensive?—He did.

2466. Gentlemanly manner and demeanour?—Yes.

2467. Did he appear to be a malingerer?—No.

2468. You considered him an inoffensive man, truthful?—Yes.

2469. Now, with the exception of not complying with those rules, he was not riotous or disorderly?—No.

2470. He smiled oftener than he frowned?—He was always apparently in good humour.

2471. Said nothing to attract the hostility of anyone in the prison?—Certainly not.

2472. From the time he entered the prison until he left it, did he get any meat diet?—When he was on first class.

2473. From what date? He was committed on the 31st, then a month from that.

2474. Did he get soup?—He did.

2475. What kind?—Table soup.

2476. What is that taken off?—It is taken off the leg or shin of beef.

2477. With the exception of a half-a-pint of that three times a week, he got no soup during the first month?—Half-a-pint of regulation soup.

2478. Did Mr. Mandeville get meat through any part of his course?—No.

2479. Did he get any rice?—No.

2480. No brandy?—No.

By the *Coroner*.

2481. Or arrowroot, or anything of that kind?—No.

The MacDermot.

2482. He went in on the 2nd of November?—Yes.

2483. His own clothes on him?—Yes.

2484. Where were you on the 4th November?—I was in Dublin.

2485. During the second month he got no meat,

The MacDermot—continued.

meat, except Sunday?—No, on that day he got four ounces.

2486. Did he get soup during the second month?—He did on Sunday.

2487. Half-a-pint of soup?—Yes.

2488. You went to Dublin on the 4th?—I did.

2489. You said you had a conversation with Dr. Ridley on the 2nd?—Yes.

2490. Had your journey to Dublin anything to do with the treatment of Mr. Mandeville?—I went to visit my board.

2491. To visit the Honourable Charles Bourke?—Yes.

2492. Was that before you inflicted any punishment on him?—It was.

2493. When you came back from Dublin you inflicted punishment on him of 24 hours bread and water?—Yes.

2494. Does that deprive him of two hours exercise?—It does.

2495. Is that under any rule (*Counsel reads rule*); what does it say there about taking his two hours' exercise from him; do not be looking across the table?—I am not looking at any one but you.

2496. He was not a disorderly prisoner, did you not say that?—I remember saying that any man who broke the rules of the prison was disorderly.

2497. Under what rule are disorderly prisoners deprived of two hours exercise; is there a word about the withdrawal of exercise?—There is.

2498. Is a prisoner entitled to two hours' exercise by the statute?—Yes.

2499. If that is a privilege, what power had you to withdraw it; do you consider it to be a privilege?—According to Act of Parliament I could withdraw a privilege.

2500. Was that privilege granted by special enactment?—Yes.

2501. Is it your reading of the rule that you can withdraw it?—I know I can do it.

2502. Do you consider the rule gave you a right?—I do.

2503. Was there anything else that gave you a right?—The Act of George.

2504. Now, with regard to the prison clothes, is there any rule or Statute entitling you to compel a prisoner to wear prison clothes, and to use physical force to compel him?—I was informed that I could make a prisoner wear the clothes.

By the *Coroner*.

2505. Except the provision that a prisoner shall wear prison clothes, is there anything in any rule or Statute entitling you to use physical force to compel him?—No.

2506. I suppose, then, that you yourself were of opinion that you were entitled to use physical force?—Yes.

2507. Now, in your judgment, do you consider you are entitled to use physical force, even though it be injurious to health?—Certainly not; if the doctor gave me a certificate I would not use it.

The MacDermot.

2508. Did Mr. O'Brien say to you that the doctor should be present at any attempt to take his clothes?—He did.

2509. Did you say you would have the doctor and that you would not have the chaplain?—I did.

2510. Was the doctor present at the time you took Mr. Mandeville's clothes? No.

2511. Describe when you entered; did you consider Mr. Mandeville was asleep?—I think he was asleep.

2512. Why was the stool taken out of his cell?—It might be in the way.

2513. Who took it?—The chief warder.

2514. At the time you took the clothes off Mr. Mandeville was he sitting on his bed or was he standing up?—He was standing up the whole time.

2515. Before you began taking off the clothes he protested against it?—He did.

2516. Did he say anything about it afterwards as a shame?—He did not.

2517. Did he say anything about taking off the shirt?—He may have.

2518. You have a discriminating memory, and I never knew a governor of a gaol who has not one; now, Governor, will you tell me, he may have complained of indecency?—Yes.

2519. Was it that you forgot that he had the protection of the sheet and quilt?—Yes.

2520. When they were taking off his clothes were they holding his hands?—They were.

2521. Will you swear he did not complain of the wrenching of his arm?—He did not.

2522. Did he resist when the clothes were being taken off?—He did not.

2523. Did you not hear Mr. Hartley swear that he resisted?—He did not resist.

2524. Now, Captain, I ask you did he make any resistance, no matter how small; you said, certainly not, is that true; did he resist to any extent?—Slight resistance.

2525. Did he twist about?—No, he twisted his arms about.

2526. Then he twisted his arms about?—He did.

2527. Did you say so to my question that he twisted about?—I dare say I did.

2528. You left him then in the cell with this sheet and quilt about him when you left the cell that night?—He had the sheet about him.

2529. When you returned next day he had a sheet about him?—He had.

2530. You returned again about five or half-past five, and took away all the bed clothes and the mattress?—Yes.

2531. Did you say, at any time, you took them away in order that he might have no mattress, unless he put on the prison clothes, and you carried out that order?—I would have carried it out till eight o'clock, by no means would I deprive a prisoner of his covering or his bed at night.

2532. That would be a violation of the rules?—It would.

2533. I think you said lock-up hour is six o'clock?—Yes.

2534. Under what rule are you entitled to take away quilts and blankets between lock-up hour

The MacDermot—continued.

hour and eight o'clock?—There is nothing to prevent me, as they cannot go to bed till eight o'clock.

2535. Then you are at liberty under the rules to withdraw prisoners bed clothes and mattress during the day?—I consider I am.

2536. Did you intend that Mr. Mandeville's bed clothes would not be given back?—No.

2537. On what date did Mr. O'Brien get the suit of clothes that was sent to him by a friend?—I do not know.

2538. Was it before Mr. Mandeville's clothes were taken off?—I think it was.

2539. On the 22nd you took Mr. Mandeville's?—I received directions to do it.

2540. Three days after Mr. O'Brien got the suit of clothes?—Yes.

2541. I presume you communicated the fact that the new garments came in?—Yes.

2542. On the 19th, was it?—On the 19th.

2543. To the authorities in Dublin?—I decline to answer that.

2544. Do you refuse to say whether you communicated with the authorities in Dublin?—I do.

2545. That was a confidential communication?—It was.

2546. After your communicating to Dublin that Mr. O'Brien had got new garments on the 19th, did you receive any letter from Dublin; did you receive any communication from the authorities to strip Mandeville?—I did not.

2547. On what date did you receive your order to strip Mandeville?—I will not answer.

2548. Now Governor, now Captain, do you decline to tell me on whose order you stripped Mandeville?—I do.

2549. Did you strip him without orders?—I will not answer.

2550. Why did you not strip him between the 2nd and 22nd of November?—I was not sure of my power.

2551. You knew the prison regulations for 20 years?—Yes.

2552. And was it not part of your duty to know the statute?—It was.

2553. When did you become sure of your power?—I decline to tell you.

2554. When was Mr. Mandeville ordered to exercise with ordinary criminals?—I cannot exactly tell you?

2555. About the date?—About four days after he came in.

2556. Will you swear that?—I think so.

2557. Did you not form a special class?—I did.

2558. Was not that three weeks after he came in?—No.

2559. Was it a fortnight?—It might be.

2560. When was he asked to clean his cell?—From the beginning.

2561. Why was he not punished for not cleansing his cell until the 28th November?—Because that was portion of the charge included.

2562. When did you first sentence him to punishment for not cleansing his cell?—On the 28th November.

2563. Why did you not sentence him before that?—Because I had the other charge.

2564. After the clothes were taken away you commenced to punish him for not cleansing his cell?—Yes.

2565. You gave him 48 hours on the 6th December?—Yes.

2566. And he got two days on the 20th December?—Yes.

2567. Who is the resident magistrate?—Mr. Smith.

2568. He lives in Tullamore?—Yes.

2569. Why did you not call on some other magistrate?—He was the only one in the town.

2570. Did you consider you were under an obligation to call in one of the visiting justices, if available?—Yes.

2571. And you only applied to one?—He was the only one that was there.

2572. Why did you not make efforts to see others?—He was the only one that was within reach of four or five miles.

2573. Why did you not write to some of them?—Because I wanted to have the punishment inflicted at once.

2574. And between the 2nd and the 22nd November you could not write?—The Doctor did not give me a certificate until then, that he was fit for punishment.

2575. Did you ask before for a certificate?—I did.

2576. And did he refuse until then?—He did.

2577. Have you any entry of the Doctor having given a certificate?—I have the certificate itself.

2578. You got a certificate on the 20th December, and you instantly wrote to Mr. Browne, and he could not come in?—I wrote to him first, and I met him afterwards.

2579. What date?—That day.

2580. Where does he live?—He has an office in the town.

2581. Did you keep a letter-book?—I did.

2582. You knew it was your duty to get one of the visiting justices if available; why did you not wait a day, and call one of them?—I considered, when I got the certificate, I should act on it at once.

2583. When he left your prison, you say he was unaltered in appearance?—I think he was unaltered, except that he was a little bit paler, that is all.

2584. Mrs. Mandeville said, that when he reached home he was thin, do you agree with that?—No.

2585. That he was bluish on the lips, do you agree with that?—To the best of my belief, he was not.

2586. Mr. William O'Brien said, that when he saw him on the day of his leaving prison, that he was wasted, shattered, and altered; you would not consider that likely to be true?—He was a good while out of prison.

2587. Dr. Rowntree and Dr. Moorhead said that he was flabby, pasty-looking, that his breathing was laboured and shallow; do you think that was true?—I do not think so, and I tell one reason for thinking his breathing was not laboured on several occasions; when I went to his cell, I found him swinging that heavy stool round his head for exercise, and if he was heavy breathed, I do not think he could do that.

2588. Do you consider that a man suffering from

The MacDermot—continued.

from laboured breathing could not be expected to wind a stool round his head for exercise?—As to his breathing, I mean.

2589. Do you believe he had sore throat?—Of course, I believe it.

2590. Is this a true account of Dr. Moorhead, "I found him walking about in his cell wrapped in a quilt and sheet, no under clothing, not even a shirt. He told me he was wakened out of his sleep by the governor and other warders, and after a struggle his clothes were taken from him." His chest, feet, and one of his arms were bare. The governor was present when this conversation took place. Now was that report by Dr. Moorhead an accurate description of what took place?—I think so; so far as the clothes were concerned.

2591. I suppose you considered that fit treatment?—I never like to punish a prisoner, and many a poor fellow I got off.

2592. Did the treatment of Mr. Mandeville give you any special pain?—No.

2593. And you knew he was a man of respectable position?—He appeared to be.

2594. And you knew he had been accustomed to the ordinary comforts of life?—I knew nothing except his appearance.

2595. Did it give you any special pain to compel him to clean his own cell?—At the time I felt it very much to have to punish him.

2596. Give me a direct answer. Did you feel it especially painful to compel him to clean out his own cell?—I did.

2597. Did you feel it painful to enter his cell at night with a body of warders, and take from him his clothes by force?—I did.

2598. Apart from the obligation under the rule, did you consider it inhuman and barbarous treatment?—I did not.

2599. When the warders make charges on the various occasions that you punished Mr. Mandeville, did they make those charges at your instance?—No.

2600. You came from Dublin on the 4th November; a charge was brought before you on the 5th by the chief warder; did you know the chief warder was about to make it to you?—I did.

2601. Did you tell him to make it?—I do not think I did.

2602. Did you, after you came from Dublin, go to the chief warder?—I may have.

2603. Did you?—I do not recollect that I did.

2604. On the 14th November he was again charged?—Yes.

The MacDermot—continued.

2605. Was he charged between the 5th and 14th by another warder?—He was charged every day by the warders.

2606. Has the warder pointed to another charge in the warder's book?—Not in his own book.

2607. Where is the charge entered in any other book, and what is the name of it?—The report book.

2608. Is it here?—It is not.

2609. Are there charges entered on which there was no punishment?—Yes; it was reported to me every day that he would not clean out his cell. What I mean by a charge is, a daily report that he would not clean out his cell or wear his prison clothes.

2610. You do not act on these reports except on the days you inflict punishment?—No.

2611. Was the entry of the charge made against Mr. Mandeville made before or after the punishment was inflicted?—In the punishment book it is after. In the report book before it is inflicted.

2612. And a prisoner is entitled to be heard on the charge?—Yes.

2613. You told me the charge was put down first and the sentence after. How do you know the charges made by the warders; the warder reported to you every day?—Yes.

2614. And you made no entries except when you punished?—Yes; on the day the charge was put down first, and the sentence afterwards.

2615. Why did not the warder put down the charges on other days?—Because I told him they would not be acted on.

Mr. *Murphy*.

2616. This report book you speak of, that is not a book prescribed by the prison?—No.

2617. It is a book for your own convenience?—Yes.

The MacDermot.

2618. You talked about the swinging of a stool over his head?—Yes.

2619. What is the weight of it?—Nine or ten pounds.

Mr. *Murphy*.

2620. At what period of imprisonment did you find Mr. Mandeville at this exercise?—About the middle of it.

2621. Did you see him towards the end of it?—I think so.

2622. Do you see this book?—I do.

2623. Was this kept by Dr. Ridley?—Yes.

Mr. James O'Gorman, J.P.; Examined by Mr. Ronan.

Mr. *Ronan*.

2624. You are a Justice of the Peace for this county?—I am.

2625. I believe you are a brother of Mrs. Mandeville?—I am; he was my brother-in-law. (*Here one of the prison books from Tullamore was handed to the Witness.*)

Mr. *Ronan*—continued.

2626. I believe, on the 10th November, you went to Tullamore?—Yes.

2627. That was the only occasion you visited it?—Yes.

2628. Did you see Mr. Mandeville that day?—Yes; that evening.

2629. Did

Mr. Ronan—continued.

2629. Did you ask him whether he had any complaint to make?—I asked him how he was, and he said he had no complaint.

2630. Did he seem in good spirits?—He did.

2631. Did you ask him had he any complaint to make?—I did.

2632. There is only one other matter that I want to ask you about; on the Wednesday after Mr. Mandeville's death had you a conversation or communication with your sister as to the desirability of holding this inquest?—No.

2633. Had you on the Tuesday?—I had. I objected to the inquest until Mr. Frank Mandeville came.

2634. After that interview with Mrs. Mandeville, did you inquire of the resident magistrate whether she had authority to prevent an inquest being held?—Yes.

2635. What o'clock was that you saw Mr. Eaton?—Ten o'clock.

2636. You stopped him on the road?—Yes; I understood it was confidential.

2637. Did you say one word about privately?—Yes.

Mr. *Harrington.*

2638. I suppose the members of your family were opposed to holding an inquest?—My sister was, until the matter of a post mortem examination was settled, and after that our family was satisfied.

2639. Did you hear her evidence here, Mr. O'Gorman?—Yes.

2640. I believe your Mrs. Mandeville had given all about the funeral arrangements into your mother's hands when Mr. Frank Mandeville came?—Yes.

The *Coroner.*

2641. I believe he was buried in his own family vault at Mallow?—Yes.

2642. After Mr. Frank Mandeville came there was no further objection?—No.

Mr. *Harrington.*

2643. You live quite close to your sister?—My farm is next to that of the deceased.

2644. I think you were saying that, naturally enough, Mr. Mandeville might not complain to you, even though suffering?—I should say so, because my sister was nervous and he would naturally make the most of it.

2645. Like any other stranger visiting him, you were restricted to the questions you should ask him?—Yes.

2646. You knew Mr. Mandeville for a very long time?—For about 14 years.

2647. He dined frequently at your house?—He dined for five years constantly at my house.

2648. Was he a man of sober or temperate habits?—I never saw him, while he was in my father's house or out of it, take anything except one bottle of porter.

2649. I suppose few persons had a better opportunity of seeing him than you?—While I knew him I always knew him to be a most temperate man.

Mr. *Harrington*—continued.

2650. Did you ever, in your whole intercourse with him, see him under the influence of drink?—Never.

Mr. *Ronan.*

2651. Do you mean that you never saw him take more than one bottle of porter in the day?—Yes.

2652. It is dinner you are speaking of?—Yes.

2653. You never saw him take any stimulants, except porter?—Never, except the time he was dying, and the doctor ordered him brandy.

2654. Is there a sort of arrangement between you and Mr. Mandeville?—None.

2655. How long is it since he was in your house?—This day three weeks.

2656. When was he there before that?—About two days before that.

2657. How often has he dined in your house since Christmas?—I should say about eight times.

2658. On your oath, on these occasions, did he drink anything but porter?—On one occasion he drank porter, and on all the other occasions he drank no stimulant.

2659. Can you give any explanation to the Coroner or the jury why that man twice took the pledge against whisky?—I never heard it until the inquest.

2660. If your account be true, can you give any reason why he took the pledge at all?—Often a very temperate man will take it. I often took a pledge myself against whiskey alone for 18 months.

2661. When did you last take a pledge against whiskey alone?—Five years ago.

2662. And it was against whiskey alone?—No; against all spirits. I could take wine. I took nothing but water.

2663. Could you tell me the cause of a man, like Mr. Mandeville, whose favourite drink was porter, taking the pledge against whiskey twice?—I don't know.

2664. Up to the last couple of months of his life, was not Mr. Mandeville in the habit of attending a lot of public meetings and demonstrations?—Yes.

2665. Were you ever with him at them?—Never.

2666. You said that after Mr. Frank Mandeville came, Mrs. Mandeville no longer objected to an inquest. When did Mr. Mr. Frank Mandeville come?—I think on Tuesday. I did not know until I saw my sister, on Wednesday.

2667. Did you tell Mr. Eaton that his brothers were going to hold an inquest in spite of her, or that anybody was going to hold an inquest in spite of her?—No.

2668. Was there anything of that sort said by you that it was going to be held against her wishes?—No; what I wanted to know was, suppose people wanted to hold an inquest against her will, could it be held?

2669. Who were the other people you referred to?—I won't answer.

2670. You did mean somebody; but you won't tell me?—Of course, I did.

Mr. JOHN THERRY, Baronial High Constable for the Barony of Condons and Clangibbons; Examined.

Mr. *Ronan*.

2671. Do you remember on the 1st of March in this year seeing the late Mr. Mandeville when he paid you some county cess?—Yes.

2672. Have you the block of the receipt to fix the date in your mind?—Yes, it was the 2nd of March.

2673. Had you a conversation with Mr. Mandeville?—Yes, a few words only.

2674. You knew at the time he had been in prison?—Yes.

2675. You asked him how he was?—Yes, I met him at the Mitchelstown post office, I asked him how he was after Tullamore, or words to that effect.

2676. What reply did he make?—He said he was never in better health in his life.

2677. Do you remember the day that Mr. Condon, M.P. was sent to gaol from Mitchelstown?—Yes, I think it was on the 7th of May.

2678. Did you see Mr. Mandeville walking with a tall man you did not know?—Yes, I was going up the street and met him.

2679. When they got up to you, did Mr. Mandeville say anything?—When they came opposite to me, he said something about the collector, and they came over to me.

2680. When they came over, did Mr. Mandeville ask you anything?—He asked me whether it was the police, or I, would be collecting the tax. I said it was I.

2681. What did he say then?—He said they would make it a little hot for me, or words to that effect, in a jocose kind of way.

2682. Did he ask you anything then?—We had a conversation for a few minutes.

2683. Did he say anything about the police collecting it?—I tried to reason the matter with him, and said surely the county has not come to that that the taxes won't be paid.

2684. What did he say then?—He told me to send him his account as soon as I could. I said I would send it the same as usual, and I was sure he would pay too.

2685. What did he say to that?—I said I would be obliged to pay it out of my own pocket if he did not pay it.

> The *Coroner* to Mr. *Ronan*.] You present this as material evidence, and relevant to the cause of death?
>
> Mr. *Ronan*.] I do, and very material, and relevant to the cause of death.
>
> Mr. *Therry*.] He said, we will give you a good passive resistance.

Mr. *Ronan*.

2686. That was before the resistance to the tax began?—Yes.

2687. How was Mr. Mandeville looking on that day?—He appeared as well as ever I saw him.

2688. Now we will go from the 7th of May to the 5th of June; did you seize four of Mr.

Mr. *Ronan*—continued.

Mandeville's cows for tax, and had them in Mitchelstown for auction?—Yes.

2689. Did you auction them that day?—Yes.

2690. About what hour that day did you first see Mr. Mandeville?—To the best of my belief, I think about 11 o'clock.

2691. When was your auction over?—At three.

2692. Was that a wet day?—It was a very wet day.

2693. Did Mr. Mandeville stop there all day until the auction was over?—Yes; I saw him after the auction, and before the auction.

2694. You previously asked him for the money?—Yes, and went to his house. He said he hadn't the money; I said I would wait for it. He said he would have to let the cattle go to be sold.

2695. Now subsequently to that, had you on several occasions to go through the country to distrain for this tax?

The MacDermot objected.

Mr. *Ronan*.

2696. Was Mr. Mandeville present on many occasions through the country when you were distraining for the tax?—Yes.

2697. And were there crowds present?—Yes.

2698. Do you remember being at Glanworth on the 18th June?—Yes.

2699. Was there a mob of a couple of hundred people there?—Yes, for a while.

2700. Mr. Mandeville and Mr. Barry, P. L. G. at the head of them?—Yes.

2701. Was there heavy rain during part of that day?—Very heavy rain.

2702. Part of the day that you saw Mr. Mandeville, had he any top coat?—No.

2703. Do you remember being in Fermoy on the 18th June?—Yes.

2704. When the mob tried to force the cattle out of the pound or wherever they were?—Yes.

2705. Was Mr. Mandeville there that day?—Yes.

2706. What hour did you see him there that day, Mr. Therry?—A little after the cattle were seized. About 12 o'clock and later on.

2707. Do you remember on the 5th of June, were cattle seized being sold in Mitchelstown?—Yes.

2708. Did you see Mr. Mandeville that day at the sale?—Yes.

2709. Was part of that day wet?—Showers, but not a very wet day.

2710. Were you around the different petty sessions here, suing people for the tax?—Yes.

2711. Used Mr. Mandeville frequent the petty sessions where some of these were heard?—Yes, some of them.

2712. Do you remember the 2nd of July, were you in the Fermoy Court-house, where you had some of these tax cases on, were you there about half-past 12, and saw Mr. Mandeville there?—Yes.

2713. After

Mr. *Ronan*—continued.

2713. After the court was over, did you see Mr. Mandeville about the town with some people you had summoned for the case?—Yes.

2714. The following morning, that is Tuesday morning the 3rd July, where did you meet your bailiffs?—About a mile from Fermoy. Beyond Granga.

2715. As nearly as you can, what hour was it when you met them?—To the best of my belief about half-past two in the morning, it may be a few minutes more or less, but certainly before three o'clock.

2716. Did you look at your watch?—I looked at my watch going through Glanworth.

2717. Did you see Mr. Mandeville?—Yes.

2718. Where was it that you saw him?—He was driving against me when I was going into Fermoy.

2719. How far from Fermoy?—About a mile or a little more.

2720. He was driving out from Fermoy?—Yes.

2721. What was Mr. Mandeville's appearance when you saw him?—He appeared a little bit tired and laughed when he saw me.

2722. Who was on the car with him?—Two others at the other side of the car.

2723. Can you say who they were?—I am not positive.

2724. Two others and the drivers?—Yes.

2725. After his car passed did you drive into Fermoy with the bailiff?—Yes.

2726. What did the car on which Mr. Mandeville was, do?—Turned around and followed us.

2727. Did you see where Mr. Mandeville's car stopped in Fermoy?—Yes.

2728. Where?—At Coleman's Hotel.

2729. Did you see him again that day?—No; I never saw him again.

2730. Tell me as nearly as you can what hour it was when you saw his car stopping at Coleman's hotel?—It must have been a little before three.

The *Coroner*.

2731. Was Mr. Mandeville on the car then?—He was.

Cross-examined by *The MacDermot*.

2732. How long did you know Mr. Mandeville?—For years.

2733. Did you ever see him drunk?—Never, nor never under the influence of drink.

2734. You spoke of a number of interviews with Mr. Mandeville, did you make any particular note in your book or mind about Mr. Mandeville's appearance or words?—No, but I remember them well.

2735. I want to know, did you pay special attention to them on those occasions?—I did, certainly.

2736. When you met him at the post office at Mitchelstown, you paid special attention to him?—I did not pay, perhaps, so much to what he said then as I did afterwards.

2737. I ask you the question, yes or no; did you pay special attention to him on the first occasion you met him at the post office?—Yes, I paid attention to him, because he made a remark that he was in such perfect health when he came out of gaol.

The *MacDermot*—continued.

2738. Had you been hearing that he had been in ill health from the treatment in prison?—I heard he got bad treatment.

2739. Did you hear that his health had been injured by bad treatment?—I don't know, except for the last few days.

2740. You said you paid special attention to what he said that day, and you give as a reason that he said he was in perfect health; was that because you heard his health was injured in gaol?—It was because I heard he got a good deal of punishment while in gaol.

2741. You said it was that made you remember it, because he got such punishment while in prison?—I remember saying that he never was better in his life, and I mentioned to my father and friends at home that Mr. Mandeville said he was never better in his life.

2742. From what you knew of Mr. Mandeville, was he a man who would be likely to inform you of his sufferings outside or inside prison?—I don't know.

2743. Don't you believe he would not?—We were always on good terms.

2744. Do you think Mr. Mandeville would be likely to inform you of his sufferings in prison or outside prison?—I cannot say, but we were always on good terms. I am sure he would answer any question I would ask him.

2745. Did he communicate to you anything about his sufferings in Tullamore on that occasion?—No.

2746. Did he communicate to you anything about a sore throat, or weak sight, or his having diarrhoea?—No.

2747. Well, you are so friendly as you were, he did not tell you much; did he tell you the number of hours he was without food?—No.

2748. A courageous man, was not he?—He was, I believe.

2749. Do you think it is the part of a soldier to complain?—No, but he looked to me well, and he said he was well.

2750. Do you think Mr. Mandeville would be likely to make a confidant of his barony cess collector?—I dont know that he would exactly make a confidant of me, but he was always friendly towards me.

2751. You never had a glass together?—Never that I remember just now, perhaps we may have.

2752. There were people present at the time; who was the tall man?—I don't know. I asked afterwards. He was not belonging to Mitchelstown.

2753. He said they were going to give you a good passive resistance?—Yes.

2754. Would you not rather have a good passive resistance than an active?—Passive very often comes to active.

2755. John Mandeville was telling you that it was to be passive?—We parted in good friends.

2756. On the 6th June there was an auction at Mitchelstown; where was the auction held?—Up at the pound.

2757. How long did you see Mr. Mandeville at

The MacDermot—continued.

at the pound?—He was there more than an hour.

2758. Did he remain there all the time?—Yes; until his own cows were sold. Yes; and there was a horse sold.

2759. If I were to jog your memory, didn't you go down several times to Mr. Ambrose Mandeville's office from the pound to see John Mandeville?—No, I did not. I went into Mr. A. Mandeville's office, and saw Mr. John Mandeville, and Mr. Gilhooly after.

2760. Did you make any note of the weather that day?—Yes; it was an awful wet day.

2761. What was the condition of the weather on the 4th June?—The 4th June was a fine day, and the 6th of June was a fine day, but it was showery.

2762. Did you keep a diary of it?—No; but I got such a wetting I remember it.

2763. How many hours were you in the open air that day?—I was the greater part of the day. It must have been raining from 11 up to 5 p.m.

2764. Were you under it all?—I was under a good deal of it.

The Coroner.

2765. Were you not under it as much as Mr. Mandeville?—I think I was longer.

The MacDermot.

2766. You went to Abercorn on the 16th June, and saw a mob of a couple of hundred of people there; why do you call them a mob?—I call any number of people who follow me and threaten me in any way a mob.

2767. Did you make a note of the weather on the 16th?—I don't know I did make a note of the weather. The bailiffs were under a wall for shelter.

2768. Did you and the bailiffs ever stand behind a wall before or since?—I dare say.

2769. And your memory is able to fix standing under a wall?—I remember a huge stone was thrown at us.

2770. Do you mean to say you are able to remember the shower by the size of the stone thrown?—It would make you remember the kind of a day it was.

2771. Do you remember that he had not a great coat that day?—He had not a great coat.

2772. We will come to the next day, the 18th June?—That certainly was not a wet day.

2773. Well, now, the 6th June at Mitchelstown you said that the day was showery; you told me awhile ago that the day was fine; which was right?—I told you the 6th of June was fine, but there were showers.

2774. Do you remember the showers on the 6th June?—I do; I remember I was afraid to open my warrants, it was raining so heavy.

2775. Was Mr. Mandeville in sight when you looked at your watch on the 6th June?—No.

2776. How many times did you look at your watch for the last month?—I could not tell you the number of times I looked at it to-day, much less for the last month.

2777. Did you look at your watch all these times?—Every appointment I have I look at my watch.

2778. Tell us some other day that you looked at your watch, and the hour?—I must have looked at it on the 5th and 6th.

2779. Tell me the hour?—I could not.

The prison doctor's book was here put in evidence by Mr. Ronayne.

Doctor James Barr; Examined.

Mr. *Murphy.*

2780. Where do you live, Dr. Barr?—In Liverpool.

2781. Are you a Doctor of Medicine of Glasgow University?—Yes.

2782. And a licentiate of the College of Surgeons, Edinburgh?—Yes.

2783. How long are you in the profession?—I graduated on the 1st May 1873.

2784. Do you mean you took out your medical degrees there?—Yes.

2785. Do you hold any public position in Liverpool?—Yes; Physician to the Northern Hospital, Her Majesty's Medical Officer, Kirkdale Prison; Medical Visitor for the Pulmonary Asylum.

2786. Is it a lunatic asylum?—Yes.

2787. How many beds in the Northern Hospital in Liverpool?—One hundred and sixty beds. There are five visiting men.

2788. And three residents besides?—Yes, four residents.

2789. This prison with which you are connected, how many prisoners on an average are detained in that?—About an average of 500, I should say.

2790. Besides that, are you practising as a physician in Liverpool?—I am.

2791. Do you remember in the month of November last being sent to visit any of the Irish prisons?—I was sent to visit Tullamore.

2792. What was the date of your visit?—Twenty-sixth of November.

2793. Did you see Mr. John Mandeville?—I did.

2794. Were you accompanied by Dr. Ridley?—I was.

2795. Where did you see him?—I saw him in his cell.

2796. From your experience as medical officer of this prison, do you know the ordinary class of prison cell?—I do.

2797. You remember the cell in which Mr. John Mandeville was confined?—I do.

2798. Was it the same, or superior or inferior to any of them you have seen?—Very much superior

Mr. Murphy—continued.

superior to any we have in Kirkdale. Also very much superior to anything they have in the Walton, Liverpool prison, and much superior to the Preston prison, with which I am also acquainted.

2799. In what respects did you say this cell was superior?—It was better lighted, it had a large clear glass window; with us the cell windows are provided with fluted or opaque glass. It was much better ventilated. The whole of this window could be thrown wide open. It was very well heated with hot water pipes. Behind the hot water pipes, there was a good large ventilator in communication with the external air, so that the air upon entering the cell was warmed. The cell had a somberly aspect, flagged, and carpeted with fibre matting. I never saw a prison cell carpeted until I came to Tullamore.

2800. As to the size, was it ordinary size?—Larger than ours.

2801. Did you make your medical examination of Mr. Mandeville the 26th November?—I did.

2802. And of other persons in the prison?—Of all the prisoners there under the Criminal Law and Procedure Act.

2803. What examination did you subject them to?—I made careful examination of them. I found him to be a strong, healthy, rather corpulent man. He was considerably over the average weight of men of his height. All his organs were healthy. Dr. Ridley told me that he had had a sore throat for which he had prescribed gargle. I examined his throat but there was then nothing the matter with it, and Mr. Mandeville made no complaint about it. He said he had a slight pain in the small of his back but that it was of no consequence. It did not seem to be of much consequence as it did not affect his movements.

2804. He was able to walk well?—Yes.

2805. Would a slight pain in the back be accounted for by the fact that a man was accustomed to sit on an easy chair and had to change?—It would.

2806. Was there anything said about his eyes?—Mr. Mandeville himself, said that the wire netting outside his cell interfered with the light, but it seemed to me a very frivolous statement. It is coarse wire netting with a large mesh. I saw no appearance of anything the matter with his eyes.

2807. You examined his eyes?—Yes. I had a long conversation with Mandeville about his disobedience of the prison rules. I urged him strongly to comply with the regulations. I told him that it could be no pleasure for the Governor or anybody else to punish him; and that when he had been so unfortunate as to get into gaol he should try to make the best he could of it.

The Coroner.

2808. What did he say?—He said he was a political prisoner and that he need not obey the rules. He also said in a jocose manner that his party would soon have the prisons under their own control, and some of the Government officials under their care, and that if they wanted to be well treated they should extend similar favours, or treat the present political prisoners well. I should remark that we all laughed at that; and Captain Fetherstonhaugh said when he was locked up he would conform to the prison rules and clean his cell. We all laughed at this statement of Mandeville's.

Mr. Murphy.

2809. Was there anything said at that meeting that he was suffering from diarrhœa, or any change of diet that he got?—Dr. Ridley told me he had been suffering from diarrhœa on the 14th or 15th of November, for which he had substituted the white bread for the brown.

2810. Did you see the mattress he had in his cell?—Yes; it was a large thick mattress. I have never seen one in a prison cell so large or so thick.

2811. Was there anything else that attracted your attention at that interview?—The carpeting of the cell.

2812. Did you, on that occasion, come to an opinion, from Mr. Mandeville's appearance, did you come to the conclusion whether he was fit to conform to the regulations of the prison?—Yes.

2813. Was he fit to undergo punishment if he disobeyed the rules of the prison?—Certainly.

2814. Was he, at that time, suffering from any shallow or rapid breathing?—No, his lungs were perfectly healthy; so, also, was his heart.

2815. Was there any blueness about his lips?—No, his lips were of a bright red natural hue.

2816. Did his cheeks look flabby or pasty?—No.

2817. Had he a pasty or flabby look?—No.

2818. Or did he exhibit any symptoms of heart failure, or want of cardiac action?—Certainly not.

2819. Did you subject him to such an examination as that you must have noticed these symptoms, if they existed?—I did.

2820. Did you see Mr. Mandeville again after that?—Yes; I saw him again on the 6th December.

The Coroner.

2821. Where?—In the same cell.

Mr. Murphy.

2822. Did you make a complete examination of him that day?—Yes.

2823. Was Dr. Ridley present?—He was.

2824. What was his condition on that day?—He was perfectly well, and he said so himself. My examination corroborated his statement.

2825. Did he then exhibit any of the symptoms I have mentioned before?—No.

2826. Had you any conversation with him. You asked him how he was?—Yes; I had a talk with him. He told me again about being a political prisoner. I may also say that the man was so well and so healthy that I would never have thought myself of making such a minute examination but for the reports of Doctors Moorhead and Roonyan, to which my attention was drawn.

2827. Was your examination of Mr. Mandeville particularly directed, by reading these reports, to the symptoms they had mentioned in these reports?—Yes; I heard something of the reports before I went there at all.

Mr. *Murphy*—continued.

2328. You say, on the 5th December, you found him perfectly well?—Perfectly well.

2329. Did you go to Tullamore again on the 14th December?—On the 14th December I again visited Tullamore.

2330. Did you see Mr. Mandeville?—I did, he was then suffering from a slight attack of diarrhœa, which he said had been in existence for two days. I examined his stool, it was not at all copious. It seemed to contain a considerable quantity of bile. I then carefully examined Mr. Mandeville. I came to the conclusion that the diarrhœa was due to an overloading of the bowel. I suggested to Dr. Ridley, in his presence, that the diarrhœa could be easily cured by a dose of rhubarb or half-an-ounce of castor oil. Mandeville said he would take no medicine for at least two days more, and if it was not then better he would. Mandeville also said to me on that occasion that he did not like to see me, because he had been punished after my two previous visits. I said I was sorry for the coincidence, but that I had nothing to do with his punishment; but that if he would not obey the prison rules I was not surprised at his being punished. He said he would never obey the prison rules. In my presence he upbraided Dr. Ridley for allowing him to be punished, and said that he should not have allowed him to be punished. I told Mandeville that Dr. Ridley could have no wish to see him punished, but that he, Dr. Ridley, had a duty to perform, and that it was only in the power of the medical officer to interpose between the prisoner and prison discipline, where his health was affected or likely to be affected by the discipline. I was told then that there was a report hanging over Mr. Mandeville. Dr. Ridley told me for refusing to clean his cell, but that Dr. Ridley had interposed on account of the diarrhœa, and would not allow him to be punished. I told Mandeville that I thought the prison officials were exceedingly lenient, and that he should not cause all this responsibility and annoyance through such trivial and simple matters as refusing to clean his cell.

2331. Did the discussion proceed any further?—I pointed out to him that every prisoner was obliged to clean his own cell, even a first class misdemeanant, according to the prison rules, could only be exempted on the payment of a small sum of money. I think that was the principal part of our conversation.

2332. Did you, upon that occasion, make a medical examination of him?—I did.

2333. What was his condition?—He was otherwise in good health.

2334. Did you, upon that or any other occasion, find him taking any exercise in his cell?—Oh, yes; on that occasion, when I went into his cell, I found him swinging a heavy stool around his head. I may also mention that upon that occasion he again mentioned about the pain in his back. He was swinging his stool about in such a manner that no man with a pain in his back could do.

2335. Could you form any idea about what the weight of that stool was?—No; it was a large, heavy stool.

2336. Is the situation of Tullamore Gaol healthy?—Oh, yes, it is very healthily situated.

2337. Now, Dr. Barr, as physician of this prison in England, are you acquainted with the dietary in England?—Yes; I have also had an opportunity of seeing the Irish dietary.

2338. A prisoner committed in England for two months, on what class of dietary does he commence his imprisonment?—He commences his imprisonment on second class diet, the same class diet as in Ireland, but it is different.

NINTH DAY.

Thursday, 26th July 1888.

DOCTOR JAMES BARR, further Examined.

Mr. *Murphy.*

2839. Is the second class diet in England and the second class diet in Ireland the same?—No, the second class diet in Ireland is the same as the English dietary, with the exception that for breakfast and supper all the prisoners in Ireland get cocoa in place of gruel; there is no such thing as cocoa for a prisoner in England until he has completed nine months' imprisonment. On the second class diet a prisoner in Ireland receives two pints of new milk daily, with the exception of three days in the week, and on those three days he gets eight extra ounces of bread for dinner instead of the three-quarters of a pint of milk. Mr. Mandeville got 18 ounces of bread and half-a-pint of soup for dinner on those three days.

2840. In England does this second class diet include milk at all?—None at all.

2841. When does a prisoner come under third class diet?—After the first month; third class diet in Ireland is rather better than English fourth class diet.

2842. A prisoner in Ireland under sentence of hard labour on the third class, what does he get?—He gets a pint and-a-half of stirabout for breakfast, and three-quarters of a pint of milk.

2843. What does he get for dinner?—Dinner varies. On Sunday he gets a pint of soup and four ounces of meat and 16 ounces of potatoes. On Mondays, Tuesdays, Thursdays, and Saturdays, he gets 14 ounces of bread and a pint of vegetable soup for dinner.

2844. On Wednesdays and Fridays?—Eight ounces of bread and 24 ounces of potatoes.

2845. And for supper on each day what does he get?—Eight ounces of bread and a pint of cocoa.

2846. In England in the same class what is the allowance for a prisoner?—I think to serve all purposes, if I just draw out what a person would get in the eight weeks. A prisoner under sentence of hard labour for two lunar months, eight weeks, on second class diet would receive in England 908 ounces of bread, 112 pints of gruel, 96 ounces of suet pudding, 248 ounces of potatoes, 18 pints of soup, and 24 ounces of meat. That is the total amount in England. The usual diet for the same period and the same class in Ireland, 48 pints of stirabout equivalent to 96 pints of gruel.

Mr. *Harrington.*

2847. We will have some of these equivalents?—How much have you down for gruel?

Mr. *Murphy.*

2848. Having regard to the quantity of material used in making the gruel, what is the relative

Mr. *Murphy*—continued.

value?—Forty-eight pints of stirabout are equivalent to 96 of gruel; 48 ounces of suet pudding, 240 ounces of potatoes, 10 pints of soup, 16 pints of vegetable soup, 84 pints of cocoa, 68 pints of milk. There is 18 ounces of meat for making soup, but I will leave that out.

2849. The quantity of food and nourishment that the usual prisoner gets in the English and Irish prisons, on which side is the advantage?—On the side of the Irish prisoner.

2850. By how much?—By 84 pints of cocoa, 68 pints of milk. Well, I won't mention the other disparities.

2851. Now with regard to the labour or industry that the prisoner has to undergo in the English and Irish prisons?—For a prisoner in Irish prisons, there is no such thing as hard labour as compared with labour in England. Hard labour in Ireland is mat making; that would be second class labour in England. The class the dietary scales are applied does not correspond.

2852. Now Dr. Barr, when you were in Tullamore, did you see this punishment cell?—I did.

2853. Did you examine it?—I was shut inside in it.

2854. On which visit?—On my first visit. It was a very comfortable punishment cell, well heated, and very much better lighted than any punishment cell that we have in England.

2855. What sort was the window; was the window composed of plain glass or stained glass?—Of clear white glass.

2856. Do you know what its cubic contents are?—I don't know. I should say 750 cubic feet.

2857. Did you observe the ventilation?—Yes; it was very good. There was a good inlet by a kind of Tobin's tube; that is, a pipe let in to the lower end of the wall, and discharging the air at the top of the wall.

2858. And there was an extraction shaft?—The inlet was quite as large, if not larger, than the extraction shaft; so that as much air could be let into the cell as would pass out of it. There could not, then, possibly be any draught in the door.

2859. Did you observe the way in which this punishment cell was heated?—It was heated by hot-water pipes running the whole length of the side wall and the end wall next the door.

2860. With the first figured, was that fit to keep up proper temperature for the health of a man?—It was.

2861. Is

Mr. *Murphy*—continued.

2861. In England, what exercise do the prisoners get?—A prisoner who is at work in his cell gets an hour's exercise in the open air. He has also to attend chapel every morning. A prisoner in the first stage gets no exercise on Sunday.

2862. What time do they spend at chapel in the morning?—About half-an-hour, except on Sunday, when they get plenty of it.

2863. They only get the one hour in the open air; in Ireland they get two?—Yes; but I think the Irish prisoners don't get any chapel.

2864. During the first stage the prisoners in England don't get any exercise at all?—No outdoor exercise at all for those working on treadwheel.

The *Coroner*.

2865. This is all from a comparison of the rules?—No; from a comparison of observations. The rule regarding the plank bed is the same in both countries; but the latter part of the rule is not carried out in Ireland

Mr. *Murphy*.

2866. What rule is that; what number?—I don't know what number. A prisoner shall be allowed the opportunity of earning by industry the gradual remission of this requirement after the expiration of one month; but after he has earned such remission he shall be liable to forfeit same on account of idleness, inattention to instructions, or misconduct. In England, male prisoners between the age of 16 and 60 have to sleep on the plank bed every night until they have earned 224 marks. If they are well conducted and industrious they earn eight marks a-day, that is the highest possible number, and they pass out of the first stage in 28 days; but if they only earn six marks a-day they have to remain on the plank bed for 37 nights. If they earn less than six marks a day they are reported for idleness, and may be kept for an indefinite period in the first stage. When they are passing through the second stage they have to sleep on the plank bed for two nights each week, until they have earned 224 more marks. They then pass into the third stage, and have to sleep on the plank bed one night each week, until they have earned 224 marks more. They then pass into the fourth stage, where they get their mattress every night. In any stage they may be reduced for idleness to the first stage.

2867. In Ireland, what period does a prisoner get on the plank bed altogether?—He gets a month.

2868. And, of course, a medical officer can exempt any man from the plank bed?—Yes, on medical grounds.

2869. Now, doctor, from your experience as a medical doctor, and from your examination of Mr. Mandeville, have you formed an opinion as to whether his health could have been injured in Tullamore gaol, considering that he was eight days altogether on punishment diet?—No, his health could have been in no way injured. I am also decidedly of opinion that, if he had had two years' imprisonment, in place of two months, he would be alive and well in Tullamore prison to-day.

2870. Was there at the time you saw him on 20th November, until the day you saw him on the 14th December, was there any apparent diminution in his size or weight. Would a man have lost three stone weight in that time, even getting prison punishment diet?—Quite impossible.

2871. Now doctor, you have been here during the evidence given by Doctor M'Craith?—Yes.

2872. Of Doctor Ronayne?—Yes.

2873. And of Dr. Croskery?—Yes.

The *Coroner*.

2874. Do you put in Doctor Moorhead?—No.

Mr. *Murphy*.

2875. Were you here when Doctor Moorhead was examined?—No.

2876. Doctor Ronayne saw Mr. Mandeville on the 15th November, and you saw him on the 20th November?—Yes.

2877. If Mr. Mandeville had exhibited all those symptoms that you heard described on the 15th, could it be possible that he would have lost them all on the 20th?—Quite impossible.

The *Coroner*.

2878. Did you examine him then?—Yes.

Mr. *Murphy*.

2879. You heard a description of the arrangement for testing the dimensions?

The *Coroner*.] It is better to go back to that at the end.

Mr. *Murphy*.] Very well.

Mr. *Murphy*.

2880. Dr. M'Craith said that the patient's tongue was swollen, and that when he depressed it with his fingers, he could only see the back part of the pharynx and part of the uvula. He said the tongue was much swollen, and he feared suffocation.

The MacDermot.] He said nothing of the kind.

The *Coroner*, reading from the depositions of Doctor M'Craith, "I observed considerable swelling under the chin."

The MacDermot.] What day is that?

The *Coroner*.] Saturday. "There was a strong smell from his breath. That did not indicate that inflammation was at work. I saw the whole of the uvula, which was inflamed. I don't think I could have seen more of the throat otherwise than by inserting the finger. There was a swelling of the pharynx. I consider there was inflammation of the tonsils. I did not consider I was treating him for tonsillitis."

Mr. *Murphy*.

2881. He found there was swelling under the chin and the glands of the throat swollen. He opened his mouth and explained his difficulty in seeing his mouth. As it was there was a difficulty in seeing far down the throat as he was only able to see the uvula. In the condition that Doctor M'Craith describes, could he, by any other means of depressing the tongue other than the finger, have an opportunity of seeing further?

Doctor

Mr. *Murphy*—continued.

Doctor Cremen said it was not very much swollen.

The *Coroner*.

2882. Having heard the diagnosis of Dr. Cremen and Dr. M'Craith, how far do you approve of the treatment?—I don't approve of it at all. There should have been a deep incision made at the earliest possible moment, made right down from underneath the jaw, to the floor of the mouth from the outside. My reasons for saying this are that in the least case of diffused cellular inflammation of the mouth there is an obstruction to the venous current of blood; this gives rise to great swelling of the tongue and palate. The swelling obstructs the entrance of air to the lungs and so gives rise to a slow process of asphyxia. The tension of the cellular tissue should at once be relieved by a deep incision, just in the same way as if a man was being strangled with a rope round his neck, the first part of the treatment would be to cut the rope, that would be the first preparatory treatment.

Mr. *Murphy*.

2883. Any other remedy that should be taken?—Then, after the incision was made, the throat should have been painted with extract of belladonna.

2884. In making this incision for the purpose of relieving the tension, how should it have been done?—Externally. There should be no incision made inside the mouth.

2885. Why?—Because you cannot easily reach the cellular tissue, and you are liable to produce uncontrollable hæmorrhage.

2886. That is ordinary language means bleeding that you cannot control. Dr. Cremen said that he did not expect the man to live to Monday?—In my opinion he did not detail one fatal symptom. He gave the temperature as 102·4, a very low temperature for septic inflammation. He said the pulse was 120, a rate at which many a man lives for weeks. He said it was soft, indicative of debility. Softness simply means low pulse tension, which accompanies nearly all feverish affections. He said the swelling was confined to the parotid gland, and to the submaxillary and sublingual glands on the right side. There is no such thing as a cellular inflammation confined to these glands. In a child with mumps he may have most intense swelling of these glands on both sides of the neck, yet parents frequently treat their children without any medical man. Dr. Cremen also stated that there was no lividity, no blueness of the nails or lips, that he was of a florid colour. If Dr. Cremen's description of the case is right, I want to know why the man died.

The *Coroner*.

2887. Perhaps you could tell us?—No, I could not.

The *Coroner*.] You have some reason for putting that hypothetical statement.

Mr. *Murphy*.

2888. The symptoms which Dr. Cremen gave, did that indicate any symptoms that ought to have proved fatal?—No; on the other hand he said he did not expect he would live until Monday. In my opinion the incisive treatment could only be justified on the ground that the man was moribund.

2889. After the symptoms exhibited as described by Dr. Cremen, would a medical man be justified in coming to the conclusion that the man's case was hopeless?—No.

2890. He said that the glands at the right side were hard and swollen, would that be any reason why a man should be expected to die within 48 hours?—No.

2891. Did you hear the description given by Dr. O'Neill of his condition?—I did.

2892. Dr. O'Neill said that on his first visit there was lividity, and that continued up to the time of his death. He said also that the man was anxious to get out of bed and restless, and his desire was gratified?—That lividity and restlessness was proof, to my mind, that asphyxia was slowly going on, and that already the right side of the heart was considerably distended.

2893. The existence of this asphyxia, as you conceive, from the description of Dr. O'Neill, and the condition of the throat, what would that indicate?—It would indicate this inflammation, obstructing the entrance of air to the lungs. This process of slow asphyxia goes on without any great embarrassment to the breathing, such as occurs in acute laryngitis.

2894. Would that condition be accounted for in a patient in the condition described by Dr. Cremen?—No.

2895. With regard to the using of the leeches in the condition described by Drs. M'Craith and O'Neill, was that a good thing to do?—They would do no good, but might do no harm.

The *Coroner*.

2896. Of course, every answer you are giving you are applying yourself to the description of things here?—Yes.

Mr. *Murphy*.

2897. The use of the exploring needle is described by Dr. M'Craith?—Well, the exploring needle is only used for diagnosis; it is of no value for treatment, but, perhaps, in that case it was better than the knife, because I don't approve of cutting in the inside of the mouth.

2898. And if it was used for the purpose of operation as distinguished from diagnosis?—It would be of no value.

2899. Would it be a proper thing to apply inside the mouth?—No.

2900. Did you hear Dr. O'Neill say it was used as a substitute for the knife?—Yes.

2901. You say that was not right?—No.

2902. It is practically useless for the purpose of operation?—It is. There is another point in Dr. M'Craith's evidence, he described it as diffused septic inflammation. He said he did not make any inquiries as to the cause of the septic inflammation. I think in all cases of the kind it is most important to make inquiry into the cause, because it may arise from some unhealthy wound about the mouth or throat, or bad drainage or sewage in his house.

Mr. *Murphy*—continued.

2903. Mrs. Mandeville told us that for some days before this affection developed he would be complaining of tooth-ache; would the inflammation extend in this way to the glands?—I don't think so.

2904. If a man were suffering from inflammation of the jaw under or over a tooth, and were to get cold, would that tend to bring on this inflammation?—A man would be more liable to inflammatory effect under the circumstances.

2905. Did you hear descriptions of how Mr. Mandeville attended open-air meetings, and spoke at them?—I heard that yesterday.

2906. If a man was suffering from delicacy of the throat, could he indulge in amusements of that sort with impunity during the winter and spring months, with an east wind blowing?—I should say not.

2907. What would be the effect?—He would be more likely to get a sore throat.

Coroner.] We are speaking of a man who has got a sore throat.

Mr. *Murphy.*

2908. Dr. Barr, this cellular inflammation; is it necessary that in order that that should be developed in a patient that he should have been in a debilitated state at the time of the attack?—Not necessary.

2909. In your opinion, could an attack of that affection be attributed in any way to his treatment in Tullamore Prison, under the conditions known of him?—It could not.

2910. Of course, there is a greater inconvenience to a gentleman who is accustomed to the comforts of life to be imprisoned than to a man who has not those comforts?—They are apt to feel the imprisonment more.

2911. But, physically, is a man who is well-nourished better or worse able to bear the privations of prison-life?—He is better able to bear it.

2912. Do you state that from your own experience?—I do.

2913. Have you had under your charge as prison medical officer men who previous to their incarceration were in good circumstances?—I had.

2914. Have you had many cases?—Oh, several.

2915. Has the prison discipline in those cases been applied the same as in ordinary cases?—The usual means.

2916. Has it been found to have any deleterious effect on the health of such persons?—No.

2917. As a fact, have these people suffered?——

The MacDermot.] I object to it.

Mr. *Murphy.*

2918. In your experience, have you found in such cases, have you found that the prisoners have suffered?—No.

2919. There was some discussion here as to a test or plan adopted by Dr. Ridley for the purpose of a test of Mr. Mandeville, in reference to the diarrhœa, was that a proper or a necessary test for the purpose of discovering the character of the affection?—Certainly.

Cross-examined by *The MacDermot.*

2920. Where were you born, doctor?—I was born in the county of Derry.

2921. When did you go to reside in England?—Fourteen years ago.

2922. Where did you begin to practise as a physician having private patients?—I began 14 years ago.

2923. Where?—In Liverpool.

2924. What date did you get your first appointment in Liverpool?—In 1874.

2925. Then you got appointed to what first?—To the Northern Hospital as one of the residents.

2926. The next year you started to look for private business?—Yes.

2927. Has your practice with regard to private patients been extensive?—I get quite as much as I care to do.

2928. Has your practice as to private patients been extensive?—I consider it is.

2929. When did it reach its highest stage of development?—The last two years I have been curtailing it.

2930. I don't want to hear that?—About two years ago.

2931. Will we take 1886?—That will do very well.

2932. May I ask what was the maximum of that year of private patients?—I have no idea; I have several hundreds on my books.

2933. In that year?—Yes.

2934. Will you tell me how much you made in 1886?—I don't know.

2935. Have you patients on your books other than private patients?—No.

2936. Is it as surgeon of Kirkdale Prison you were sent over to Ireland?—It was on account of my connection with the English Prison Service.

2937. Was it as surgeon of Kirkdale Prison?—We don't call them surgeons, medical officers.

2938. Was it as medical officer?—It was.

2939. When were you sent over first?—I left England on the 24th November 1887.

2940. Who sent you?—Sir Edmund Du Cane, Chairman of the English Prisons' Board.

2941. Have you learnt that you were sent over at the instance of Mr. Balfour?—I believe I was.

2942. And on that mission you went to Tullamore?—Yes.

2943. Was it part of your instructions to ascertain whether Mr. Mandeville could bear punishment?—No.

2944. Had your mission any reference to Mr. Mandeville?—Very little.

2945. Had it reference to prisoners charged under the Crimes Act?—It had.

2946. Including Mr. Mandeville and Mr. O'Brien?—Yes; Mr. O'Brien was the chief prisoner.

2947. Were you sent over in respect to Mr. John Dillon, later on?—Yes; lately.

2948. Was it not part of your duty to ascertain whether any of the prisoners were fit for punishment?—I had no instructions at all with respect to punishment; my instructions were very general.

2949. Do you mean you had a large discretion to

The MacDermot—continued.

to do what you liked?—No; I had no discretion at all, but to make my report.

2950. Did the general instructions give you a large field of action?—They gave me no action whatever.

2951. They gave you power to make a report?—Yes.

2952. It gave action to get materials for the report. Is it action to take your seat in the punishment cell on the 25th November, to see what it was like?—Yes; that was a physical act.

2953. Was it in reference to the political prisoners you examined that cell?—It was very accidentally that cell was examined; it was not in reference to the prisoners I examined it. Dr. Ridley took me in to see the cell as we were passing through the yard.

The *Coroner*.

2954. What cell is this?—The punishment cell.

The MacDermot.

2955. You went in with him accidentally?—I was taken in by him.

2956. How long did you remain in it?—Not long; I should say certainly not five minutes.

2957. Had you ever seen it except on that occasion?—Never, except on that occasion.

2958. And on that accidental visit during those five minutes, you made yourself master of the ventilation, the heating, the lighting, and pretty much of the size of the cell?—Yes; I could do that in a couple of minutes; I am accustomed to them.

2959. You could do it all in two minutes?—I could.

2960. And preserve the memory of it to the day of your death?—Yes, especially if it were well fixed.

> The *Coroner*. I have it taken that it was fixed in his memory because he stated it to Captain Fetherston-Haugh.

The MacDermot.

2961. On that occasion you ascertained that the cell was warm?—I said it was well provided with hot water pipes.

2962. Were you in court when it was sworn here that upon the 31st December, when Mr. Mandeville was in it that he was chilled and cold up to the knees?—I was not in court when it was said.

2963. On the 25th November you saw him. Will you tell me what was the thickness in your opinion of the mattress?—About four inches.

2964. Is that what you call a thick heavy mattress?—Yes, it is nearly twice the thickness of our own.

2965. Did you hear Mr. Bardley state that the thickness of it was about three or four inches?—Yes.

2966. Don't you think he had more opportunity of knowing the size of it than you?—Of course he had.

2967. What would you say was the weight of the stool Mr. Mandeville was swinging about his head?—I don't know.

The MacDermot—continued.

2968. How many pounds weight do you wish to convey to the jury?—A stone, or somewhat under 10 or 14 pounds.

2969. Did you hear Captain Fetherston-Haugh state that it was seven pounds weight?—No.

2970. You call a fibre matting a carpet?—Of course I do; it is not an aesthetic one.

2971. You examined the patient's eyes, and you thought them all right?—Yes.

2972. Is not it a singular thing he took to wearing glasses after leaving prison?—I did not test his eyes beyond a superficial examination. I occasionally wear smoked glass myself.

2973. You observed no indication of sore throat?—No.

2974. You know he was treated frequently in hospital for sore throat?—He was not in hospital at all.

2975. Is not it an extraordinary coincidence that six weeks or so before he died, he was treated for sore throat, that he had been wearing a muffler, and that he died from a sore throat, and that you saw no appearance of a sore throat?—Nothing extraordinary.

2976. He went into prison without having a sore throat; complained of it after coming out; got remedies for it and died of it?—Yes.

2977. You went into the room on one occasion, and he was swinging a heavy stool on that occasion; he complained of a pain in his back?—Yes.

2978. Did you consider he was shamming?—No, I considered the pain was of so trivial a nature that it was of no importance; in fact he said so himself.

2979. Did you ever state to anybody that you thought he was shamming?—I stated in my reports just what I saw, believing that this pain was a very slight one.

2980. What was the word you did use. Did you convey by the report that you thought he was shamming?—I conveyed that this pain was of no importance.

2981. Did you convey by this report that he was shamming?—I did not.

2982. Did you ever convey outside a report, or say to anybody he was shamming. Did you ever speak abusively of him?—No.

2983. Did you ever say he did not get half enough punishment?—No.

2984. Did you convey so much?—I may have.

2985. You stated that on the 24th November on your careful examination of Mr. Mandeville, that he was strong and healthy, and by all the tests which you so carefully applied in thoroughly good health?—Yes.

2986. How did it happen that on the 28th November, after you left, he was punished. On the day after the punishment began, the 29th November, Dr. Moorhead, a doctor, a magistrate, and gentleman, an official medical officer of the Board of Trade swears he had tremor in both his hands?—I don't believe him.

2987. Did you believe Dr. Moorhead perjured himself on his oath?—He gave it as a matter of opinion.

The MacDermot—continued.

2988. Do you believe he perjured himself?—Perjure is not a proper word to apply to any man. I believe that that was not true.

2989. Does it strike you as a little astonishing that that statement of Dr. Moorhead's was made in presence of the governor and written in the journal of the gaol from dictation?—Not a bit. It would not be the more true of that.

2990. Did that cell on that day look healthy?—Yes, some of his food was sprinkled about the floor.

2991. Is it true what Dr. Moorhead swore to on that day; the excrements had not been removed, the smell offensive?—They were removed before I went in.

2992. What hour were you there?—I entered the prison shortly after eleven o'clock and I would leave about two o'clock. It was some time between these hours.

2993. Did you state, upon any of your visits, before you left, that in your opinion, he was fit for punishment?—On my last visit, that was the 14th December, he was suffering from diarrhœa, and the medical officer told me there was a report hanging over his head, and that he would not allow him to be punished. I told him to exercise his own discretion entirely in the matter.

2994. What do you mean by saying that you told him to exercise his own discretion?—That I would not advise him in the matter.

2995. Did you say anything on that occasion that would indicate the contrary of what you say now?—I told the Governor that day if he was in an English prison he would be punished.

2996. Did you that day in presence of Dr. Ridley convey in any way that he ought to punish him?—No.

2997. Did you say to Mr. Mandeville in his presence that where a prisoner violated the rules, and was in good health, it was not proper or within the right of the doctor to interpose?—I used words to that effect.

2998. Did you not say on that occasion that the man was in good health?—I said he was in good health with the exception of a slight attack of diarrhœa.

2999. And I think you said the slight attack of diarrhœa did not disqualify him from punishment?—I say so now.

3000. And said so then?—I dare say I did.

3001. Didn't you say all he wanted was half-an-ounce of castor-oil or some rhubarb?—Yes.

3002. Now, having regard to what you have just told me, did not you, in fact, tell the doctor in Mr. Mandeville's presence that it was his duty to punish him?—No.

3003. You said it was not in his right to keep him from punishment, if the prisoner was able to bear it?—I say so still.

3004. You said on that occasion that he was fit to bear punishment, did not you thereby say, in fact and substance, that it was not in his right to prevent punishment?—Yes.

3005. Did not you tell him that the doctor had been too lenient?—Yes.

3006. And you thought so?—Yes.

3007. You were aware at that time that the only rule that he had failed to observe was the rule about cleansing his cell?—That was the rule; I thought there was something about refusing to exercise.

The MacDermot—continued.

3008. Your observations applied to the rule about cleansing his cell?—Yes.

3009. When you saw Mr. Mandeville on that occasion, and he said that he would never obey the prison rules, did not you know Mr. Mandeville was only speaking of the rule about his cell?—He was doing no work; that was another rule he was breaking.

3010. There was no charge brought against him for that?—No.

3011. Was he ever called upon to perform work?—If he was not, the prison officials were neglecting their duty.

3012. Were not you in court when Captain Fetherston-Haugh swore that with the exception of refusing to clean his cell, to associate with criminals, and to wear the prison garb, he violated no rule, and gave no annoyance. Having regard to that answer, have you the smallest doubt when Mr. Mandeville said he would never obey the prison rules, that it could have any meaning but to cleanse his cell?—Oh yes, I think Mr. Mandeville's view of the case would be that— —

3013. Were you discussing any rule but that with him?—We were not discussing any particular rule.

3014. Did you consider he was in a general state of rebellion against all the rules?—No.

3015. I daresay you considered it followed in every rule?—No.

3016. Did the Governor not tell you of the violation of the rule?—Yes.

The *Coroner.*

3017. Was that the only rule that you were told was violated by him?—That is the only rule that was told me.

The MacDermot.

3018. I think you said the diarrhœa he was then suffering from. I think you used the phrase that his bowels were overladen?—Yes.

3019. Would you consider that arose from undigested food?—Yes; an accumulation of food.

3020. He was suffering on the 14th December from an accumulation of food within him?—Yes.

3021. Well, now on this 14th December, Mr. Mandeville upbraided Dr. Ridley for allowing him to be punished?—He did.

3022. He told the doctor to save him from his punishment?—I don't know whether you would call that an appeal or not.

3023. Did you consider it an appeal?—No; I considered it more a complaint of Mr. Mandeville against Dr. Ridley for allowing him to be punished.

3024. He addressed that observation to the doctor?—He addressed it to us both.

3025. Was his upbraiding Dr. Ridley an address to you. Did he upbraid you also?—Yes, by saying he was punished after each of my former visits.

3026. Mr. Mandeville was then suffering from diarrhœa, and do you ask the jury to believe that his complaint to the medical officer had not more reference to the state of his health than to politics?—He was not undergoing punishment at all at the time.

3027. W—

The MacDermot—continued.

3027. You say he upbraided you?—Yes.

3028. You were there three times?—Yes.

3029. After the first occasion he got 24 hours on bread and water?—Yes.

3030. You were there on the 26th: when did you get back to England?—On the 27th.

3031. And on the 29th he was placed on bread and water?—Yes; but my report could not reach Dublin sooner than the evening of the 28th, and go to the Castle on the morning of the 29th.

3032. You visited again on the 5th December; when did you return to England?—On the 6th.

3033. And on December 8th he got 48 hours?—So I believe.

3034. Another singular coincidence?—My report in that case probably would have reached Dublin on the morning of the 8th.

3035. You visited again on December 14th, and by another extraordinary coincidence he got his other punishment of two days in the punishment cell in which you had been sitting on the 26th November?—Yes.

3036. You sat in the cell, examined it, and the next person who inhabited it was Mr. Mandeville?—Yes.

3037. You say that from what you saw on the 14th December Mr. Mandeville could not between that and the date of his leaving have fallen into the state of health described by the witnesses?—He could not have lost two or three stone in weight.

3038. I ask you now could he have got pale and ghastly afterwards?—He could not.

3039. Could they have disappeared?—They were not there to disappear.

3040. Then you do not believe one word of Dr. Ronayne's evidence about that?—I do not.

3041. You do not believe a word of it?—There might be some odd statements.

3042. You believe that that was false?—Yes.

3043. Invented?—Yes; and I stated so much about Dr. Moorhead's evidence before.

3044. You know Dr. Ronayne is a medical gentleman; a medical officer; you have heard that?—Yes.

3045. You have heard that he was in practice as he stated over 30 years, and you have given us your view that he invented this statement?—I did.

3046. It was stated by Mrs. Mandeville that when her husband came out of prison, as a matter of fact she swears he was pale, thin, bluish on the lips, tremour in his hands, so that he could scarcely write at all for a month. Weak in the sight from the time he came home from prison, in your opinion, could that have happened between the day you saw him on the 14th December and the 24th December?—It could not.

3047. Then you consider that she also has sworn falsely?—I consider this statement is false.

3048. Drs. M'Craith and O'Neill both swore that he was thin, worn, altered, and one of the two swore that he saw a bluishness of the lips; that is Dr. O'Neill; on Mr. Mandeville's leaving prison. Do you say that this statement could not be true also?—I do.

The MacDermot—continued.

3049. And you are a medical gentleman?—Yes.

3050. Before I come to the medical part of your evidence, am I right in saying that you have been taking a very active part in this case?—I have.

3051. And a very prominent part?—And a very humble part, I should say.

3052. In your humble way, you devoted a good deal of your time to instructing counsel in this case?—I gave them information on medical portions of it.

3053. Was it confined to medical?—Yes.

3054. Was that for the cross-examination of members of your own profession?—Yes.

3055. In your experience of the 13 or 14 years that you have been engaged in the medical profession in prisons, hospitals and asylums, have you ever in any court of justice seen a medical gentleman of eminence writing on slips of paper for the cross-examination of other doctors?—Oh, yes; but not to the extent to which I went in this case.

3056. Tell me the name of any medical gentleman you have ever seen pursuing that course?—I won't give you any names. I will give you my own.

3057. Why would not you give me the name of any medical man, would it be discreditable to him?—No; because the questions would be chiefly on points in criminal cases where the barrister would see a medical man for his opinion on medical points.

3058. Will you tell me the name of any doctor you ever saw instructing counsel for the cross-examination of members of his own profession. Give me the name of any doctor?—Yes, I will give you several names. At one of the late Liverpool Assizes, there was a railway case on, and there were several medical men for the plaintiff and several for the railway company. I and two other medical gentlemen were for the railway company, and I think the whole three of us gave instructions.

3059. Give me the name of a doctor who did it, except yourself and the doctor on that occasion?—Dr. Davidson and another in Liverpool.

3060. Who were the witnesses examined?—Mr. Banks, Mr. Harrison, and Dr. Robinson, and some others.

3061. If this be true, why did you refuse to give their names a few minutes ago?—I was just thinking of which case I would bring up.

The Coroner.

3062. Did they give evidence for the purpose of discrediting other doctors?—It was for the purpose of bringing a conflict of the evidence.

The MacDermot.

3063. Don't you think the doctors seeing a patient who was called in two days before he died, who saw his condition at the time, watched the progress of the disease. Don't you consider they have a better opportunity of forming an opinion than the doctor or surgeon who did not see the patient?—Certainly; they have a better opportunity.

3064. Now, assuming the diagnosis which was given us by these three doctors is true, do you consider

The MacDermot—continued.

sider the treatment was bad and wrong from the beginning?—I do.

3065. As a matter of fact, do you consider that the death of Mr. Mandeville lay at the door of the doctor's treatment?—I say he did not get a chance for his life.

3066. You an official of 13 or 14 years standing, prison doctor of Kirkdale, and attached to an hospital and an asylum, you undertake to say to that jury, that Dr. Cremen, of Cork, Dr. M'Craith, of this town, and Dr. O'Neill, of this town, all holding important employments, and having private patients, you tell them they did not give their patient a chance for his life?—Yes, I have arrived at that conclusion after a careful examination of the evidence.

3067. In point of fact and in substance, you have arrived at the conclusion that if you had been there you would have saved the life of the patient?—No.

3068. You say his life could have been saved?—It was quite possible.

3069. Do you think it was probable?—I think it was. He certainly would not have died so quickly.

3070. You consider that he died not of failure of the heart's action, but of asphyxia?—Oh; every one dies of failure of the heart's action.

3071. Is there a medical difference between dying of syncope and dying of asphyxia?—Yes.

3072. Do you consider he died of asphyxia?—Yes.

3073. That means suffocation?—It does.

3074. You heard the three doctors, who were there on the spot, swear that he did not die of asphyxia. You differ from that, of course?—Yes.

The Coroner.

3075. Did you hear the post-mortem symptoms?—There were no post-mortem symptoms.

The MacDermot.

3076. You say Dr. Cremen, having sworn that he came to the conclusion upon the symptoms, he saw that Mr. Mandeville could not live till Monday. Dr. O'Neill having come to a corresponding conclusion, and the patient having died on Sunday. You say that if he were otherwise treated his life could probably have been saved?—You say it for me.

3077. Don't you say it?—Not exactly in those words.

3078. Do you say so?—Probably he could.

3079. Then, in addition to accusing a large number of persons, including medical gentlemen of your own profession, of absolute falsehood, you accuse the three gentlemen of absolute incapacity?—I do.

3080. I have only one word more to ask you. Have you ever seen any medical gentleman taking so active a part in a case as you have taken in this case?—I have never seen anyone who had to do with such a case before.

3081. Have you ever seen a medical gentleman taking so active a part in a case before?—No.

3082. Have you ever seen or heard in court a gaol or hospital official of 13 or 14 years' standing, state on oath that three medical gentlemen of long standing were guilty of absolute incapacity and thereby gave a patient no chance for his life on the treatment of the case?—No.

3083. Did you say to any gentleman in Liverpool that Mandeville was a great scoundrel and deserved what he got?—No. I may have used words to that effect.

Warder MOONEY, called in; and Examined.

Mr. Rowan.

3084. You were warder in Tullamore prison when Mr. Mandeville was confined there?—Yes.

3085. Do you remember the evening that Mr. Mandeville's clothes were taken away?—Yes.

3086. Was it you brought the suit of prison clothes to the cell?—Yes.

3087. Now, when you went to the cell with the other warders was the gas lighting in the cell?—Yes.

3088. How long were you there altogether?—I suppose about five or 10 minutes.

3089. Was there any serious resistance on Mr. Mandeville's part?—No.

3090. Now, on the 22nd of December did you enter the cell where John Mandeville was confined, with Dr. Ridley?—Yes.

3091. Did you see the doctor attempt to examine Mr. Mandeville?—I did.

3092. What did Mr. Mandeville do?—He would not allow him to examine him, and said that there was no necessity to consult him.

Cross-examined by Mr. *Harrington.*

3093. You are a long time in the prison service?—I am over twelve years.

3094. When the governor and warders proceeded to Mr. Mandeville's cell where were you?—I think I was around within the cell.

3095. Did you close the door, or had you the clothes with you?—I brought the clothes with me from my own stores.

3096. When were you informed that an attack was going to be made on Mr. Mandeville?—I think it was some time before 8 o'clock, I was told I was wanted in the prison.

3097. You had gone off duty for the evening?—Yes.

3098. What hour?—Six or half-past 6 o'clock.

3099. And some of the other warders had gone home?—Yes.

3100. Were you asleep when you were called?—No, I was not asleep.

3101. Was the gas lighting in the rest of the gaol as well as Mr. Mandeville's cell?—Yes, it is never put out till 8.30.

3102. Now, will you swear that this was not after half-past eight?—Yes.

3103. How

Mr. Harrington—continued.

3103. How do you know?—Well, I know the gas was not out; that is one good reason.

3104. And was it that you had an opportunity of seeing the gas in other cells besides this?—Certainly.

3105. How did you know?—I knew it was not up to the time for putting it out.

3106. Had you an opportunity of seeing whether the gas was or was not lighting in any other cell?—I did not go into any other cell, but I could see the gas from the outside; of course it is not necessary for me to go to any cell to see whether it is in or out, for I know when it is put out.

3107. And is that your only reason for being convinced that the gas was lighting?—It is.

3108. Will you pledge your oath that neither the governor or chief-warder Bartley approached the door before you went there and lit the gas?—I will, because we all went there together.

3109. Were you on parade?—Yes.

3110. Was it on the parade you got the clothes? No, I had them on my arm on parade.

3111. Who opened the door of the cell?—The chief warder.

3112. The governor swore that he was next the chief warder, was it true?—I think I was next the door.

3113. On your oath, is there hard labour in Tullamore?—There is oakum picking.

3114. Twenty-four oakum in the day?—Yes.

3115. Do prisoners who are not on hard labour get that work?—Yes.

3116. Is there not stone breaking in Tullamore?—No.

3117. Is there crank work in Tullamore gaol?—A crank pump.

3118. And that is considered hard labour?—Hard labour prisoners work it.

3119. While Mr. Mandeville was being stripped, did you hear him say anything about any particular article of his clothing?—No.

3120. He did not like to part with them, and he said nothing about the indecency of taking off his shirt?—I did not hear him say anything.

3121. Who removed the articles from the cell?—All the articles I saw removed was the stool by the chief warder.

3122. Why were these articles removed?—I cannot tell.

3123. Is it because they were in the way?—I suppose so.

3124. Was it not that they were afraid that the prisoner might defend himself?—I know I was not a bit afraid.

3125. Was Warder Wilson engaged in that party?—Yes.

3126. You never heard him discussing how Mr. Mandeville should be treated?—I never heard anything about it.

Mr. John Pierce, J.P., called in; and Examined.

Mr. Ronan.

3127. You are a visiting justice of Tullamore Prison?—Yes.

3128. Do you remember two or three months ago being in the Imperial Hotel, Dublin?—Yes.

3129. Did you see Mr. John Mandeville at breakfast?—Yes.

3130. I believe you saw him on one occasion in the prison?—Certainly, once.

3131. When you went over to him what did he say to you?—I said I was very glad to see him there and well in good.

3132. Did he receive you with politeness?—He did.

3133. Did you breakfast together?—Yes, at his suggestion.

3134. Were you talking to him about his prison treatment?—Yes.

3135. Did you ask him if he had any complaint?—I did. I knew that during his incarceration he never made any complaint, but that, perhaps, after his liberation he might say what he would not say while in.

3136. What did he say then?—He said he had no complaint.

3137. Did he say whether he attached blame to anyone?—None whatever.

The Coroner.

3138. What did he say?—He said any punishment he got was brought on himself.

3139. When you were there at breakfast, did some of his friends come in?—A great number.

The Coroner—continued.

3140. Did he introduce you to them?—He did.

3141. How did he introduce you?—As one of the cruel justices of Tullamore Gaol, or some words to that effect.

3142. Did you part on very friendly terms?—Certainly.

Cross-examined by *The MacDermot.*

3143. How many visiting justices are there?—I don't know.

3144. Tell me those whom you know?—Mr. Charleton, Mr. Digby, Mr. Browne, Mr. Goodbody, and Mr. Fosbell.

3145. Is there a Catholic amongst them?—I think not.

3146. Where do you live?—In Tullamore.

3147. Where does Mr. Browne live?—In the town.

3148. Where does Mr. Fosbell?—Five or six miles from the town.

3149. Mr. Goodbody?—He lives about six miles.

3150. Where does Mr. Ridley live?—He lives in the town.

3151. Where were you on the 19th November?—I cannot tell.

3152. You are accustomed to be examined in courts of justice?—Often examined as a land valuer?—Yes.

3153. Was anyone present when Mr. Mandeville chatted at breakfast?—A lot of people.

The MacDermot—continued.

8154. Can you tell me the name of any?—I could not.

8155. Was it before anyone came in that you began the chat about the prison?—The moment we met.

8156. Were you here in the Court for the last three or four days?—I was here.

8157. Do you not know that statement of yours that he had made no complaint, was not true?—No.

8158. Do you know that he complained in prison that they called on him to clean his own cell?—I heard it.

8159. Do you know he complained of being compelled to wear prison clothes?—I heard it.

8160. He said to you, of his own accord, that he had never made any complaint in prison?—He never complained to me.

The MacDermot—continued.

8161. Did he say to you that he never made a complaint in prison, or that he never complained to you?—I asked him had he any complaint to make of us as justices, and he said he had not.

8162. He said any punishment he got he brought on himself?—Yes.

8163. He described you as one of the cruel justices of Tullamore?—Yes, in a joking way.

8164. He told you he had no complaint to make?—Yes.

8165. And the substance of what he said was that he had no complaint to make against you as justice?—Yes; I wanted to see myself right. He never made any complaint to me of his treatment in prison. I believe the reason we are appointed as visiting justices is because we are the justices close to the prison, and most likely to attend.

Mr. Brown, J.P.; Examined.

Mr. *Ronan.*

8166. You are also one of the visiting justices?—I am.

8167. Do you remember about the 8th of November seeing Mr. Mandeville when Mr. Ridley's father was with you?—I saw him about that time in his cell.

8168. Did you ask him whether he had any complaints to make?—I did.

8169. What did he reply?—Nothing whatever.

8170. Had you and Mr. Ridley a conversation with him on general subjects?—We had.

8171. And the only other occasion you saw him was on the 6th December?—Yes.

8172. You were then in company with Mr. Ridley, Mr. Goodbody, and Mr. Digby?—Yes.

8173. Did you on that occasion also ask him if he had any complaint to make?—He said he had none whatever, but he asked me about my arm, which he saw was unwell.

8174. On both these occasions did you see him in fair health?—Yes, so far as I saw.

8175. Did you see anything different in him then from the time you saw him first?—No.

Cross-examined by Mr. *Harrington.*

8176. He did not appear to you to be in any extent altered?—No.

8177. When you saw him first, was he in his own clothes?—Yes.

8178. And the prison clothes made no alteration in him?—None whatever; physically speaking.

8179. From what you saw of him do you think he would be likely to complain if he had not proper reason to complain?—No, I should not say so.

8180. Did he appear to you to be that description of man who would be fond of malingering in gaol?—Oh, I could not say.

8181. Were you sent for by the governor at any time?—I received a letter requesting me to go to the gaol.

8182. Where did you receive the letter, do you remember?—I was collecting rents at the time.

8183. Do you recollect the reason of your being sent for at the time was to enforce Mr. Mandeville to clean his own cell?—I do not.

Mr. Reginald Digby, J.P.; Examined.

Mr. *Ronan.*

8184. Were you with Mr. O'Brien on the 2nd November?—Yes.

8185. And with Mr. Mandeville on the 8th December?—Yes.

Mr. *Ronan*—continued.

8186. How was Mr. Mandeville looking?—Well.

8187. Was he asked in any one's presence had he any complaints to make, and what did he reply?—That he had no complaints whatever.

27 July 1888.

Mr. JAMES P. GOODBODY, J.P., of Clara; Examined.

Mr. *Ronan*.

3188. You are one of the visiting justices?—Yes.

3189. I believe the first occasion you saw Mr. Mandeville was about the 10th November?—I think that was about the date.

3190. He was in his cell?—Yes.

3191. As far as your observations would go, he appeared to be in good health?—He appeared to be in good health. I had a considerable chat with him.

3192. Did you ask him if he had any complaint to make?—I did.

3193. What did he say?—He said he had none.

3194. Did you see him about the 19th November?—I did.

3195. Did you inquire if he had any complaints?—Yes.

3196. What reply did you receive?—I don't know, but I know he only complained once on that occasion; we had a conversation about diarrhœa.

3197. When you had the conversation about diarrhœa did he say anything about treatment? I particularly asked him had he any complaints to make about the doctor or the governor, or were they kind to him; and he said they were.

3198. Did you see him again about the 1st December, and again on the 6th December?—Yes.

3199. On both of these occasions did you ask him had he any complaints?—He said he had no complaints.

3200. Did you see him again on the 19th or 22nd?—I was there both on the 19th and 22nd.

3201. On that occasion was he in the punishment cell?—No, I never saw him in the punishment cell.

3202. On that occasion had he a complaint to make?—No.

3203. Did you observe any change in his appearance?—No; I thought he was a very fine man when he went in, and the last time I saw him I thought he was a very fine man.

Cross-examined by Mr. *Harrington*.

3204. Visiting justices, Mr. Goodbody, are not in the habit of sending to the press anything about their visits?—No; I never sent anything to the papers for political purposes.

3205. Did you ever send any communication to a friend in connection with Mr. Mandeville's treatment to be used for political purposes?—I don't think I did.

3206. Did you write to any political friends in England any letters about Mr. Mandeville's treatment in Tullamore?—I don't think so.

3207. Did you know Mr. Albert Pease?—I never saw him in my life. I heard of Alfred Pease, but I did not know Albert.

3208. Do you know that a communication was published in a York newspaper, giving you as an authority as to the treatment of prisoners?—I never heard of it.

3209. Direct or indirect, did you hold any communication with him?—I never heard of the man. I don't know the man anyway.

3210. Do you know Mr. Alfred Pease?—I do.

3211. He is a member of the same family. The uncle and he, you are aware, don't agree in politics?—I believe they don't.

3212. You know Mr. Albert Pease is a Gladstonian Member of Parliament?—(*Reading from the newspapers.*) Yes.

3213. Do you know that Mr. Alfred Pease is opposed to his nephew in politics?—I know that he is not a Gladstonian.

3214. Had you ever any communication with Mr. Alfred Pease?—I don't know that I ever wrote him a letter on such a subject.

3215. Have you ever written him a letter at all?—I have.

3216. Did you ever get a copy of the "York Herald"?—To my knowledge I have never seen the paper.

3217. Did you ever write to Mr. Alfred Pease of the treatment of political prisoners in Tullamore?—I don't believe I did.

3218. And it would not be true if he had given you as his authority for the treatment of prisoners in a communication which he sent to the "York Herald"?—I could not answer that question, but I wish to explain that I believe I never wrote a letter to him on political subjects, but I will not swear.

3219. Do you remember the Lord Mayor of Dublin having been present in Tullamore?—Yes.

3220. Has it come in any way to your knowledge that a statement attributed to you with reference to the treatment of prisoners in Tullamore, was used in a York paper?—No.

3221. You had correspondence with Arthur Pease?—I think I had about half-a-dozen letters from him.

3222. Now, would you pledge yourself that none of these letters you made any reference to the prisoners in Tullamore?—To the best of my recollection, no.

3223. You visited the gaol on other days beside those you mentioned?—I did.

3224. Did you visit Mr. Mandeville whilst on punishment?—No. I visited him every time I went to the gaol, except once. I don't know whether he was on punishment or not.

3225. Is not it customary with the governor to tell you when a prisoner is on punishment?—Not when visiting a prison.

3226. Do you know any of the justices who visited Mr. Mandeville while in the punishment cell?—No.

Mr. *Ronan*.

3227. Did you ever use information derived by you in your capacity as visiting justice for party or political purposes?—Certainly not.

3228. You said that you did not know that Mr. Mandeville was on punishment. You mean by that that when you visited you did not know he was on punishment?—Yes.

TENTH DAY.

Friday, 27*th July* 1888.

Dr. Moore; Examined.

Mr. Murphy.

3229. You are a physician practising in Dublin?—I am.

3230. What are your qualifications?—I am a Doctor of Medicine of the University of Dublin, a Fellow of the King and Queen's College of Physicians, &c.

3231. Have you any public appointment in Dublin?—I have the Meath Hospital and County Dublin Infirmary.

3232. How many patients are there in that hospital?—One hundred or one hundred and twenty.

3233. How long have you held that position?—Thirteen years.

3234. Besides that, have you held other public appointments in Dublin?—For the same period I have been one of the physicians to the Cork-street Fever Hospital, Dublin.

3235. I believe you also edit the only medical journal published in Ireland?—Yes.

3236. I believe you had some connexion with the late Dr. Ridley?—He was related to my first wife.

3237. You knew him?—Yes.

3238. Did you read any newspaper reports of the evidence given at this inquest?—I read the medical evidence throughout.

The Coroner.

3239. From the daily papers?—Yes.

3240. No particular paper?—The "Express" and "Freeman's Journal."

Mr. Murphy.

3241. Have you also read a shorthand note of the evidence given here up to this?—I have.

3242. When was that transcript submitted to you?—Wednesday afternoon.

3243. You read the evidence of Dr. M'Craith?—I did.

3244. Dr. M'Craith said that on *Friday*, 6th July, Mr. Mandeville arrived at his house in the town at about two or three o'clock in the day with muffler round his neck. He asked him what was the matter with him, and he said he was suffering from sore throat. He said he ordered him a gargle, recommended him to go home, inhale warm water, and take nourishment. He says the following morning he went to Mr. Mandeville's house. He could not articulate; he had to write what he had to say. The glands were hard and swollen. He drove back to town and brought out some leeches. They applied leeches to his neck, and they afterwards sent to Fermoy for leeches. You have read all this?—I have.

3245. Dr. Cremen arrived at 2.30 on Saturday. They gave the iron tincture, muriate of iron and potash, and other sweating draughts. He said that on Saturday night or Sunday morning he was punctured with an exploring needle. Did you read also the evidence of Dr. Cremen and Dr. O'Neill?—I did.

Mr. Murphy—continued.

3246. Now, have you from reading the evidence formed any opinion as to what he was suffering from, and how he should be treated?—I have no hesitation in saying, from the evidence of these men, I am able to form an opinion as to what he was suffering from.

3247. Now, dealing with the evidence that you have read and Dr. M'Craith's statement, and Dr. O'Neill's, you say that you know what the nature of the case was, and the remedies that ought to be applied in your opinion?—The case, I believe, was one of diffuse cellular inflammation about the mouth. It is also called phlegmonous erysipelas.

3248. What were the symptoms as described by these gentlemen that led you to that conclusion?—First the complaint of sore throat; second, the swelling in the back part of the mouth; third, the enlargement of the glands in the upper part of the neck.

3249. Having considered the evidence of these gentlemen, what in your opinion would be proper treatment of the case at the stage described by Dr. M'Craith on Friday?—I would have put the patient on strengthening or tonic-supporting and stimulating treatment, and I would have had the benefit of a surgical operation. I would have advised at once the making of free incisions where the tension was externally greatest.

3250. Have you had patients of that description under your charge?—I have.

3251. Did you as a physician endeavour to find out what the cause of Mr. Mandeville's death was?—Most undoubtedly.

3252. Dr. M'Craith said some short time before this Mr. Mandeville came to him and complained of sore throat, and he gave him a gargle, without an examination. Now was that a proper thing for a physician to do?—I am sorry to say I think not.

3253. Mr. Mandeville asked him for a cough mixture, and he gave it to him without examination; was that right?—No.

3254. On Saturday, 7th July, Drs. M'Craith and O'Neill applied some leeches to this poor gentleman's mouth, inside under the tongue, was that proper treatment under the circumstances they described the patient at that time?—I do not think so, for two reasons: First, it is always difficult to check the bleeding from leech bites inside the mouth, and especially so when the parts are congested, and with the swelling as described the second application of leeches was contra-indicated. You see this throat affection is a marked form of erysipelas.

3255. Did you approve of the using of leeches?—Yes, certainly.

3256. Besides the danger of leeches, would the

Mr. *Murphy*—continued.

the use of the knife be more effective?—It would not, inside, but outside the objection to the use of the knife internally in the mouth is the risk of hemorrhage which could not be controlled.

3257. Dr. M'Craith says he was swollen under the jaw; Dr. Cremen says the swelling was at the parotid gland. Upon this Saturday you read the description by Dr. Cremen and Dr. O'Neill, what, in your opinion, would that indicate?—A serious interference with the blood; in other words, the blood would not be there in its proper quantity.

3258. What would that indicate with respect to the throat through which the air gets into the lungs?—That the air was getting in with great difficulty.

3259. You read the account of the temperature and breathing and pulse of Mr. Mandeville, described by those doctors; what would they indicate in your opinion?—I was struck by what is called by the word correlation. That correlation showed that the patient was suffering from fever of medium intensity.

3260. Having read the evidence of Dr. Cremen, were there any symptoms which as described would indicate a fatal termination of the case?—I considered that Mr. Mandeville was dangerously ill but not hopelessly.

3261. Would you not consider whether the incisions ought to have been applied before or after that period?—Before that period.

3262. Now, Doctor, can you indicate from your reading of the case when they ought to have been applied?—On the earliest opportunity on Friday, and even then perhaps it was too late.

3263. What is the technical term for an affection of this sort?—Angina.

3264. What does it mean?—Strangling.

3265. Did you consider whether or not the mode of getting rid of this is to remove the pressure?—Certainly.

3266. It was said here that like a man who was being strangled that the right remedy was to cut the rope; do you agree in that?—The analogy of Dr. Barr is a good one.

3267. Men sound and healthy are liable to this form of disease that you have described?—They are.

3268. And what are the predisposing causes? —Epidemic influence, contagion, defective sanitary arrangements, bad habits, over drinking or over eating; these are the predisposing causes. An exciting cause is the introduction into the system of certain virus or poison.

3269. In your opinion, could this virus or poison exist from November to July without being developed?—Nine days is the period of incubation; I tested it in my own practice.

3270. Would, or would not, exposure to cold tend to develop this affection?—I mentioned only four of these predisposing causes, and there are many others.

3271. Nine days is the period of incubation of this virus?—Yes.

3272. Mr. Mandeville was in Tullamore prison, and discharged on the 24th of December. In your opinion, having regard to the account of his fatal illness, could that have any connection with his imprisonment?—In my opinion, it had no possible connection with it.

3273. If a gentleman had over-exercise in public speaking, would that be any cause of a disease of that sort?—Over-exercise in public speaking might be another predisposing cause.

3274. Now, it has been proved that Mr. Mandeville was out for a considerable portion of the night of Monday, 2nd of July; would that, in your opinion, have any effect in causing this disease of which he died?—I have no doubt it would develop the disease, and have a very prejudicial effect.

3275. Now, it was proved here also, that some days before that he was complaining of toothache; would that indicate that a particular virus was still working in the system?—That was one of the symptoms characteristic of erysipelas about the throat.

3276. Mr. Mandeville was incarcerated on the 31st October. About the 7th November he weighed 16 stone 2 lbs., and about the 15th he weighed 16 stone; if this treatment was causing any real mischief to his system, could he have kept up his weight to that standard?—No.

3277. Mr. Mandeville was a man of large physique, and in your opinion are such men good subjects for these inflammatory attacks?—Certainly not, but this is simply an opinion.

3278. I presume that in a man of his habits there is more matter to be affected than there would in a spare man, and the inflammation would cause greater tension, would it not?—Yes.

3279. There would be more matter for the inflammation to operate on, and it would cause greater pressure?—Certainly.

3280. In that case, the remedies applied should be more prompt than in the case of a spare man? —Undoubtedly.

3281. Dr. M'Craith said that either on Saturday night or Sunday morning he opened some portion with an exploring needle; was that an operation that should have been performed?—For diagnostic purposes, perhaps yes, but for other reasons, not.

3282. Assuming that an operation of that portion of the throat was necessary, would an exploring needle be the proper instrument to use for it?—He could not see the pharynx; the swelling must have been so great as to conceal it from view.

3283. As a matter of fact, is not the pharynx behind the uvula?—Certainly.

3284. Is there such a word as the pillar of the pharynx?—I do not know.

3285. Have you ever heard of it?—I heard of it here to-day.

3286. Not before to-day?—No.

3287. From the evidence you have heard, what conclusion have you drawn as to what caused this poor gentleman's death?—I should think that he died of interference with the air supply of the blood, which would affect the brain, the heart, and the various systems generally.

Cross-examined by *The MacDermot*.

3288. Will you tell me what is meant by the pillar of the pharynx?—The outside portion in front of the tonsil.

The MacDermot—continued.

3289. The pillar is the outside portion of the internal formation?—Yes.

3290. I suppose you say, Doctor, a medical gentleman who attended a patient from the time he got ill up to his death could form a more adequate opinion than a man who had not that opportunity?—Certainly, as a rule, yes.

3291. You said that when Dr. M'Craith gave a gargle to a patient that he knew previously as a patient he did wrong in doing so without an examination. Did he act injudiciously?—Certainly.

3292. In giving a simple gargle?—Yes.

3293. Or giving a cough mixture?—Yes.

3294. You say if you had been there and if you had the benefit of surgical opinion you would have made free incisions on the outside?—Yes.

3295. If the surgeon was there and advised it not to be done, would you do it?—Under no circumstances would I operate myself. I am a physician.

3296. If there was a surgeon there who gave it as his opinion that it was not advisable, would you do it?—I would not do it.

3297. Would you direct him to do it?—No.

3298. You said you would adopt tonic treatment, I suppose beef-tea, brandy, milk, preparation of iron?—I say my treatment would be threefold.

3299. Do you think if when a patient is suffering considerably this treatment is always necessary?—It is not necessary, as a rule.

3300. It was sworn to by the doctors who attended the patient that the application of leeches gave great relief. Are you sure that it injured the patient?—I am sure it did.

3301. Why?—First of all, the hemorrhage depressed him, although it gave him relief. It gave relief to the veins of the blood, but it ultimately had an injurious effect.

3302. I think you said the description given by Mrs. Mandeville was very important?—Yes.

3303. You said that that was a symptom of the disease?—Yes.

3304. I suppose, in addition to that first complaint of sore throat and difficulty of swallowing, did you consider that a collateral symptom?—Yes, it would indicate that the disease had commenced.

3305. Now, supposing three physicians swore they saw a portion of the pharynx, would you take it on yourself to say they did not?—Only one of them swore it.

3306. Now, doctor, supposing a man was broken down in health, would he be more susceptible of that disease?—It does not follow.

The MacDermot—continued.

3307. But as a rule? As a rule, yes; but the strongest are sometimes prostrated by that disease.

3308. Each of the three doctors swore that he had not died from suffocation. I suppose asphyxia would be the proper name for suffocation?—Yes.

3309. You say that interference with the air supply to the blood had the effect of affecting the brain?—Yes.

3310. Would that cause wandering of mind?—Yes.

3311. Now, if any of the medical gentlemen swore he did not die of suffocation would you contradict them?—I wish to explain that the interference with the blood supply to the brain has a great influence over the supply of blood to the heart, and this may lead to a stoppage of the heart's action. Interference with the blood supply to the brain has a paralyzing effect on the nervous supply of the heart, tending to stop the heart's action.

3312. What would you consider a very rapid decomposition of the body to indicate?—It indicates the presence in the system of some very violent poison.

3313. Would the presence of very violent poison in the system, render disease more dangerous than a less violent attack?—Certainly.

3314. Have you not said rapid decomposition indicates the presence of very violent poison in the system?—I may have; there are many causes of decomposition, one of them is the presence of violent poison in the system, and one is intemperate habits from which may be indicated chronic disease, and it may indicate the presence of blood poisoning known as uremia. It would also indicate that a person has been exposed to high temperature. The causes of decomposition are numerous.

3315. In this case did I not indicate the presence of very violent poison in the system?—Yes.

Mr. Murphy.

3316. You said you would call in a surgeon to perform the operation in these cases?—Yes.

3317. Are you certain that that is the course that ought to be taken?—Yes.

3318. You have no doubt but that would be the proper treatment?—No doubt.

3319. When you refer to a surgeon who would operate, you are a physician who do not operate?—Yes.

3320. If Mr. Mandeville complained of sore throat in Tullamore in November and December 1887, would that have any connexion with the sore throat of which he died?—None whatever.

Gentlemen of the Jury,—At the end of this rather protracted inquiry I should first express my great regret that Mr. John Mandeville, a gentleman I had not the pleasure of knowing, except by repute, but who, from all I can learn, was a man of splendid physique, and was socially a very estimable character, should have been cut off in the prime of his life by the disease which caused his death on the 8th July. Gentlemen, you are empanelled here for the purpose of ascertaining the cause of Mr. John Mandeville's death; and gentlemen, if it were not for a tragic occurrence that occurred on Friday last, I should be disposed to characterise the opening of this enquiry as a grotesque farce in which my learned friend, The MacDermot, was acting a leading part. Gentlemen, Mr. John Mandeville died on the 8th July, and he died beyond all question of diffuse cellular inflammation of the throat, and you have heard a great deal of medical and other evidence, as to the nature of the affection and how it operated on Mr. John Mandeville; and, gentlemen, you can have no doubt that the true cause of death was this cellular inflammation of the throat. It appears to me, that the farce The MacDermot is taking a leading part in, is that Mr. John Mandeville, having died by the visitation of the Almighty, The MacDermot is appealing from that decree of the Supreme Being to you as a jury assembled here in Mitchelstown; because, gentlemen, when you come to weigh the evidence, and when you give your verdict, having regard to the fact that you are giving it on your oath, and that you cannot give it for the purpose of satisfying the wishes of Mr. William O'Brien, or of Mrs. Mandeville, or of any other person, but that you must find your verdict satisfied on your oaths as to the cause of this man's death. Gentlemen, if you weigh the evidence I have no doubt as to the conclusion you must come to, and the only verdict you can find is that Mr. Mandeville died on the 8th July, from the inflammatory attack in his throat. I think, when you come to weigh the evidence, you must come to the conclusion that nothing that occurred in the treatment of Mr. Mandeville in Tullamore Prison, or elsewhere, had the slightest effect upon his general health, and I hope to demonstrate to you that that is so. Gentlemen, we have had a great deal of medical testimony here. We have had the evidence of Dr. M'Craith, and I regret extremely that Dr. M'Craith was not here to listen to the evidence that was given as to his treatment of the patient. I don't for a moment wish to impute to Dr. M'Craith that he wilfully maltreated Mr. Mandeville. I am quite certain that he and Dr. O'Neill treated Mr. Mandeville according to their lights; but my case is, that the lights of Dr. M'Craith and the lights of Dr O'Neill, in reference to the particular affection from which Mr. Mandeville was suffering, were very dim lights indeed. Gentlemen, Mr. Mandeville, subsequent to his incarceration in Tullamore Prison, was here moving about amongst you. You saw him. You know I have no doubt what an active life he led. You know the leading part he took in any political movement going on in your own district. You have heard from Mr. William O'Brien the leading part he took at several meetings addressed by Mr. William O'Brien. You know he was a speaker at several meetings, and I have no doubt you are aware of other meetings he attended which were not included, because we were not keeping up espionage on the conduct of Mr. Mandeville since he left Tullamore Prison; but beyond all question Mr. Mandeville was going about as he used before he ever went to Tullamore, taking part in the movement against the Leahy Tax, and taking an active part in it. Well, what happens? On Monday, 2nd July, Mr. Mandeville, then suffering from an affection deposed to by his wife, Mrs. Mandeville, this pain in his jaw or in his tooth. Of course, anybody who has a pain in the jaw it is localised over or under some tooth, but beyond all doubt Mr. Mandeville, on the 2nd July, upon the testimony of Mrs. Mandeville was suffering in this way. He goes to Fermoy; and, gentlemen, it is a singular thing that none of the persons who were associated with him from the early morning of the 2nd July until the early morning of the 3rd July have been produced here to account for his movements or conduct during that interval. He was met at two o'clock or half-past two o'clock in the morning, apparently returning to Mitchelstown. Having been met by Mr. Tharry he returned to Fermoy, and we have the evidence of Mrs. Mandeville that he did not reach his own home until an advanced hour of the morning, considerably after four o'clock, because I know it takes at least an hour and 20 minutes to drive from Fermoy to Mitchelstown. Having had that pain on the 2nd, and previous to the 2nd, he had it on the 3rd Mrs. Mandeville tells us, and on the following day he was prevented going to the Board of Guardians, and on the next day he felt so affected that he goes to Dr. M'Craith. Now, Dr. M'Craith had a fortnight previously prescribed a gargle for some affection of Mr. Mandeville's throat; and he had done that without taking the ordinary precaution which a physician of experience ought to have taken of examining and trying to discover what cause of the evil he was then endeavouring to remedy. There are several affections of the throat, and one treatment may be suitable for one affection, and it may require a totally different treatment for another. But Mr. M'Craith, in an off-hand sort of way, dealing with Mr. Mandeville who, he would say, was in a debilitated state, he treated him without making the most superficial examination of the affection with which he proposed to deal. A few days afterwards Mr. Mandeville, apparently having some affection which caused him to cough, applies to Dr. M'Craith to give him a cough mixture. I submit to you that Dr. M'Craith was wanting in his professional duty to Mr.

Mandeville if he prescribed without examining what was the exciting cause of that particular affection; because, gentlemen, knowing before that he had complained of his throat, this mixture which was supposed to work on the system would have been useless. Giving a prescription of gargle for his throat, his asking for a cough mixture, would excite in any man's mind an anxiety to know what Mr. Mandeville was suffering from. Upon the Friday Mr. Mandeville feeling a swelling in his throat goes to Dr. M'Craith, and Dr. M'Craith gave him an examination which he described here, and all the doctors who have been examined here, have agreed that it was the first duty of a physician, dealing with an affection of that sort, to have put certain queries to the patient to ascertain what was the origin of the affection which he proposed to treat, and how he could have acquired it; I got a very singular answer from Dr. M'Craith when I asked him had he made this inquiry. He said no, and I asked him why he did not, and he told me he did not like to insult the man by asking whether he had been out the night before. What was the meaning of that as showing the condition of the mind of Dr. M'Craith at the time he commenced to treat Mr. Mandeville for this throat affection. Does it not show beyond all question that from the time Dr. M'Craith commenced to treat Mr. Mandeville, that he attributed his then condition to some exposure to cold, and his failure to make any inquiry as to whether he had been suffering for any length of time from this affection, his failing to make any observation on the condition which he describes Mr. Mandeville to have been in from the time he left Tullamore until the 6th July, is proof conclusive to my mind, and I think it will be proof conclusive to yours, that on the 6th July, when Dr. M'Craith commenced to treat Mr. Mandeville for this affection, that he was satisfied from his abstaining to make inquiry into the cause of the disease, and his saying that he did not want to insult him, that the man exposed himself by being out at night. It is proof conclusive to my mind that Dr. M'Craith was satisfied that the peculiar acute affection from which he found Mr. Mandeville suffering on that occasion was due to exposure, and nothing else. He very properly sent Mr. Mandeville home to keep his bed. I don't quarrel with the treatment of Dr. M'Craith in sending Mr. Mandeville home, but what I do say is this, that from the diagnosis made by Dr. M'Craith on that occasion, taking it now with the evidence of the other medical men that you have had, including Dr. Cremen, I will submit to you that if anything could have been done for Mr. Mandeville the omission was on the part of Dr. M'Craith when he made that first diagnosis of Mr. Mandeville's case, and he ought then and there have adopted the remedies which were since suggested as the proper remedies by Dr. Barr, by Dr. Moore, and joined by Dr. Cremen. Dr. M'Craith does not appear to have had sufficient confidence, or to have had sufficient knowledge of the particular subject with which he was dealing. He then calls in upon the following morning, instead of taking prompt remedies that night as would have been the proper course for an acute affection of this sort. He waits until he is sent for the next morning. Mr. Mandeville had rapidly grown worse during the night, and Dr. M'Craith instead of adopting those prompt measures suggested by the other physicians when he found the nature of the affection, if he was aware of the character of the remedies, or how they ought to be applied at all, but—I am rather doubtful—but I think you will be satisfied upon the evidence now, that at all events, Mr. Mandeville would have had a chance for his life if these remedies had been applied when Dr. M'Craith first saw him, and you must be satisfied with the evidence of Dr. Cremen that when he saw him his condition was a hopeless one. Remedies may be good if applied at a certain time, but no good when the patient has gone too far. But now we have the evidence of the three doctors who attended him. Dr. O'Neill was called in on the morning of Saturday, and I think the most painful thing that has occurred during this inquiry, is the way Dr. O'Neill gave his evidence here. I cannot see how any gentleman could commit himself to the statements he committed himself to. He purported to read from his note book things taken on the spot. Gentlemen, that means that he took the notes from which he purported to read at the bedside of the patient. He subsequently qualified that by saying that he did not take them on the spot, but that he commenced writing his notes on the evening of the Saturday after he returned home, and after he had been at least three times with the patient. Gentlemen, when you come to consider the evidence of Dr. O'Neill, and what weight you ought to attach to it in considering the cause of Mr. Mandeville's death, you will have to consider the nature of the evidence he gave with reference to the note on which he relied for the purpose of giving his evidence here. Now, what was that note. He swears to you he wrote on the Saturday evening in his notebook the condition in which he found Mr. Mandeville: "I saw him for the first time in his fatal illness on Saturday morning." Did you ever make an entry in a book of an occurrence which occurred on the date in which you were making the entry, and did you ever make an entry describing a case which had not occurred for two days afterwards. He states, he saw him for the first time in his "fatal" illness on Saturday morning. He swears that was made on Saturday evening. Nobody could believe that Dr. O'Neill's statement as to that is accurate, and the occurrence is of so recent a date no possible mistake could have been made about it, and the only thing is, Dr. O'Neill has made a statement which cannot be supported as true. "I saw him on Saturday morning the 7th instant, &c." That portion, he says, gentlemen, was written on Saturday evening. Now, this illness, describing Mr. Mandeville's illness as a fatal illness, upon Saturday evening. I think after you give it an examination in your own minds, you will say it is impossible that any gentleman of ordinary intelligence could have used such a statement on Saturday evening, and the man alive at the time, because no illness is fatal until a man is dead, and no person making the entry on Saturday could describe the occurrence in the way that Dr. O'Neill does, as having seen him on Saturday morning, 7th instant. He would simply say Saturday. Saw Mr. Mandeville at such a time. Having

Having made use of the remedies he could not be certain whether he would die or not. He could not be sure that the remedies which ought to have been applied and which were not—the absence of the remedies—would have allowed Mr. Mandeville to die on the Sunday. He goes on then to recite how upon that date he met Dr. Cremen at 3.30 upon the Saturday, but he had met Dr. Cremen before the period at which he said he wrote this note, and if he wrote this on the Saturday evening, do you think he would omit to mention the visit he paid to Mr. Mandeville on the day Dr. Cremen attended.

Then we have also a statement that Dr. O'Neill made: first, that he kept a diary and that he had left it at home, because the particular book he produced was one bearing the date of 1878, and when he came to be tested further he had no book at all at home. It may be, that this old gentleman's memory is not as accurate as it might have been, but he comes here to give an account of what he knows about Mr. Mandeville and makes statements that cannot of reality be as accurate as they might. Finding that, you may receive a good part of his evidence with great suspicion. Dr. Cremen appears on the scene at half past three on Saturday, 7th July. He tells you that on that occasion he came to the conclusion that Mr. Mandeville would not live longer than Monday. He also tells you the treatment to which Mr. Mandeville had been subjected was good preparatory treatment. Now, Dr. Cremen came to the conclusion on the Saturday that the man could not live. He came to the conclusion that the symptoms had arrived at that stage that nothing could be done to save his life, and though he tells you he agreed with the treatment of Drs. M'Craith and O'Neill up to that particular time, he describes them as good preparatory treatment; but it is rather late to say that it is good preparatory treatment when, gentlemen, the man was in that condition which showed that something more than preparatory treatment should have been applied long before Dr. Cremen came upon the scene at all. Drs. M'Craith and O'Neill told us that previous to the coming on the scene of Dr. Cremen there was no suggestion made as to the propriety of resorting to any surgical operation, that is an incision in the throat for the purpose of relieving the tension caused by the swelling from which Mr. Mandeville was suffering. Dr. Cremen says that he, in his own private practice, would have preferred the use of the knife to the use of leeches, and I think what may be drawn from Dr. Cremen's evidence is this, that having been called into consultation with these gentlemen and then finding that the case was hopeless, he has been endeavouring to let them down as lightly as he can, and not to denounce as possibly he might, if he had not been in consultation with them, the treatment that they failed to subject Mr. Mandeville to in his last illness. Now, you have had the benefit here of evidence given by Dr. Barr. Dr. Barr, gentlemen, is a physician practising in Liverpool. He is physician to a large hospital there. He also is that upon which my learned friend, I have no doubt will harp, he holds the position of physician to one of Her Majesty's prisons in Liverpool. He, I would venture to say, sees more cases in the course of a year in Liverpool than probably would come under the notice of Dr. M'Craith during the course of his life in Mitchelstown. Gentlemen, he has given you his opinion grounded upon the statements of the symptoms exhibited by Mr. Mandeville from which any medical man could form an opinion. Dr. Barr has given his opinion on the symptoms at the different stages in Mr. Mandeville's case, and he has furthermore given you the grounds upon which he has formed those opinions, and I think he has explained to you in the clearest manner the course that should be adopted, and explained to you why that course should be adopted, and done it in language that is intelligible to any ordinary man. You have had to-day the benefit of the opinion of one of the leading physicians in Dublin, a gentleman who has held for about 14 years the position of physician to one of the leading hospitals in Dublin, the Meath hospital, a gentleman who holds the highest degrees in medicine that can be held by any man in this kingdom, a gentleman who is surgeon for 13 or 14 years to the Cork-street Fever Hospital, the largest in this country, at all events. He has held every office which he has mentioned to you, which shows that he would not have been selected for those offices unless he possessed a large and extended experience. He has described to you the treatment to which Mr. Mandeville should have been subjected by the gentlemen by whom he was first seen; because gentlemen, I think it has at least been the evidence of Dr. Cremen, he finding and considering that the man was moribund, practically, that the failure to treat him occurred at an earlier stage of the illness. It may be, that he was so far gone that even those remedies would have been vain when Dr. M'Craith saw him; but what I submit to you is, that Dr. M'Craith says by his not treating this that he was entirely ignorant of his business. Now, I have to complain that at the early part of this inquiry certain matters were introduced here in the evidence of Mr. O'Brien, which could have no bearing on the questions which you have to decide. The opinions of Mr. O'Brien as to whether prison punishment was, or was not proper, or, whether he would submit to it; they were introduced under the sanction of The MacDermot, with a view of possibly catching the opinions of some of you gentlemen who may sympathise with views Mr. O'Brien is known to entertain, but I am sure in the discharge of your sworn duties here you will cast out of your mind any of those views so evidenced by Mr. O'Brien, and you will deal with this question upon the evidence so far as it is evidence, and not upon the views and opinions of Mr. O'Brien, whatever they may be. A great deal of evidence has been given by Mrs. Mandeville in reference to her husband after he left Tullamore prison, and gentlemen, that is subject to this criticism, I think. Mrs. Mandeville appears to be a lady of great intelligence, and appears to have had considerable affection for her husband, and gentlemen, if Mr. Mandeville were in the condition which she has described, if he were in this emaciated and debilitated condition which she would have you believe, it is inconceivable that she would not in that period, from the 24th December up to July, have insisted on her husband

husband consulting some medical man as to what course he should adopt to restore him to his ordinary health. She tells you he was not able to wear his boots, he complained of their weight. He complained of the weight of his top coat, but notwithstanding that, she does not suggest that she asked him to take the advice of Dr. M'Craith or any of the numerous physicians in Cork or Dublin, who would have suggested to him what course of treatment might have resulted in his complete restoration to health. The absence of any anxiety upon her part as to his health—because if she felt that anxiety she would have insisted upon his taking advice—the absence of that is, to my mind, and I think it ought to be to yours, evidence why you should discount largely the statement of Mr. Mandeville from the time he left Tullamore prison until the time this fatal illness came on him. You were told he was unable to write his name after coming out of Tullamore gaol. It is a singular thing that not a particle of his writing before or after have been produced here to verify that statement. Statements of that kind can be easily made, but a specimen of the handwriting should have more weight with the jury than any statement of that kind. Mr. Mandeville, subsequent to his discharge from prison, was going about his ordinary business—going into Mitchelstown, going into Fermoy, taking part in the agitation for the purpose of getting rid of the obligation cast on the people in reference to the Leahy Tax. In all these matters he took an active part, and during all that time Mrs. Mandeville does not appear to have suggested to her husband the propriety of taking rest in order to restore him to the condition which he had fallen from, or getting advice to see if he really had anything wrong with him. It has been suggested, and of course will be suggested by The MacDermot, that everything from which Mr. Mandeville suffered during his last illness was attributable to the treatment he got at Tullamore. Mr. Mandeville, beyond all doubt, before he went to prison was a man of splendid physique, and you have the testimony of the doctors that a man in that condition, disagreeable as would be the privations of prison life, still that gentleman in that condition would be less likely to suffer any real injury from the privations to which he would be subjected in prison. It is an inconvenience always to a man who has enjoyed the comforts of life to have his liberty taken away from him, to be reduced suddenly from good food to diet where he had not meat or anything of that sort which he had previously enjoyed. But, gentlemen, a change of that sort is entirely consistent with entire and complete health. It may be of course that a sudden change of diet will cause a temporary change, in the shape of diarrhoea; but I think you must be satisfied that a change like that caused by a change of diet is not an affection that will greatly affect a man's health or constitution, or debilitate him in any way. Mr. Mandeville went into Tullamore Prison with a fixed determination that he would not submit himself to the prison discipline. Gentlemen, in this country, notwithstanding the fantastic theories of Mr. William O'Brien, The MacDermot will tell you, we are all bound to obey the law. Portion of the law is that when men render themselves liable by their conduct to penal restraint, to the punishment of a prison, that they must submit to the discipline of the prison, and the only way to escape from that is to avoid committing an offence to which the law attaches the penalty of imprisonment. Outside the prison we must all submit to the law, and when we get into prison we must submit to the laws of the prison. Mr. Mandeville was fully aware of the conditions to which he would be subjected when he went to prison, and he determined he would resist being subjected to those conditions to the utmost. He was quite prepared to take the punishment attached to such resistance. The most anxious care appears to have been exercised by Dr. Ridley—the unfortunate man who has since gone to his rest—for the health of Mr. Mandeville while he was in prison. We have the prescription book bearing on the face of it prescriptions ordered for the minor affections under which he was labouring while in prison. We have the prescription for diarrhoea. He appears to have been suffering from some pain in his back; we have the prescription for that. Dr. Ridley was a man who for several years had charge of that prison, and a man of whom Mr. Mandeville himself never complained. Dr. Ridley was a man of whom Mr. O'Brien has given a high character in reference to his treatment of himself while he was in prison; and, gentlemen, Dr. Ridley was the man who was responsible for the health of Mr. Mandeville, as he was for the health of every other prisoner confined in Tullamore Gaol; because under the prison rules, every rule of discipline is subject to the will of the medical officer exercised upon medical grounds. It is for the doctor to examine a prisoner when he goes into the prison first. He has to examine him day after day—almost every day—and he has to say if a prisoner refused to submit to the ordinary prison discipline, whether he is a fit subject for punishment or not. Mr. Mandeville being a man of splendid physique, no doubt he suffered to some extent from diarrhoea. The prescription book shows that he was treated for that, and there is no evidence in the case to show that while he was suffering from diarrhoea or any other affection he was subjected to any punishment. The only punishment to which Mr. Mandeville could be subjected was putting him on bread and water for a limited period. It appears that Mr. Mandeville was subjected to eight days' bread and water while he was in Tullamore. He went on the 2nd November, he was discharged on the 24th December; and, gentlemen, you have the evidence of Dr. MacCabe, an experienced gentleman who has held several public appointments, who is himself a member of the Prisons Board, who came there in the anxiety that nothing wrong should be done to any of the prisoners confined in that prison, and who himself examined Mr. Mandeville. I will ask you to believe, on the evidence of Dr. MacCabe himself, that he did not come down for the purpose of ascertaining if Mr. Mandeville was a fit subject for being subjected to cruelties, but for the purpose of seeing whether Mr. Mandeville had maintained his health, because it was the anxious desire of every one connected with the vindication of the law in this

this country that though the law should be vindicated, that no evil results should attach to any of the persons who had rendered themselves subject to the punishment which the law accords for a breach of the law. Dr. MacCabe came down and examined him, and you have had the benefit of his opinion. Not satisfied with that, the Government sent down Dr. Barr. Dr. Barr is a gentleman who I think by his evidence proved to you he knows his business. He subjected Mr. Mandeville on three occasions to a minute examination. He is accustomed to examine men in the condition in which Mr. Mandeville was, and you have had his opinion that Mr. Mandeville was entirely fit to be subjected to the punishment to which he was from time to time subjected by order of the Government and the resident magistrate. Captain Fetherstonhaugh is a gentleman whom you have also seen, and I think you will come to the conclusion from the way in which he gave his evidence here that he is a gentleman of kindly disposition. He upon several occasions tried to reason with Mr. Mandeville, to point out that the course he was taking was not really a justifiable one, and that no disgrace attaches to a man by reason of his complying with the regulations which affect everybody who becomes liable to such punishment. He endeavoured to persuade Mr. Mandeville, before he inflicted any punishment on him, to comply with these regulations. He did not desire to inflict punishment on Mr. Mandeville; if he did would he have resorted to this? Captain Fetherstonhaugh having endeavoured to persuade Mr. Mandeville to comply, had a duty to perform. It was his duty to see that the discipline of the prison was observed. Prison life must be kept very strict. If one man is allowed to disobey the prison rules or disregard the prison rules the thing may quickly extend, and prisons, instead of being examples of discipline, would become regular pandemoniums. Some of the persons who go into prison are not estimable characters, but whoever goes in must be made to submit to the laws of those establishments. A great deal has been made here of the fact that on the 22nd November the clothes in which Mr. Mandeville was arrayed were taken from him, and that he was coerced to put on the prison dress. Under the Acts of Parliament, which bind prisoners as they bind everybody else, it is prescribed that the prison dress shall be worn. The statute of George IV. prescribes what that is to be, and that it shall be worn by every prisoner sentenced to imprisonment above a month, and it imposes the obligation. The prison rules also state that every prisoner shall wear this dress. Captain Fetherstonhaugh appears to have taken a great deal of trouble with Mr. Mandeville to get him to comply with the regulations. He took precautions to get a suit of clothes that never had been worn before, he had them aired, he brings them to Mr. Mandeville, and asks him to put them on. This thing has been made great capital of by my friends on the other side. They have laid great stress on it. Mr. Mandeville seemed to think, acting on the advice of the person who incited him to institute the action, that he had great cause of complaint, and Mr. Mandeville lodged an appeal in the High Courts in Dublin. He brought his action against Captain Fetherstonhaugh on the 28th November. They filed a statement of claim, setting forth the cause of complaint against Captain Fetherstonhaugh, and he put a statement on the file justifying his action. If Mr. Mandeville had a cause of complaint against Captain Fetherstonhaugh, it was open to him to have prosecuted in that action; but Mr. Mandeville was better advised, and the action was allowed to drop. He came to the conclusion that the action of Captain Fetherstonhaugh on the 22nd November was justified by the authority he held as governor of Tullamore Prison. If Mr. Mandeville considered in his lifetime that he had any cause of complaint or had been subjected to any ill-treatment in prison, he might have commenced an action against the prison officials, and if he had done so he would have had a better opportunity of discussing what are here described as the cruelties and atrocities of prison life, than they can be now afforded that he is gone to his own account. I think it is a melancholy thing that this inquest has been forced on the relatives of Mr. Mandeville, because, I think, it is plain on the evidence of Mr. William O'Brien that he is the man who is responsible for this inquiry. He is the man who has insisted on the remains of his poor departed friend, John Mandeville being discussed here, in order that he may fling them against the authorities for whom he has such a hatred. Mrs. Mandeville appears to have had an objection to the holding of an inquest at first, but she was persuaded by Mr. O'Brien. Was it in the interests of Mr. John Mandeville that that was done. Was not it in order that a jury of Mitchelstown men would find whether with or against the evidence that the death of John Mandeville was attributable to something beside the act of God. I do trust that you in examining this case will not allow yourselves to be made the instruments of such a conspiracy as I say has been concocted here for the purpose of drawing the Prison's Board into odium. Every act, every circumstance, that occurred during the imprisonment of Mr. Mandeville has been disclosed here. Every act and every circumstance of that imprisonment is justified under the law as it stands, and my friend, The MacDermot, who a short time since held office under the Crown, had the same prison law in force then that was in force when Mr. Mandeville was subjected to his imprisonment, and it never became necessary while he was in office to amend the prison rules. There has been no violation of those rules in reference to Mr. Mandeville. Mr. Mandeville has had punishment inflicted on him of bread and water, and two days in the punishment cell; but being a man of the physique described, Dr. Barr, who has experience in such matters, and Dr. MacCabe, who himself was the man who settled with Dr. Robert M'Donnell and Dr. Grimshaw, the prison dietary have established beyond all doubt that the treatment to which Mr. John Mandeville was subjected, while in that prison, was not calculated to injure and did not injure the health of Mr. John Mandeville. It has been said by some that when Mr. John Mandeville returned

from

from prison he was wasted, shrunken, flabby, and all that sort of thing. Gentlemen, the weights told their own tale. Mr. Mandeville was 16 stone six, according to the scales when he entered gaol. It is shown that those weights were in error, and that his real weight was 16 stone three lbs., and on the subsequent times he was weighed up to 22nd December he had only lost three lbs. A man of corpulent frame and the change of diet would account for the failure of three lbs.; but it is absolutely false to say that he had wasted two or three stone when he came out. Gentlemen, one witness has been produced here, and that is Mr. Goulding, and I think he is a nice sample of the evidence upon which you are asked to find a verdict in this case. Mr. Goulding was in the prison during the incarceration of Mr. Mandeville; and, gentlemen, he is produced here for the purpose of giving a description of this suggested outrage on the 22nd November; and, gentlemen, it is a curious thing how Mr. Goulding has been procured. Mr. Goulding continued a warder in this prison after Mr. Mandeville's discharge, and after this outrage was committed he continued a warder up to the 5th July. Upon that date he was dismissed from Tullamore Prison for lying. By some strange coincidence it became known in Mitchelstown upon the 11th July immediately after the death of Mr. Mandeville, that Mr. Goulding had been discharged from Tullamore Prison for this lying. Mr. Ambrose Mandeville seems to have thought at once that he would be a valuable witness on this inquiry. Well, I think he has not lost his reputation of lying, by the evidence he has given in this Court. If anything is proved it is that Mr. Goulding has lied upon the most material points. Goulding's evidence is, that at eight o'clock on the evening of the 22nd November, he, with others, were summoned by the governor. He says, that on that occasion the light in the cell was out; the gas had been extinguished. The time *for* turning off the gas is half-past eight o'clock. He says they went to the cell at eight o'clock, for the purpose, as I have said of exaggerating the outrage, which he alleges. He says that the gas was then out, and that the warders stole into the cell in the darkness, and so caused a shock to Mr. Mandeville's *feelings*. If anything is proved it is that that is a lie and a distinct lie on the part of Mr. Goulding. It is proved by the governor that the gas was not extinguished, it is proved by the chief warder, it is proved by Warder M'Calla, and warder Meaney, that on that occasion the gas was lighting. Now, why did this fellow concoct that lie? It is for throwing discredit on the officer who caused his dismissal from Tullamore gaol. You must bear in mind that he was not dismissed in connection with any of these prisoners who are supposed to be political prisoners, he was dismissed for having told a lie with regard to his duties as night warder in that prison. He not only told that lie, but he introduced that blasphemous statement that the stripping of Mr. Mandeville reminded him of the stripping of our Lord by the Jews. Well, he occupies in that transaction the position of the impenitent thief. During the whole course of his imprisonment Mr. Mandeville upon frequent occasions had opportunities of complaining to Dr. MacCabe, to the gentleman you saw examined here yesterday, Mr. Goodbody, Mr. Browne, Mr. Digby, and the other visiting justices. These were gentlemen whose duty it was to go into the prison and converse with the prisoners, to see whether they had any complaint to make of the officials, or of their treatment in prison; and, gentlemen, it won't get rid of the fact that he made no complaint to these gentlemen fearing the governor would make a handle of it. Dr. Moorhead, who in my opinion, has been guilty of gross breach of his duty professionally, and the etiquette of his profession, he did not fear to make the most ample complaints to him, and the same observation applies to his complaints made to Dr. Ronayne. Gentlemen, it is not a fact that he was unwilling to complain when he had complaints to make. He appears to have complained to Dr. Barr, who was not a visiting justice, whom he thought was not in sympathy with the party with which he was connected, but he had a complaint to make, and he made it to Dr. Barr. He complained that Dr. Ridley allowed him to be punished, but the ground that he put his complaint on was, that he was allowed to be punished as an ordinary prisoner, instead of being treated as a political prisoner, but he never complained that Dr. Ridley neglected his duty and allowed him to be subjected to punishment when he was physically unfit. It was no reason, according to the law or the prison rules, why Mr. Mandeville should not be subjected to punishment when he declined to comply with the regulations, because he was a political prisoner. There is no distinction recognised in the law or the prison rules. The only way a man can escape is by keeping out of prison, and if he does that he won't have to complain of the prison rules. These rules are made for the purpose of enforcing strict discipline in the prison, and the prisons of the country are necessary to the preservation of public order and public peace. Discipline must be observed in every public institution. Gentlemen, it is proved beyond all doubt that Mr. Mandeville on the 14th December weighed within three pounds of the weight he was when he went into prison, and it has been proved by Dr. Moore that such a condition of things is positive proof to his medical mind that no such impairment of his constitution had been effected, as has been suggested by Dr. Moorhead or Dr. Ronayne. It is worthy of note, that these gentlemen being magistrates, have availed themselves of their position of magistrates for the purpose of impugning the conduct of a brother professional. It is a curious coincidence that Dr. Ronayne himself, in dealing with the treatment to which Mr. Mandeville was subjected by Drs. M'Craith and O'Neill, was not satisfied that it was quite correct. There is one very singular thing in connection with this case. One of the principle items of complaint stated by Mrs. Mandeville was that her husband after his discharge from Tullamore Prison was suffering from his eyes. He consulted a gentleman in that district, Dr. Ahern, and it is a wonder he was not brought here to tell you what that affection of his eyes was. Dr. Ahern the evening before the man's death saw him, and he is not here to tell you of the causes which he

then

then saw, and the treatment Mr. Mandeville had been subjected to at the hands of his medical advisers. Gentlemen, that is a very singular thing that Dr. Ahern has not been brought here. Why is not he here? He is a member of the family of Mrs. Mandeville. He knew Mr. Mandeville before either Dr. M'Craith or Dr. O'Neill. Neither Dr. M'Craith nor Dr. O'Neill ever treated Mr. or Mrs. Mandeville before. Dr. Moore has described to you the nature of the affection. He attributes the affection described by Dr. Cremen to a poison got into the system at a period nearly approaching the time that the unfortunate gentleman died. He has told you that that virus takes about nine days to mature, and he has told you that the course of living adopted by Mr. Mandeville travelling at night would have an important effect of developing the disease of which that virus was the origin. He has himself subsequent to his discharge from Tullamore Prison, borne to unfortunate Dr. Ridley his testimony as to the care and attention he paid to him during his incarceration, and he having done that I respectfully submit to you that no person less capable have need impugn the treatment of Mr. Mandeville by Dr. Ridley while Mr. Mandeville was under his charge. It is proved by Dr. Moore that the disease from which Mr. Mandeville died was not an affection that could be lurking in the system for the period suggested, and if it was not lurking in the system Tullamore Prison has no more to do with Mr. Mandeville's death than any other circumstance in his life. Every day that a man lives brings him nearer to his grave, and the fact that he was two months in Tullamore Prison brought him nearer to his grave in the same way that our being here to-day brings us nearer to our own end, but we could not, if we died in eight or twelve months, attribute our death to being in Mitchelstown now. I submit to you that the biliousness from which Mr. Mandeville occasionally suffered is a matter to which no weight can be given as tending to show that his constitution was in any way affected by his incarceration in Tullamore, because it has been proved on the last occasion he suffered from anything of that sort he declined to have any remedy for it, knowing his own constitution, and being desirous that it should run its course for a few days after. A man may be suffering from biliousness and a clearing of the system would not be prejudicial to him. He knew that he would be likely to suffer from this, and suggested that no steps would be taken to stop it for two days after he was speaking to Dr. Barr. If that is so it disposes of the suggestion that the diarrhœa had or could have any effect upon his general health. If that is so, what is the other suggestion about his being subjected to any treatment from which he could suffer any real injury. It is suggested that he had a pain in his back. On the particular occasion he complained of that he was found by Dr. Barr, as he had been on previous occasions found by the doctor, swinging for exercise this stool over his head. Any man suffering from a serious affection in the back could not indulge in that sort of exercise. Any man accustomed to live in a well-furnished house where he will have his arm chair to sit in in the evening, when he has to sit on a stool without a back to it he will suffer some inconvenience, which may give rise to a slight pain in the back, but to think that any such affection as that could have any effect upon a man's general health is the merest nonsense. Nothing has been shown to you that would enable you to say that Mr. Mandeville's death was due to anything in connection with his imprisonment.

ELEVENTH DAY.

Saturday, 28th July 1888.

ADDRESS of The MacDermot for the Next of Kin.

Gentlemen, addressing you at the end, or towards the end of this prolonged inquiry, I have only one cause of regret, and it is a strange regret for an Irish Counsel to express to an Irish jury. I regret, and I shall continue to regret that I have not an opportunity of placing the facts of this case, of submitting them to the investigation and review of, of an English jury. However, it is my duty to give you some inadequate description of the event which you have to investigate upon this inquiry which my friend the Counsel for the Prisons Board called a farce. He said there was not a shadow of necessity for this inquiry; yet, gentlemen, this great Executive Department which my friend Mr. Ronan, I think, called a Department of State, has sought protection and shelter from this farce in strange and curious ways to shelter themselves and their officials from this so-called farce. They sought safety during some part of this inquiry in casting aspersions upon the habits and social character of Mr. Mandeville. They sought shelter by inquiring to as first falsehood professional in capacity and invention. No witness on our side whom I will not insult by comparing them with theirs, have sought to impute falsehood to an inoffensive lady whose widowhood we lay to the door of Tullamore Prison. In other ways they sought shelter a few summer showers, a drive on a summer night addressing a meeting for about ten minutes were referred to by the Prisons Board with the view of showing that John Mandeville was not killed by their treatment, but that it was the drives, the speeches on a summer's night that did it. These are the strange contrivances pursued. I ask you have you ever heard or seen a farce so encountered?

Gentlemen, turning to a more important feature of the case, and upon that feature I lay great stress, and to it I attach great importance. I would remind you before I refer to the details of facts that every doctor on both sides have come to the conclusion that Mr. Mandeville died from this acute disease which has been described as diffused cellular inflammation; and whether the period of incubation of that acute disease was late or more than nine days is no part of our case. The immediate disease which killed John Mandeville in a few days had existed in its acute form from the time he left the prison at Tullamore. You have been told there are three sets of causes connected with disease: the predisposing cause, the exciting cause, and the last fatal attack. The exciting cause would mean as described by Doctor Moorhead the introduction into the system of that immediate violent poison which killed him later on. It will be my duty to show you as plainly and unanswerably as ever was shown in a Court of Justice that the death of John Mandeville lay as clearly at the door of the Prison Board as would the death of a man who had had for some time a dangerous life would lie at the door of his own evil acts: I will show you that. I will show you that Tullamore Prison played the same part in the destruction of John Mandeville. John Mandeville was known to you all. It has been proved in evidence that he lead a good and excellent life. He has been proved to have carried within the walls of that prison an untouched constitution, accustomed to the healthy exercise of athletic mankind. He enters that prison, the gaol of Cork, carrying with him all those qualities that ensure a long and healthy life to enable him to resist disease, and to encounter any attack on his constitution. No doctor ever treated him for illness; no affections of the throat ever interfered with the happiness of his life; no tremor in his hand; no diarrhœa cut down and carried away that constitution; his sight was the sight of a strong man till Tullamore Prison carried away that sight. No members of his family were ever attacked by any evil effect from the sanitary arrangements of his house. His wife was more within doors than he was, and never suffered from the sanitary arrangement of the house in which Mr. Mandeville resided. I presume some showers fell before John Mandeville went to prison. I suppose they fell on John Mandeville. I suppose he was sometimes out at night. John Mandeville went to prison cheerful and healthy. The Governor of Tullamore tells you that he was a gentleman, courteous and inoffensive, not a malingerer, not an inventor of suffering. He tells you that in the whole of that period of time John Mandeville maintained and carried away with him the good opinion of the Governor, and on terms with all the officials. There seemed to be only one man who formed a bad opinion of him, the emissary of Mr. Balfour, Dr. Barr. He was sent to this country, chosen, selected by the Government as one who had a great important duty to discharge, a duty for which intelligence was required, a duty for which impartiality was required. No man of a malignant mind ought to have been sent on such a mission; no inconsiderate man ought to have been sent on such a mission. He came to a country where party feeling ran high, where due circumspection in every word and act was of the greatest importance, where men, even though they were Irishmen, ought to have been judged honourably. And he came from Tullamore Prison, and he states that he may have said Mr. Mandeville was a scoundrel, and that he deserved all the punishment he got. Where did he learn this? Where did he get the information that justified him in saying Mr. Mandeville was a great scoundrel? Was it because of his want of truth? Was it because of his shamming? Gentlemen, he enters the prison of Tullamore; but before he enters it I have to draw your attention to this. He was taken to the prison at Cork; the first or second night of his imprisonment his own clothes were taken away without resistance, and a suit of prison clothes was put in place of them. John Mandeville offered no resistance. Later on that night, or on the 1st November, a sudden message came to the Governor, and about 3 or 4 o'clock the prison cell of Mr. Mandeville was invaded, and he was directed to rise. Is this the light which it has been held the prison regulations give to everything, so that the scenes that disgraced our prisons in past times should never occur again. From the time of Howard down the tendency is that the light of day should be on everything done in prison. In our prison, how much in keeping with that, the invasion of the cell at this hour to hurry a prisoner off. Why and wherefore was all this strange mystery? And, gentlemen, by one of their rules, three rules by which I shall ask you to come to the conclusion, this man's constitution was shattered. One of these rules is that the doctor of the prison should certify as to the health of a prisoner before he is moved from one prison to another. Without the doctor being called in, Mr. Mandeville is hurried on by a special carriage, with blinds down, policemen guarding the road stage by stage, until we find him delivered into Tullamore Prison. They began by the violation of a rule, and it could not have a good end, and had not a good end. Now, gentlemen, when Mr. O'Brien reached Tullamore Prison; you will allow me to tell you a word upon what I think is evidence to guide you in this case; and what I think ought to be the prison life of a prisoner. You were told in this case, and it is true, that the doctor of a prison has the power and duty of acting and caring for the health of his prisoners. He can give them meat if they require it; he can give them wine if they require it; he can send them to hospital if they require it. Prisons are intended for punishment, not to destroy the life of anyone. No punishment is to be awarded where health is in danger, and therefore it is there is an hospital.

Mr. Mandeville went into that prison carrying with him all that health and strength that you have heard of. Before many days he was suffering from diarrhœa. He was treated by the doctor for it on the 3rd of November, on the 4th of November the Governor went to Dublin. Now, there were the prison rules, there was the prison surgeon, the hospital there were all appliances, and now I have to draw your attention to another feature in this case. You remember the communications Captain Roberts confessed to having received, one by telegram and two by letter on the 1st of November, marked private and confidential from the Prisons Board. Does it seem to you that the light of day is cast on what occurred in Cork Prison if there are private and confidential communications which the counsel for the Prisons Board would not produce in this inquiry. Why did the Prisons Board refuse to submit these private and confidential communications and leave all in the dark? Why should there be stealthy communications affecting John Mandeville and which are concealed, although they were called on to produce them they were not produced. They declined to produce them, so important was it for the Prisons Board that their production should not be had. We find the Governor, in November, going to Dublin, having an interview with the Prisons Board, returning and after he got back on the 6th of November Mr. Mandeville got his first punishment on bread and water. In that cell, whatever may the quantity of cubic feet of air, there was that cell, and in that cell he was placed for 24 hours. Mr. Mandeville had been accustomed to comfortable quarters. He had led a life in which there was proper food, proper housing, you were told that ordinary prison treatment breaks down the constitution of some men and breaks down the mind of others, but ordinary punishment was not enough for Mr. Mandeville. He got 24 hours bread and water following the return of the Governor, so far for the 6th of November. Was there another attack made on him? I believe that on the 8th November Dr. Ridley described him as unfit for punishment. Why was he unfit for punishment, was it true or untrue, or is it that Dr. Ridley had a little more of the human heart and a little less inhumanity than those who were pushing him forward, or was it that Mr. Mandeville was unfit for punishment on the 8th of November. Another indication of the attack on the health of that strong man, which attack we say had terminated in his death, I find that he was again treated medicinally on the 10th November. Again, another indication of the growing ill-health of Mr. Mandeville under this treatment, I have other indications and I shall tell you what they are. Dr. Moorhead tells you that on the 10th of November he found his breathing embarrassed, and so early as that he found him complaining of sore throat, you were told that Mr. Mandeville was a cheerful man, and you find him on the 10th November suffering from sore throat, on that day a change to hospital was recommended by Dr. Moorhead. I will tell you now who these doctors were. Dr. Moorhead was a member of the College of Physicians, he was a licentiate of the College of Surgeons in Ireland. He was also medical officer of the workhouse. Dr. M'Craith had the diploma of the College of Physicians and Surgeons in Edinburgh. He was a dispensary doctor in this town, and he was also physician to the constabulary. Dr. Ronayne was a physician and surgeon. He was medical inspector for the Board of Trade, and he was for some years a visiting justice to the Youghal Bridewell. Dr. Cremen was a member of the University, a physician to the North Infirmary, and he has been 30 years in practice. I have already referred to the medical certificates of the doctor, and I find that on the 10th November he was suffering from sore throat, I want to tell you that one of the rules is that the linen of a prisoner is to be changed every week, and I find that on the 10th November complaint was made to Dr. Moorhead in the presence of the Governor, "sore throat, no change of linen, supply of flannel recommended, and a larger and better cell." He said that he considered this essential and he made an entry to that effect, and he made a note of that entry. On the 12th his eyes were suffering, and he recommended that he should be sent to hospital on that day. He tells you Mr. Mandeville's health

was

was failing, and he recommended as essential a change to hospital. Now, Gentlemen, put these facts together: sore throat, embarrassed breathing on the 10th. No change of linen. On the 12th, two days later, his eyes sore; a change to hospital recommended. You have the sworn evidence of Dr. Moorhead that he is a member of the College of Surgeons, and in the performance of his duty, which is to go there and see the prison, he recommended the hospital as essential. You will remember that from the beginning to the end poor Mandeville was not allowed anything. Punishment cell, punishment diet, were the remedies by the prison authorities for restoring and maintaining the health of Mr. Mandeville. It was their duty not to injure his health; it was their duty, even if he were in fault, to stop short when they found his health was going. He was prescribed for on the 12th November. Now, having regard to the evidence of Dr. Moorhead of his condition on the 10th. I ask you to come to the conclusion that he was unfit for punishment on the 11th, 12th and 13th. On the 14th a charge of not complying with the prison rules is brought by a warder against Mr. Mandeville. You remember all the hedging by by that respectable governor on that point. He admitted at last that when the warder made the charge he was ordered to make it. That punishment was devised to break the strong will of that man by breaking down his strength of body. Here you have a record of his condition on the 8th, 10th, 12th, and on the 14th that most terrible sentence is pronounced upon him. The warder makes his charge, the doctor gives his certificate, and the governor sentences him to 72 hours bread and water, no exercise.

Well, Gentlemen, the sentence was imposed on him. It appears Mr. Mandeville took his privation inoffensively and quietly. On the 14th he endured that sentence; on the 15th he endured that sentence. On the 16th it was found necessary to take him off this, but I must draw your attention to why he was taken off. I find him using a gargle for sore throat on the 14th. That was the first day of the 72 hours of terrible punishment to a man who was unaccustomed to such a life. Again, I ask your recollection to the bed-clothing and the mattress being carried out of the room lest he should sit down and take a little repose during the course of the day, the regulations, which ought to be hung on the walls of an ordinary cell, removed, nothing left him but the walls and a few necessary utensils; and there was where they placed Mr. Mandeville for his sore throat under medical treatment. Unfit for punishment on the 8th; suffering on the 10th from embarrassed breathing; on the 12th from feebleness of sight, and recommended for hospital. We find him in this cell using a gargle for his throat on the 14th.

Now, Gentlemen, have you ever heard of a patient so treated? Have you ever heard of a human being dealing with a man for days in that way, a man who ought to have been in hospital. To find him expiating the non-performance of this prison rule at the risk of his life. Dr. Moorhead found him on punishment diet using a gargle for his throat, and recommended his immediate removal to hospital. On the 16th he says I found him in his cell on punishment diet, and suffering from diarrhœa, and getting thin, and rapidly losing weight. That evidence was given by Dr. Moorhead here; and now, Gentlemen, I have brought this under your notice, hear now what he has on his notes: "I consider this treatment calculated to endanger the life of any man." You see, looking back with what prophetic knowledge this doctor spoke, the cell was most unsuitable for a patient suffering from diarrhœa, and the hospital a suitable place; do you concur in all that? You were told the cell was calculated to produce a pernicious effect on his constitution, and you were told the hospital was a suitable place. Gentlemen, on that same day another report was made which I must draw your attention to.

Now, gentlemen, let me tell you what Dr. Ronayne said; Dr. Ronayne, this member of the College of Physicians, medical officer of the Board of Trade. He tells you he had formed a bad opinion of his appearance, flabby, bluish lips, suffused eyes, marked symptoms of heart failure, want of proper oxidation of the blood. No open air exercise ordered by the doctor; suffering from weakness of sight, sore throat, and diarrhœa. The voice showed that something was wrong with the throat. Mr. Mandeville, in presence of the governor, turned to the doctor, and said, I have been attacked from diarrhœa twelve times since three o'clock. He was put on this punishment the day before. There you have sore throat, feebleness of sight, diarrhœa. What was the opinion of Dr. Ronayne to the governor? He says, Poor fellow, this is a sad and distressing case; take care you do not have a repetition of the scandal of Kilkenny here. Here, again, we have it stated no change of linen since his imprisonment. The rules still violated.

Mr. Ronan.] The linen was left with the other clothes.

The MacDermot.] Would Dr. Ronayne complain that he had no change of linen if he had linen? No, he goes on to say he is losing his right complexion, short in his breath, and ought to be put in hospital, with a view to mitigate his suffering and curing his malady. None of that has been denied by the governor as having occurred; but what does occur next day, the 16th, the last day? They were compelled to take him off, and did take him off, punishment. There was the treatment of Mr. Mandeville on the 14th and 16th of November. They were not satisfied. You remember Mr. Joyce came on the 11th November. He was sent down on the 11th November. We have Dr. Moorhead's report of the 17th: "Made a report, in which I complained that he was suffering from diarrhœa, and should be removed to infirmary for medical treatment." Now, gentlemen, you have the condition of affairs down to the 23rd of November I may also mention to you that on the 16th November, the day before this report was made by Dr. Moorhead, he was prescribed for by the surgeon of the hospital, who gave him a mixture of opium and ammonia. And now we come to the 23rd November. On the 23rd November you remember the punishment he has been receiving up to this. You find a patient suffering from diarrhœa, debility of sight, suffering from weakness; still, notwithstanding all this suffering, not sent to hospital. On the 23rd of November a surprise was made, to which I shall have to call your attention, for so gross, so inhuman, so merciless as ever happened, made upon an honest prisoner; the time, the mode, the character of it. The governor admitted to me that in Mr. O'Brien's case that, although he did not promise the presence of the chaplain, he did promise the presence of the doctor if any raid was made upon him. On this night, the 23rd, there was a lock-up at six o'clock. The hour of darkness had come; Mr. Mandeville asleep in his cell. See what happened. Warders summoned back to the prison, paraded. Not a word of this was denied, and there they are, and there is the governor of twenty years' standing, the prisoner asleep; and there on parade the governor addresses and tells them the duty they are going to perform, a hard duty even the governor and the warders acknowledge; it is a hard duty, acknowledging the potent force of humanity, acknowledging the attack on that sleeping, defenceless prisoner; but, "Men," he says, "do your duty; lead on." And on they went till they reached that cell, where Mr. Mandeville was awakened by the unlocking of the door or by the men walking into his cell. It does not matter whether he was roused by the unlocking of the door, by the turning of the keys, or by all together; and then they proceeded, seven men against one. We are told one of the corporal works of mercy is to visit the prisoners. Here is one of the works of mercy performed. They proceeded to rouse him from his sleep, and they proceed to drag off garment after garment of his clothes. The indecency of stripping off his shirt is committed, and the governor directs a sheet to be given to him. If a prisoner be disobedient, there are rules which enable the prison authorities to do many things, but there is nothing in the rules or in the statute about physical violence; and, God knows, John Mandeville had been receiving punishment enough for his disobedience. From morning until night in that dreary cell, with that hard stool, God knows he had got punishment enough, and all that night, to enforce the rule, for which he was punished over and over again, these men came and dragged off his garments, and left him there in his cell. The governor said it was a hard duty to perform. He said to me it was a painful duty; but still he did it, and from that until five o'clock next day we find this gentleman in that desolate cell. Then they come back and take away the quilt, blanket, and mattress, and everything that might make a room comfortable, in order to drive that patient man on to surrender. Dr. Moorhead describes him with his chest bare, with his neck bare, trying to cover his large and splendid figure with a paltry prison sheet and quilt. There he is left to perish or die of disease. In the report made of this matter by Dr. Moorhead, which the governor admits to be true, he says, "I found him in his cell wrapped in the quilt and sheet, no underclothing, not even a shirt. He complained that his clothes were forcibly taken the preceding evening. He protested against the treatment and demanded his clothes. His legs, chest, and one of his arms were bare. I visited him next day, he was then attired in prison garb." This, the governor admits, is a true description of Mr. Mandeville on the 23rd November, in Her Majesty's prison at Tullamore. Now, gentlemen, we come to an important date. Upon the 19th of November it appears that Dr. MacCabe came here, and Dr. MacCabe, who appeared to me to give his evidence with a considerable amount of what I would call self-esteem. He gave his evidence in what I would call a number of little speeches. Now, gentlemen, I say that Dr. MacCabe having been examined, a remarkable incident occurred, a remarkable incident quite in keeping with the rest of the evidence in this case. He was a medical member of the Prisons Board. He told you he was a member of that Board, and I pressed him to inform me why he came down to Tullamore. For a long time he would not allow that the Executive had anything to do with it. I asked him was he sent down there, and he said no, he believed that Mr. Bourke knew of it, and that Mr. O'Brien knew of it. I pressed him, because it appeared to me that, from the whole proceedings of this case, that every punishment that was inflicted on him was urged from external sources. I asked him whether he had had any communication with any person forming a Member of the Government. He said he believed he had had a communication with Mr. Bourke. I asked him whether he had any suggestion from Sir West Ridgeway, and he said he had no explanation to offer, and then he admitted that he was deputed by the Government to come down, a matter which he denied the day before. He is sent down at the instance of Mr. Balfour, and Ridgeway, and when he came down he examined Mr. Mandeville. He took him to the window and told him that his eyes were all right. Well, while he had been admittedly suffering from his eyes, this clear-sighted doctor could see nothing wrong with his eyes, and said he was fit for punishment. Surgeon MacCabe, who tells you he is a Fellow of the College of Surgeons, tells you he could see nothing wrong with the throat. Mr. Mandeville asked him to give him his finger, and he would draw his attention to it, and he asked him to put his finger into his mouth at the right side of his throat, and MacCabe could neither see or feel anything hard; and remember this, that the right side of his throat was the side that was punctured by Dr. McCraith, and so early as the 19th of November we find Mr. Mandeville getting Dr MacCabe to put his finger into the right side of his mouth. Of course, Dr. MacCabe could see nothing and find nothing, except that John Mandeville was fit for punishment. Now, in addition to this 19th November, I find that on the 25th November another very remarkable person came on the scene. Now, on the 25th November, Dr. Moorhead describes his condition: "On the 25th November I found him in his cell complaining of rheumatism. I am not surprised to hear this. He told me that he had been 24 hours from the time his clothes were taken off until he put on the prison clothes. He told me he complained of rheumatism, for which the prison doctor had not prescribed. His cell was close and offensive smelling, due to the presence of excreta not removed. He was ordered by the governor to take exercise with criminals, and he refused to do it. A continuance of such treatment would break down the strongest man." Gentlemen, that is the state of affairs on the

20th. If you remember, that until the prison clothes were put on him there is no evidence of his having been called upon to clean his own cell. The prison clothes were not put on him till the 23rd, and it was only then we find him asked to clean offensive matter out of his cell. Now it was resolved to enter on another campaign against him, and to compel him to clean his own cell; and just as they removed the quilt and mattress to drive him by prison suffering to put on the prison clothes, now they seek to destroy his health by having that offensive matter in his cell for 24 hours, and they tried to add to the degradation of wearing prison clothes the cleaning of this offensive matter out of his cell. Was that calculated to injure the health of a man who had been ill during the whole time? Do you agree with Dr. Moorhead that it would break down the health of the strongest man? What could they have done that they did not do? Where was the relaxation in this case? Everything that could be done to break down his health was done in that prison. Well, on that day, and in the midst of this state of things, a remarkable man arrived for the first time, that was Dr. Barr. Dr. Barr came there, and he tells you John Mandeville was healthy, that John Mandeville was strong, and fit to undergo punishment. Dr. Mac'abe said that if Mr. Mandeville had been suffering from diarrhoea the food would be improper. This gentleman said on cross-examination that that treatment on punishment diet would have been highly improper; that a patient of that kind should get good food. He also told you that the act of depriving a man of his clothes was highly improper. He was asked whether the patient could have been flabby, pasty, blue under the eyes, lips, and so forth. He said no. He (Dr. Barr) said to me on cross-examination that after having seen the patient on the 16th, that every word of that statement of Dr. Romayne was false and unfounded. Dr. Romayne was a gentleman, a surgeon, a physician of the Board of Trade. Dr. Romayne had been magistrate of the county. Dr. Romayne was well known to many, and yet this gentleman swore here to swear that the evidence of Dr. Romayne was false. So far for the 26th. He (Dr. Barr) came there again on the 6th December. He came there again on the 15th December. In his evidence he said he had nothing to do with the punishment of the prison. Now I will ask you, is that true? I pressed him about a remarkable coincidence; that he came on the 26th, and on the 28th Mr. Mandeville was punished for refusing to cleanse his cell. He came there on the 6th, and on the 8th Mr. Mandeville got 48 hours for not cleansing his cell. He came on the 15th December, and on the 20th Mr. Mandeville got two days in a punishment cell. Apart from these coincidences, this man, who dares to swear he had nothing to do with the punishment, he tells you that he did say he was fit for punishment. He tells you that he did say the doctor had no right to refuse a certificate for punishment where the prisoner was in good health. He tells you that Mr. Mandeville was fit for punishment and deserved all he got, and yet in the face of all that evidence he dares to swear that he had nothing to do with the infliction of punishment. Now, notwithstanding all that was said about the 15th December, notwithstanding that this gentleman said the prisoner was fit for punishment, I find that on the 16th Dr. Ridley certified him unfit for it. He went away; his report had not yet gone up. Next day, the 16th, in spite of all that poor Dr. Ridley, who has expiated with his own life any offence he could be charged with being guilty, on the 16th this man, who described Mr. Mandeville as a great scoundrel, in spite of that certificate, reported that Mr. Mandeville was fit for punishment. He tells you that he told them in Tullamore that he had come from the Government; so he had come from the Government. There was poor Ridley, there was the governor, there were the warders, and they were dealing with the representative of the Chief Secretary in this country sent to Tullamore clothed with all the authority that he had, and for the first time, 20th December, four days before Mr. Mandeville had left the prison, for the first time he is put in the punishment cell. Who had been the last inhabitant of that cell? Barr, on the 26th November. This Surgeon Barr was in that punishment cell to inspect it, and he came here to hold it. He tells you he visited many prisons in Ireland, and he tells you he spent five minutes in this cell, and that in that time he could take all its bearings. He tells you he will remember it until the day of his death. Does he remember everything, the ventilation, the mattress, the stone, and all about that until the time of his death? Why, his mind must be like a beehive, it must be all cells. Do you believe that? You might find the reason why. He had not yet made his report; he was preparing to make it for the gentlemen who entered it on the 20th of December, and would have entered it long before but for the struggling opposition of poor Dr. Ridley. He was put in there for 24 hours, into this cell, the floor of which was covered with what this surgeon of Kirkdale Prison dignified with the name of carpet. A stool 8 or 10 lbs. weight he called a heavy stool. Well, strange to say, that cell has been boarded since, and it appears the second day after Mr. Mandeville going in they had to put bags to keep out the draught. I will just read for you the evidence that has been given by Dr. Moorhead regarding the condition of that cell: "I visited the prison on the 29th of November. I saw Mr. Mandeville in his cell. I observed his condition, and I made a report in the visitors' book. I found Mr. Mandeville chilled from the use of bread and water. He also had a distinct tremor in both hands, and he complained of the long confinement in his cell, now four days, without exercise. He pointed out to the governor that he had power to relax the rules. I am aware my recommendations were disregarded." Now, in that report, entered in the prison's book, he tells you that Mr. Mandeville had distinct tremor in both his hands. Now that is of the greatest importance. We have a distinct tremor in his hands sworn to by Dr. Moorhead, yet this audacious Dr. Barr ventures to swear on his oath that that statement of Dr. Moorhead was untrue. He saw the tremor in both his hands, yet Dr. Barr swears that that statement was untrue. Here is what I find in the evidence of Dr. Moorhead: "On the 21st December I found him in a special cell for

for special punishment. He was the only prisoner I ever saw in a punishment cell. It was situated on the ground floor. The cell opens into a small yard by an iron door." Now, by the rule no person could be sent to a punishment cell for such a period as 48 hours unless the sentence imposed upon him be passed by a justice of the visiting committee, and if that justice is not available, by some other justice, under the rule. The words "if available" are to be found in the 109th section of Geo. 3, which is not interfered with by the Prisons Act. (*Here there was an altercation amongst counsel as to the authority by which visiting justices are appointed.*)

The governor said, in answer to my question whether by the rules it was not his duty to be acquainted with the statutes and rules, and, further, I asked him whether it was not within his knowledge that he could not call in a visiting justice unless that the members of the visiting committee were not available, the jurisdiction was transferred to the visiting committee by statute, and the governor said to me that he knew that was the rule.

Mr. Ronan.] The jurisdiction of the board of superintendence was transferred to the visiting justices by statute.

The MacDermot.] A few days before Mr. Mandeville left prison they called in not a visiting justice; but this governor goes to an executive officer, a paid official, a removable officer, instead of going to Mr. Bowen, Mr. Joyce, or any other person; he goes to a paid official, and it is said that he had at that time with regard to the fact whether he was to be punished for not cleaning out his own cell, in all fairness and justice, pending that appeal, which was not denied by the governor, pending that appeal by the suffering prisoner, and having been on bread and water for seven or eight days, broken in health, tremor in hand, my substance wasted, are you going to put me in a punishment cell now for 48 hours? Surely you are not going to perform this last act of cruelty! All this he would say to a visiting justice; but no, the resident magistrate is called in instead of the proper tribunal. Is that not the legal aspect of the case? It is easy to see that, though Mr. Mandeville had gone through every form of punishment, they would not let him out to his Christmas dinner until he had 48 hours in a punishment cell. Gentlemen, there is the treatment of Mr. Mandeville in Tullamore. I shall now proceed to point out to you the consequences, and why I undertake to prove a case so unanswered and unanswerable that no jury can doubt that the illness and destruction of his health, which was mainly carried on in Tullamore, stuck to him until he was called away on Sunday the 8th of July. Gentlemen, I have been dealing up to this chiefly with the treatment of Mr. Mandeville in Tullamore Prison. I might, perhaps, remind you that during the time he was in that prison, according to the evidence of the Government, the quantity of meat which he received amounted altogether to 18 ounces boiled in soup, and the quantity of meat soup he received in those two months amounted to two pints of such soup as they give in prison. Mr. Mandeville, you know, was a large man and a strong man, and you have to put to the credit of the prison authorities the 16 ounces of meat and the six pints of soup. Perhaps I am not entirely accurate when I say all the meat he received amounted to 18 ounces only, because I neglected to mention the scrap of meat he received from the charitable warder. You have the evidence of Hartley, the chief warder, that Mr. Mandeville lost no weight while he was in prison, or only a matter of three pounds. I ask you to come to the conclusion that that statement is absolutely and entirely unfounded. He told you that Mr. Mandeville had told him what he weighed in Cork Prison, and he told you he took him from his cell on a day when he was undergoing punishment and weighed him; but, gentlemen, you have a conflict of evidence which makes it utterly and entirely impossible that the evidence of this warder could be true. For that purpose you are not confined to the evidence given of while Mr. Mandeville was in prison. Listen to the evidence of the condition he came out of prison, and ask yourselves whether he retained all his weight. Did Mrs. Mandeville, when she gave her evidence before you, strike you as one who was likely to exaggerate her evidence? The inquest was not held altogether at her will, because she felt a repugnance against having the sanctity of death invaded on the husband she loved. She tells you in language plain, quiet, and ladylike, of the condition of her husband when he reached his home. She told you the hand that guided the pen in writing a fair good hand for a month could scarcely write at all. Remember the evidence of Dr. Moorhead, that he observed tremor in both hands of the prisoner, Mr. Mandeville. Here you have added to the evidence of the doctor the evidence of the wife, that from this impaired and broken-down nervous system the same hand that had a distinct tremor on 28th November could no longer guide the pen, except with the greatest difficulty. Of course, if you believe the statement made by Dr. Barr, that this statement of Mrs. Mandeville and that statement of Dr. Ridley were false and untrue, don't act upon them, but you have to be the judges between the view of the Birkdale surgeon and the evidence given you by Dr. Moorhead and the evidence given you by his wife. She tells you he was thin, and very thin; she describes to you the outside coat he was accustomed to carry, he could no longer carry without fatigue. This was on coming from prison. This giant of physique used to carry her upstairs. She told you of his feebleness and debility, and he told her that he had never recovered his strength since he left the prison. A matter that I think will strike you is this: I have gone more into detail than I wished, into all that occurred in prison and after he came out of prison, but there was an observation made by Dr. Moore which struck me. I asked him, on the assumption that a complaint of a pain in the tooth and a complaint of a sore throat had existed outside the nine days, because he said the maximum period of incubation was nine days; I asked him, if that had existed, what conclusion would he come to, and he said that would be, in his opinion, a previous attack. If it occurred within the nine days, it would be a stage

in

to the same disease; if it occurred outside the nine days, it would be a fresh attack. The last attack came on within nine days, but it was the disease knocking at the door, and the strength of the constitution enabled him to resist the first attack. Assault number one, and the man recovers. Assault number two: weakened, prepared, predisposed for it, he may recover on the second occasion; and then comes the last fatal attack, and it kills him. There is the true history of Mr. Mandeville's case.

Now, gentlemen, I would say one word in conclusion; as the life of John Mandeville has been unselfish and self-sacrificing, adorned by many virtues, blemished by no vice, stained by no crime, and one-ided by what everyone will admit he considered the path of public duty, so, perhaps, in the ways of Providence the death of John Mandeville, and the manner of that death, may be a benefit. In the days of Imperial Rome, Christian martyrs were tortured and slain in the presence of Imperial Rome, or cast to the lions in the amphitheatre. Much, perhaps, in the olden language of Rome, might then have been called a grotesque farce; but, gentlemen, the blood of martyrs was the seed of Christians, and if this inquiry, shedding a light on prison life, tends to put an end to that baleful system of political persecution which has been choosing amongst us the best and the noblest as its victims, if it puts an end to that system, then the death of John Mandeville, more than his life, will not be in vain. The tomb in which he now rests, his last home, will not be again disturbed by the warfare of disputing parties; but, gentlemen, it is our duty and your duty, that no mausoleum, no crypt, no catacomb shall screen from the view of civilised mankind the heroism with which he endured, and the sufferings he bore.

The Coroner, in addressing the Jury, said:—

At this stage of the proceedings it becomes my duty to give you a few remarks on the law and facts of the case, and I have to stand up to address you on account of the bad arrangements in this court. Before I proceed to the consideration of the facts of the case, I would wish to return you thanks for the prompt and regular attention of the jury during the inquiry, and also for the close attention and consideration, and manifest anxiety you have evidenced throughout, in order to form a correct estimate of the evidence that was brought in so extensive a manner before you on behalf of the Prisons Board, and on behalf of the next-of-kin, and all other persons concerned. I feel that it will be quite unnecessary for me, after the manner in which the evidence has been already addressed before us in this case, to go into the details of the inquiry, which I should otherwise feel disposed to do, because we have not only had occasion to take the evidence carefully and deliberately, after question and answer from counsel and witness; we have had to take them down in writing, and to read them afterwards, so that you have heard not only the evidence given viva voce here, but you have heard the evidence given, so far as I could possibly have taken it, with care and accuracy in the interests of all persons concerned. You have also had the advantage of being addressed at great length by Mr. Murphy on behalf of the Prisons Board, who treated the subject very ably, and ably, and exhaustively on his side. You have heard the distinguished address of The MacDermot, the leading counsel for the next-of-kin, and both gentlemen have engrossed your time with so much details of this case, that I feel it will not be necessary for me to go into every minute detail of the evidence, and only so far as counsel on either side, whom I invite for that purpose, shall deem it necessary to draw your attention from me to the case. I shall not feel disposed to go through the entire evidence again. Before proceeding further into this protracted inquiry, and everyone will admit that it has been protracted to no greater extent than the grave circumstances of the case required, and the immense mass of evidence produced before us for our consideration, I feel it my duty, as I say, to at once take the earliest opportunity to relieve the characters of all persons concerned in the case, of persons unnecessarily assailed before me; and my first duty in that respect, which I hasten to perform, is my duty towards the deceased gentleman. There is no doubt it was quite manifest at the early stages of this inquiry to asperse the character of that gentleman in one respect, and to asperse it was the duty of counsel. It was their peculiar province from their instructions in a matter that may be put forward as one of the matters which are for your consideration as to the cause of death. The question was put quite palpably that that gentleman was a man of intemperate habits. There is no evidence whatsoever, in fact, on the contrary, there is all the evidence produced, on one side as well as the other, going directly to upset, to remove even the slightest scintilla of suspicion that this gentleman was addicted to intemperate habits, but quite the contrary, that he was a gentleman of temperate habits to an extreme degree, and it was thought to be relied upon as a reason for exposing that aspersion, which is a grave aspersion, the fact of his having taken a pledge. The explanation given was manifest to you, as it is manifest to persons in the adjoining towns, that children who have never taken a drop of drink take it as a matter of caution against drink, rather than a necessity arising.

Mr. Ronan.] Mrs. Mandeville gave as the reason, "to save expense."

Coroner.] Her evidence was to this effect, and it is entirely corroborated by the evidence of her brother, that on the occasions on which he dined she never saw him partake to any excess. Then, again, gentlemen, before I formulate to you in legal shape the issues to be determined in this case, I think it is necessary for me to refer to the character of the medical gentlemen, which certainly has been subjected to, I don't say on the part of counsel unnecessarily, to an attack of a very trying character. The data upon which medical opinion is formed are of a very variable, eternally changing, constantly going and re-going sort. What is an effect at one stage becomes a cause in the next, and it is obvious to a medical man that it is highly improbable that anything but an approximate opinion could be obtained. It is necessary, therefore, that there should be a diagnosis to the eye of the truth, and that there should be a history of the previous habits and previous life and constitution and health of the patient upon which medical opinion is sought to be operated. Although it may happen that to one doctor coming in at one particular stage of a disease which he was called upon to investigate a particular marked effect would be apparent, causing him to form a particular opinion. The next time, a different doctor would be called in and he forms a diametrical opinion. As to the gentlemen who attended at the end of this poor man's life, there was not a disapproval on the part of any of them of the treatment adopted at any particular stage. On the contrary, that most distinguished and eminent physician, Dr. Cremen, from Cork (whose demeanour and conduct in the chair here would at once strike any intelligent observer that he was a man of more than ordinary ability, as he stated, he was a man of vast experience, and he gave his evidence with the greatest amount of care, and usually after hesitation, as a man showing sufficient competence and ability in the discharge of his duties, and that he acquired a knowledge of the evidence), stated that though he would adopt other means, and this is only in one particular portion of the treatment, the application of the leeches, he found as to their having afforded relief, and it was doubly odd that that was a mode of treatment prescribed by medical authority. He says doctors differ, and though differences occur in all sciences, there is none in which it is so difficult to address a set of circumstances so unchanging in their nature upon which you can come to a definite conclusion as in the medical science. He did not disapprove of the treatment; he approved of it as a preparatory treatment. Dr. O'Neill is a local gentleman here; he gave his qualifications to you. Dr. O'Neill, as I am aware, is a surgeon of the highest possible significance and experience, both by his scholastic qualifications, his experience here, and one which is rather of a family matter, as you are aware. He belongs to a family which produced some of the most eminent men in the medical science. There is one case in which he exposed himself, I won't say voluntarily. You are aware that he has suffered from a paralytic affect, which made him produce his evidence here in such a manner as left him open to remarks on the part of counsel that it was not evidence that could be relied upon. There was his note-book, which was produced here, which would appear to be a contradiction of the state of things. I say, so far as I am concerned and responsible here for the protection of character so far as that character has been assailed, these gentlemen leave this court, so far as I am concerned, free from the statements of their incompetency, as stated here by Dr. Barr. As for Dr. McCraith, it is unnecessary for me to say very much. He may not have the experience of Dr. Cremen, but he is highly qualified. At all events, there is nothing in the case before us to show that at the final stage of this gentleman's illness that he was so treated that his life was shortened by a single span, or that any other treatment would prolong it. It was only given here as a possibility that it may have been prolonged; not even Dr. Barr pushed this case further than that life might have been prolonged, but he does not go so far as saying that life could have been saved. He went so far as saying that there was no chance given for the man's life. Dr. Barr occupies a very peculiar position here which I can't avoid animadverting to. He has occupied a very unique position, a very conspicuous or bold position. I have had some experience myself of evidence in courts of justice personally, and I have read a good deal of what transpires in courts of justice in the course of my professional life, and I have never known a case where a doctor assumed the position that Dr. Barr assumed here, and that is not resting with what he was perfectly entitled to assume as his position has been to go in contradiction and conflict to all the opinions of other doctors, those gentlemen I have referred to in the case; but he went further than that, and did not allow for that difference of opinion which was permitted and sworn to, as may be permitted in the case of a medical man; but he went further, and stated that the statements made by Dr. Moorhead were utterly false. I may be wrong in his meaning in making that assertion, but he was asked with emphasis that left him as a free, intelligent gentleman no excuse of not understanding the meaning of the question, and he stated that not only Dr. Moorhead but the statements of other witnesses were made deliberately with a knowledge of their being untrue. That is a very serious and a very advanced and bold position to take. Departing from these observations that I felt it necessary as one entrusted with the conduct of this court to make, I have to invite your attention to the real facts and circumstances of the case, and, with Mr. Murphy, I ask you with all the deliberation I possibly can, if it be at all necessary to disabuse your minds of any feelings of sympathy on the one hand, or antipathy on the other, sympathy arising from any statement that may have been made here even from that sad and mournful statement made by the widow of deceased, or from any sympathy arising from any feeling that he may have had on the part of the deceased gentleman, or feelings of the opposite because of any official, from the Chief Secretary down to the warders of the prison, comprising the Governor and Dr. Barr, or any other person. You will not have conscientiously discharged your duties if you allow any feeling of that kind to operate on your mind. You have got to bring your judgment to bear on the facts before you, which facts are not to be received by you in the nature of statements unless they are facts amounting to proof as deposed to here as facts, and you will allow those facts alone to operate in forming your judgment on the issues I will now formulate for you. The first is the immediate cause of death. The immediate cause of death could not from medical evidence here be obtained, and it is not for you to investigate whether the brain first failed, or the heart first failed, or what was the last part that ceased to moulder; but the cause of death here is quite manifest to us, and the cause of death that I will take in the case is this diffuse cellular inflammation, and whether the heart failed or the brain failed I think it is not exactly what we are strictly to ascertain. At this stage of the inquiry it was mentioned by Dr. Moore, a very eminent physician, and whose evidence is to be received by you with all the amount of respect and all the amount of credit that is due to a gentleman of his vast experience, that in hospitals there was no serious case of important holding of any serious kind without a post-mortem examination. In hospitals medical men for a statistical purpose often where there is no inquest at all hold post-mortem examinations. The reason a post-mortem examination has not been held in this case first of all, it was not asked for by any representative of the Crown or Prisons Board on the one side, and consequently as it was sworn to be unnecessary and useless by the doctors who attended before and at the death, and from the usual post-mortem symptoms after death, Dr. Cremen agreed with the other gentlemen that it would throw no light on the subject. As far as I can see, the question was whether it would throw light on the previous treatment in the prison; and the answer of Dr. Cremen was that it would not throw light. It has also been stated by Mr. Murphy that this inquiry originated from a conspiracy. So far as I am concerned, there is not one particle of foundation for that statement, and so far as I am officially concerned, I need not say that I would receive no instructions or intimation from any source whatsoever except from a source which would be entitled at any hand to the consideration of the advisability of holding an inquiry. When a member of the profession called upon me, and in a peremptory manner brought before me the necessity of holding an inquiry, I not only yielded to his request, but I came to this town and called on the district inspector, and had an interview with the medical gentlemen who attended him in his last illness, and then I found it was a case in which I would have completely abandoned my duties if I did not thereupon issue a precept for the purpose of holding an inquiry.

Well, gentlemen, after the extensive and exhaustive evidence produced before us from every direction, I will not admit that it was not in its nature a fit and proper and necessary subject-matter of inquiry. I will not refer you to the charges under the sub-commission for the purpose of holding the different matters that come under the heading of causes to be investigated, but this above all others is one of the cases, our only limitation is that the death must have occurred within a year and a day of the direct cause from which it originated. So far as individual criminality in this case by your verdict here is concerned, I am of opinion that the circumstances of the case are not of such a nature as to allow you to find that any particular person—on the assumption that you find no person guilty—that no person would be individually responsible in this case, or would be individually responsible for the death of Mr. Mandeville. Gentlemen, the cause of death has been diffuse cellular inflammation, or this class of sore throat. It is for you to ascertain to what that owed its origin, or whether any treatment of any person in the past was the cause of that. Now, the evidence which you are to consider is of a different class on both sides. You have the scientific evidence of the medical gentlemen, and you have the ordinary evidence of the officials connected with the gaol, the internal evidence and the external evidence of the persons connected with the deceased gentleman, either by kindred or friendship, as the case of Dr. M'Craith and Dr. O'Neill and others. The medical evidence adduced here on behalf of the next-of-kin as to the effect that that particular class of throat affection is of such a nature as that it may be superinduced by a lowered or depressed condition of the patient, and they go further than that. Dr. M'Craith says that the germ of the disease must have originated in Tullamore, but he did not mean by the germ anything that is meant by the germ theory, but that it owed its origin to the treatment in Tullamore. Dr. Cremen was asked in this sense, that is, on the assumption that the evidence given here is correct, would he ascribe the presence of that disease to the prison treatment, and his answer, gentlemen, I will read for you: "I did not consider that any different course of treatment would restore him to health. I thought him a gone man. I should say that the succession of conditions as deposed to here, that is, the succession of conditions involved by his imprisonment and the too great changes in life, had lowered his condition and rendered him less capable of resisting." He went further then, and said he never knew an instance where that class of disease would be induced for the first time, unless from a wound, but in men whose constitutions are lowered by morbid conditions of the blood, &c. All these causes would predispose to this disease. "Any cases I saw of it were broken-down constitutions, and I never saw a case of it except in case of a poisoned wound. It is quite possible that a man whose constitution was not broken down may be subjected to it. The disease he was subject to would not be caused by sleeping in the open air, but other causes would. If the leeches had not been used before I came, I possibly would have made an incision at the external surface of the jaw." I only mention this for the purpose of character, because it is altogether outside our consideration on legal grounds. Unless the treatment was of such a character or so indifferently performed as to be apart from medical skill, it would not exonerate the person from responsibility for an injury committed by him in the first instance, and that afterwards would be the cause of death. A person is responsible for his original criminal act. The case mentioned by The MacDermot here was a very exceptional case, in which a principle was clearly laid down, and a principle clearly maintained. Dr. M'Craith, Dr. O'Neill, and Dr. Cremen gave similar evidence as to the predisposing cause, and they reflected the predisposing cause back as a matter of fact to the time of the prison treatment. Doctor Moorhead gave evidence as to the treatment in the prison, but I won't refer to his immediately until I deal with the evidence on the opposite side. Doctor Moore, that distinguished gentleman who was examined here, and Dr. Barr, both say that it was a perfect impossibility that the disease this gentleman died

of

of could have any connection with the treatment he received in the cell. Dr. Moore states that the process of incubation would be a period of nine days; but he applies the process of incubation to poison in the system, and that being introduced into the system, that it was an impossibility as a matter of medical science that it could extend over nine days, and that was contradicted by the evidence of other gentlemen who were examined in this particular yet other gentlemen say that the constitution of Mr. Mandeville was so lowered and so depressed by previous treatment that it made him more liable to that, so that, gentlemen, you are left now independently to form your own judgment as to whether the treatment of Mr. Mandeville in prison had anything to do with this final disease of which he died. Even though you trace it to have a connecting link from the first of this man's ill-health down to the final stage to which he succumbed, you have still to consider whether that treatment was treatment of such a nature as would not be justified by the discipline of the prison, or by the law under which that discipline, and the system of dietary, and other measures that have been used in the case of Mr. Mandeville have been carried out. Of course it is unnecessary for me to say that prisons as an institution must exist in every civilised country, under every form of Government, whether Conservative or Liberal, or otherwise, and that as a necessary institution it is essential for their proper management and control that there be laws laid down for the proper order and regulation of the inmates; and it is also a matter of legal right to the officials entrusted with the management of those institutions that they are entitled to the fullest extension and the most considerate application of the laws in the form of discipline, and in their attendance to the necessary wants and requirements of the persons placed under them. They are entitled to every protection, the same as any other person entrusted with Executive functions, so long as they discharge these duties only according to law, and the rules for their guidance in those prisons. But their duties must be performed carefully. Their duties are entirely statutory. The restriction of the liberty of any subject is a restriction that must take place by law, and being restricted of his liberty, as in the case of Mr. Mandeville, for offences that you and I have nothing to say to here, he is entitled still, under such circumstances, to be treated in a manner in accordance with those laws, and not in excess of them; but it is for you entirely to consider whether that treatment has been in accordance with the rules and regulations, and consistent with the discipline of an institution of that kind, or whether it was treatment that affected the treatment of this gentleman to such an extent as rendered him liable to be subject to this diffuse cellular inflammation which terminated in his death.

Mr. *Harrington.*] There may be punishment which the rules would justify but the exercise of which would be cruel.

Coroner.] Yes, prisons are essentially necessary institutions in all civilised countries, so also I say that persons having control of those institutions are supposed to be vested with a certain amount of authority, which authority is carefully and vigilantly watched in order that those entrusted to their care may not be exposed to either harsh or bad treatment of any kind that would affect their health, because while it has been his duty, when it clashes with health, the punishment must in my humble judgment give way, and there are means adopted for discovering that, that is there is a doctor appointed for the purpose of examining into the health of the prisoners daily, and to certify as to their fitness for a particular class of restrictive punishment and other matters of that kind. It is necessary, I would say, for the well-being of those institutions in every sense, and it is essential in my mind for the proper discharge of the duties of the officials and in the interests of all inmates and all concerned that those persons should be allowed, having once been entrusted with so responsible an office, freedom of exercise, especially in the case of medical gentlemen in the discharge of their duties. It would appear to me that neither the governor nor the medical officer whose untimely end we deplore, were allowed a free exercise of their functions in this case as would be supposed to be vested and is vested in institutions under ordinary circumstances, for we find with the governor that there was a question of the enforcement of rules entirely confined to himself by consulting a doctor, and going and passing judgment. He went to Dublin for advice on the matter; from whom he got it I don't know.

Mr. *Rowan.*] He went to Dublin to know his powers.

Coroner.] He was asked whether he was bound to know his powers under the statutory rules, and he said he was. At all events we have the deceased gentleman overruled by Dr. Barr in the prison cell, and we find that there is a sort of discussion as to whether a complaint made by the deceased gentleman was one that should be entertained or not, and his previous theory, and the manner in which he put it would lead me, at all events to suppose, having to absolutely interfere, that there was a controlling influence over the discretion supposed to be vested in the local doctor. To my mind it seemed to be an ill-advised matter that a stranger should be brought in to perform duties that would more properly devolve on a local physician. For these reasons persons like Mr. Mandeville are naturally sensitive, very suspicious, very distrustful, and even on the evidence of this gentleman himself, Dr. Barr, to prescribe for a patient and ascertain the cause of his ailment, you want an examination and an anterior knowledge of his ailments. It would appear to me that it would be very essential indeed that in these cases a prisoner of that class should be approached with the utmost delicacy which humanity would suggest. No doubt Dr. Barr said he suggested to him the advisability of complying with the prison rules, but he did it in such a way that he spoke of them as very trivial matters. They may be in a disciplinary way trivial matters, but trivial matters are sometimes attended by the strongest principles, and it would be advisable on those occasions that the persons in that position ought to be visited by persons in whom they would have confidence. I confess that if I were suffering I would not trust examination tention and prescription to a man whom I did not know at all, but who was introduced, as in Mr. Mandeville's case, by the Government who had deprived him of his liberty.

Mr. *Murphy*.] It is only right to say that Dr. Barr never prescribed for Mr. Mandeville.

Mr. *Harrington*.] No, it was with a view to punish him.

Coroner.] Consequent on his visits, Mr. Mandeville was sentenced to punishment. Dr. Barr does not admit that it was he who was the cause of it; his reports could not have reached in such time as he could be punished on them, but he stated freely that there was nothing in Mr. Mandeville's health that would exempt him from punishment; and he went further, gentlemen, and he stated that this is a matter as to whether the treatment in any sense had any connexion with the death of Mr. Mandeville—he says if he was incarcerated for two years he would be alive to-day. As to the predisposing causes that have been given here, there are only one or two of those causes which will admit of being introduced before you as evidence, and that is the exposure of Mr. Mandeville to the night air. It has been stated that Mr. Mandeville was in the habit of going freely around to meetings, and that his speaking in the open air, and being found on one occasion early in the morning, or late at night, out in the open air, that that would be one predisposing cause which would account for the final cause of death. If there was a primary cause which eventually led to his death, a person affected by that is entitled to go about in the ordinary course of his business, performing his ordinary duties, and it would be no excuse for the person who originated this cause that the person in the ordinary exercise of his calling got a wetting, and that that developed what had previously existed, unless he unduly exposed himself to that inclemency of the weather, and brought on disease which had not existed. In that case it would be very unreasonable to suggest that an original cause existed, and that the person who caused it was responsible. There is no evidence of excess in eating or drinking, no bad habits, or starvation, no other exciting cause such as was deposed to here. The case as to intemperance has to be entirely abandoned. The case of being out at night is a matter for your consideration. Mr. Therry was out on all occasions that Mr. Mandeville was there. There was one day a very wet day, and Mr. Mandeville had not his top coat, Mrs. Mandeville states, and I don't wish to go into all the particulars of the case; you are bound to take a broad comprehensive view of this case, an open intelligent view of the case, as common-sense men not inclined to form an opinion to satisfy any person. You are to satisfy your own consciences according to your oath. You are not to be guided by any desire except of doing strict justice, because it is to your consciences you will be responsible, not to any particular class. Mrs. Mandeville informs you of the condition of her husband after his release. You recollect her referring to his inability to take his coat and boots. His complaint on the occasion would not be evidence of what he suffered in Tullamore Prison; but as to after his dinner when he dined in his father-in-law's house, when he expressed a desire to go home on account of his inclination to sleep, which would be another proof of debility. You had an array of the visiting justices here, and the sum total of what they stated here is that he made no complaint to them. You are to take another explanation for that; the character given of Mr. Mandeville, of his weight, and given generally by all the witnesses that came here, Mr. Mandeville's particular disposition to avoid complaining at all. He was a reticent man, and it was inconsistent with a man of his character that he should make a complaint, especially when he asserted freely that he would brave whatever punishment was put upon him. There is no other way of accounting for it, because that statement would be more or less inconsistent with other facts of the case, as showing that there was some cause of complaint on the part of Mr. Mandeville. Even the evidence of Dr. Barr himself shows that he made a complaint in his presence. That would be contrary to what was stated by the visiting justices; in fact, the evidence of one of them, that gentleman who performs the functions of court valuer, he said it was their desire; and also you are to take that state of things in connection with his meeting Mr. Mandeville at the hotel in Dublin, because there again he had no reason to complain. Well, it is quite possible that a man having manly feelings had not occasion to complain unless he had necessity to seek redress from a source in which he was entitled to demand an inquiry as to the cause of his treatment. Dr. Moorhead stated the different courses of treatment from time to time that he objected to; and Dr. Ridley, from the first time he met him in his cell until he found him in his punishment cell, and this being put before you as showing that there was a harshness and severity and departure from the ordinary mode of treatment of prisoners in the case of Mr. Mandeville, especially in bringing Mr. Mandeville before an external magistrate, as he called him, a removable magistrate. Well, there was some difference about when he could be called in, and he has, according to the construction I put on it, found no fault with the visiting justices. At all events, the evidence is that the governor found it his duty to call in a visiting justice, and right and, coming from them, it would come with more leniency than from a stranger.

You have the whole course of treatment. Mr. Mandeville complained in presence of Dr. Moorhead, and Dr. Moorhead made certain reports produced here in evidence, that Mr. Mandeville was suffering from diarrhoea on various occasions. That he, during that time, was deprived of exercise. That he was subsequently stripped forcibly of his clothes. That he was obliged to cleanse his own cell. That he was sought to be made associate with ordinary criminals, and by reason of his refusing to do so was put upon certain punishment, and that immediately before his release was put into a military cell in a place in a ground floor compartment, a plank bed; he complained himself of being cold, from which he suffered, and that he was there subjected to punishment diet. Now it is only right to say with regard to the prison dietary, in order to explain that no undue severity was exercised on Mr. Mandeville, a gentleman, a high official, a superintendent of prisons, was brought before us, but so far as the evidence he gave, he might as well have been left at home. He stated there was no difference between the dietary in England and in Ireland, and that, on the contrary, the dietary would be in favour of the Irish prisoner. Dr. Barr gave you a full account of the dietary; however, it is well for your consideration that, so far as the rules are concerned, and so far as the provisions made for the treatment of prisoners are concerned, there is no difference between the treatment in both countries; and if there be any, then it is in favour of the Irish prisoner; and you are to take it that the authorities would be favourable to give them more under the head of diet. You had, first of all, a man of splendid physique, full of health and vigour. You will find him incarcerated in Cork Gaol, on the 31st October, and you find there that he subjected to what exposes him to punishment, that is the wearing of prison dress. You will find that that dress was afterwards restored to him, and you will take into consideration that, under directions that were sought to be given in evidence, and which I ruled admissible, that no official in the land could exempt an official from the responsibility of any loss of life by any act that might have the effect of depriving that person of their life, and the highest potentate, if I may put it, the most influential official would be responsible for the loss of life, if by act or commission it could be directed to him, and on the grounds that Major Roberts, the official in Cork Gaol, having the care and custody of prisoners under his control, on the ground that he got certain orders, and in such a way as to affect the treatment of prisoners once I ascertained that state of things; Major Roberts would not be exonerated more than any official in Tullamore or any other gaol would not be exonerated on the ground of any document, private or otherwise, because the person who commits a criminal act is responsible for it, and because these instructions are in accordance with the law of the land. You are to take then into your consideration the mode in which the prisoners were treated on that occasion, their removal from that gaol at that particular hour in the morning, which was described here in a manner which you are not, of course, to be affected by. It was described very graphically by Mr. O'Brien, the hurried manner in which they were taken away in the early morning, they were then admitted into Tullamore Prison. It appears that persuasions were exercised by the Governor, who appears to me to be a man who would not unduly exercise any functions intrusted to him either towards the treatment of a prisoner or otherwise, if allowed to act on his own individual responsibility. Dr. MacCabe, who appears to have a very persuasive manner about him, wanted to reason with Mr. Mandeville about the advisability of donning the prison clothes, but he and the Governor rallied altogether on discipline, as it would appear to me to be paramount to a requirement of health; but when health is in question it is to be considered in preference to discipline. Dr. Barr spoke, the prison justices had come, but Mr. Mandeville felt that he was upholding a principle, and that was his reason, because he was a political prisoner and not a criminal in the ordinary sense of the word. Dr. M'Cabe, when pressed as to the frequency or not of the act, he would not say it was inhuman or barbarous, but he did not like it, and he would wish very much if there was some means adopted for the purpose of enforcing obedience of the rules without affecting the feelings of such men, and which was obnoxious to them. It would appear that the prison officials observed some principle of that kind, because they formed a class for exercise. About his being deprived of his clothes, you have the evidence of Goulding and the other six who were engaged, and it is for you to consider both. You have the taking off of the shirt, and it was described that there was no change of linen. It was asserted on the other hand, that when the clothes were taken away there was a whole new suit left in their place; however these are minor details. The case is put before you in the true sense. It is the mode in which the enforcement took place, the means adopted for making him comply with prison discipline; it is in that sense it is produced for your consideration. It is admitted at all events that it would have the effect of giving a severe shock an entrance under these circumstances, and the rapid manner in which they disposed of Mr. Mandeville's suit, and left him there more or less exposed to the cold of his cell. Against that he had his own clothes, and it cannot be stated that the consequences of his being exposed was one in which the person who stripped him would be responsible, because they left him a substitution. It is the mode in which the clothes were abstracted, and the means afterwards adopted which were put before you as an undue course of treatment which you will consider among all the other circumstances. The bedclothes being removed, they were restored that night, and as far as the evidence of the warders, one was that he had the prison dress on at night. It is for you then to consider how far, for the purpose of ordinary discipline, measures were adopted whether as to dietary or punishment, or restriction of dietary, that were not in excess of the powers of the officials acting under certain rules and Acts of Parliament for their guidance and control, whether there was not an excess of the means resorted to for the enforcement of that discipline on their behalf as would have affected the health of Mr. Mandeville, and which effects would have remained in his system, and so have affected it afterwards, so that it would have terminated fatally. You have the evidence of Dr. O'Neill; you know him personally; of Dr. M'Craith, the evidence of his widow, and of Mr. O'Brien, and all these will go to show that Mr. Mandeville was a completely altered man; that he was broken down, that he must have lost in bulk at all events, if not in weight, and one person went so far as to say that it might be three stone. You have the evidence on the other side of Mr. Therry, of the visiting justices, who saw him after leaving prison, and they say they saw no perceptible appearance, and Mr. Therry states that he even inquired about his health, and that he stated he did not suffer from his incarceration; but again you are met with the evidence of Doctor Moorhead. Doctor MacCabe states, while he was in prison on the occasions he visited that he did not consider it necessary to discover what was the state of the heart by using the stethoscope, and that he was so much struck by the robust health that he said it was ridiculous to examine him. Doctor Barr formed the same conclusion. You are to weigh all the evidence on one side and the other; but I cannot put it to you to say how far. It is for you to say. It is for you to say which side of the evidence you believe. You have the evidence of Doctor Ronayne, who saw his eyes affected, &c. He considered he was affected by the prison treatment. At that time Doctor Moorhead also saw him. However, it has been stated of them that they gave a colouring to their evidence. It was the inevitable duty of Doctor Moorhead, as a justice of that prison, to see to the health of every prisoner there, including Mr. Mandeville, and he would be guilty of a dereliction of duty if he did not expose it to the public. Doctor Ronayne gave a statement of how he found him. He was suffering from diarrhoea; he was suffering from sore throat. It was prescribed for. As to the test used in the former instance, there was a discussion about that, and Mr. Mandeville himself complained. There was a defectiveness of sight, which was evident, having to consult Doctor Ahern, who made no examination of him, and he was introduced here at the last of the proceedings, which would necessarily imply that he was an adverse witness, and which, if I were acting for the next of kin, would say nothing about it. The man had an interview with Doctor Cremen, the purport of which we have not the slightest evidence, and it would not be advisable for those having charge of the case for the next of kin to produce Doctor Ahern; but I would receive any evidence that would throw light on the matter. He wore glasses, and after that he suffered from diarrhoea. Do you believe Doctor Moorhead and Doctor Ronayne's evidence he was suffering from the effects of a broken-down constitution, and bore all the symptoms of a person who suffered severely in constitution? Against that you have the hypothetical evidence. What would be your opinion? The symptoms would be not only inconsistent, but false, and only made by a person with a knowledge of their being untrue. As to the matter, as being interested by the evidence on either side, I will say nothing to you. Gentlemen in the highest positions have put their evidence in conflict, especially in the evidence of Doctor Barr, in a painful degree, to say the least of it, and it is for you to say who is more interested. It transpired in evidence, and that was the first I had heard of it, that a good deal of public comment was made during the time Mr. Mandeville was in Tullamore. It was at that time that Dr. Barr arrived on the scene to investigate matters for himself, and if he brought to bear the same disposition that he seemed to manifest here, it is for you to say how far any man assuming that egotistical, dogmatic position, as being infallible, is interested, or how far he feels the treatment of the prisoner in Tullamore was responsible. I think I have, as far as I can with the time at my disposal, given you my view of the evidence; but it was unnecessary, on account of the clear way it was put before you by counsel on both sides. I think I have touched on all the matters that will be brought before you in a pretty general way. In treating this subject you are not to take into consideration small matters of detail, but a broad, common-sense, comprehensive view of the treatment *in globo*. There is one thing I may mention to you, and that is the weight. It has been alleged here that by a tested scales, which was first wrong, and afterwards by another scale in Tullamore, that the weight of this gentleman was taken, and if that was true it would be inconsistent with the evidence given here. It is for you to say whether that would be evidence by a person so interested in the case, and though you are to receive the evidence made from external observation, it, of course, would not rank in equal degree with the evidence of a man having scales and weights. Taking that range generally, and the previous life and history of Mr. Mandeville from a medical point of view. His good habits, his previous health and strength, and taking then the course of his treatment down to his release, and from that to the time of its final termination, it is for you to consider whether the prison treatment had the effect of so operating on his constitution as was proved generally in the manner described here, as to make him a fit subject for that disease, and as an effect of that disease, and the lowering of his system not only being capable of receiving the disease, but not of resisting it, and that in the ordinary course of events he would not have been subjected to this disease if he had not been incarcerated in prison. There is no evidence of any serious throat affection until the time Doctor M'Craith was called in on Friday. There is nothing incompatible in Doctor M'Craith giving a gargle without going to trouble the man, or asking any detail what brought this on. I have often myself bought gargle. I have merely said I have a sore throat, and I would get it at once. There is nothing wrong in doing that. I know of a great many people in public life going to a doctor for a cough mixture for a person who was not present. The doctor may or may not see what sort of a cough it is; it is only evidence that the thing was so slight that it did not appear necessary for the doctor to be observant. Gentlemen that was put in here in a very distasteful manner. There was an attack made which has not been borne out by the evidence here.

Mr. *Ronan*.] That matter was sworn to by Dr. Moore.

The *Coroner*.] There was a severe attack on the character of a medical man here, and I need not say that the character of any honourable man is his life; deprive him of his character, and you might as well deprive him of his life. There is nothing to bring discredit on the conduct of any of these gentlemen. If there be any discredit whatsoever, it would seem to me to be tendered in a manner not fair or right. I again enjoin upon you that you will leave out of the jury box all considerations whatsoever, except the anxious and earnest desire that you have displayed throughout this case of doing your duty honestly. When we have departed from this

this scene your conscience will remain. It is that alone will be your guide in this case. You have sworn here to do your duty to the best of your skill and ability according to the evidence. You are not to take into consideration the value of poor Mr. Mandeville's life, either to the public or his widow, or anybody else. You are to deal with him the same as with the meanest subject of the realm. You are dealing with the existence of a fellow-being, and you are to account on your oath why that existence has been terminated, either by ill treatment or absence of proper treatment while in the prison in Tullamore. Of course, it is a solemn and a very serious thing. You are to take the matter in a broad honest general way, and you are not to be actuated by any considerations as to what will be the effect of your verdict to please any person whatsoever. You are to please your own consciences. You are not to take into consideration whether the punishment imposed on Mr. Mandeville, in the first instance, was under any particular Government; whether it was under Liberal, Tory, Parnellite, or any other Government whatever. You are then to assume that he was properly in prison, and taking into consideration his physical, and even his intellectual and social position, would you, placing yourselves in the position of the officials, find you would be responsible for the death of Mr. Mandeville, if you treated such a man, having regard to the health of that man and being bound to carry out the rules of prison discipline, do you find the circumstances of the case of such a nature as to find any person criminally responsible, and in the manner in which you have been addressed by the next of kin, it is put in that way, whether you attribute it to the imprisonment the cause of death of Mr. Mandeville. Of course that inferentially would be a terrible consequence, for any individual criminality would be a great responsibility on the prison authorities; and should you find, assuming you were in their position, that your treatment ought to be condemned here by a jury under the circumstances disclosed in evidence, taking into consideration all the evidence brought before you, and the facts and circumstances of the case, then that treatment you would describe as causing the death of Mr. Mandeville. If you do you will find your verdict accordingly; if not, you will find, if you can find consistently with your duty, that the cause of death was diffuse cellular inflammation; but if you believe, on the other hand, that the treatment was connected with it, you are bound, in the interests of the public, regardless of the consequences, to find a verdict accordingly.

Mr. *Ronan.*] I wish to make an observation, Mr. Coroner. I wish to know will I make it now or after the jury retire?

The *Coroner.*] What is it, Mr. Ronan?

Mr. Ronan.] What I would wish to say is this, that the question you leave to the jury now is an abstract question as to whether the prison treatment had anything to say to the death of Mr. Mandeville. What we want to know on behalf of the Prisons Board with a view to future action.

Mr. *Harrington.*] Future action!

Mr. *Ronan.*] What we wanted to say is this; the real question here is, is anybody to blame?

The *Coroner.*] I only gave them my opinion, and said, if they found the prison treatment had the effect of in any way leading to the death of Mr. Mandeville, that that was a thing they ought to adhere to.

Mr. *Ronan.*] I wish you to tell them that they won't have discharged their duty by saying the prison treatment had anything to do with it, except they go farther, and say the Prisons Board, Dr. Ridley, or somebody else, is to blame. If anyone is to blame let it be boldly stated. Let my learned friend not shelter himself behind abstract statements.

Mr. *Harrington.*] You would like a verdict against a dead man.

The MacDermot.] I have already stated here yesterday, and I understand it was with the consent of the Court. I was asked what I considered a proper question for the jury. I consider the proper question for the jury is what this gentleman died of. The question I want to have left to the jury is whether his death was caused by unjustifiable treatment during his imprisonment in Tullamore prison. I want to have you or no to that. It has been asked by my learned friend, Mr. Ronan, to tell the jury to go further and attempt to discover the particular individual or individuals who are responsible for that treatment. I tell my friend, Mr. Ronan, that it is not that I am afraid of that, but the Prisons Board have made it impossible. Men were there, and men were not there. No human being at the end of this inquiry could put the blame on any person, because it would be impossible to discover under what thimble the pea was. As you have already put it to the jury, the question is was it caused by the unjustifiable treatment in Tullamore gaol; they may say a particular individual was responsible or they may not.

Mr. *Ronan.*] Captain Fetherstonhaugh was governor of the gaol during the entire time of Mr. Mandeville's imprisonment. The supreme, absolute, unappealable authority who had the absolute power of determining what diet, what lodging, what punishment, what dress Mr. Mandeville should get, was Dr. Ridley.

The *Coroner.*] Before you came in I mentioned that to the jury, because we had it in evidence that Dr. Barr came under very peculiar circumstances to the prison, and that he had given expression to his feelings in the prison.

Mr. *Ronan.*] I repeat to you to tell the jury as a matter of law, that there is no evidence to go before them that Dr. Barr had anything to say to the treatment.

The *Coroner.*] I cannot do that. If the jury find they cannot, from the circumstances of the case, fix the responsibility on any particular person, they will find a verdict to the effect as to whether the immediate cause of death was occasioned by ill-treatment.

Mr. *Ronan.*] They are to try to ascertain the people responsible.

VERDICT.

VERDICT.

The Jury then retired at 5.40 p.m.; at 6.15 p.m. they returned into Court with the following Verdict :—

"We find that John Mandeville died on the 8th July of diffuse cellular inflammation of the throat as defined by the Doctors, brought about by the brutal and unjustifiable treatment he received in Tullamore Gaol;

"That we enter our solemn protest against the system of the present Government in awarding similar treatment to Irish political prisoners as to common criminals, and the cruel methods by which the rules are enforced;

"That we condemn the vile aspersions of Dr. Barr on the Doctors who attended Mr. Mandeville in his last illness."

The [illegible] thanked the Coroner for the way he had conducted the proceedings, and was sure everyone connected with that inquiry was satisfied with the way the proceedings were carried out.

Mr. *Ronan*, B.L.] On behalf of the Prisons Board I must compliment the Coroner on the very accurate note he took during the entire proceedings, which may be of use to us in another Court.

www.ingramcontent.com/pod-product-compliance
Lightning Source LLC
Chambersburg PA
CBHW030631270326
41927CB00007B/1393
* 9 7 8 3 7 4 2 8 1 6 8 2 5 *